GOING BACK

GOING BACK

How a former refugee, now an
internationally acclaimed surgeon,
returned to Iraq to change the lives
of injured soldiers and civilians

Munjed Al Muderis
with Patrick Weaver

ALLEN&UNWIN
SYDNEY·MELBOURNE·AUCKLAND·LONDON

Allen & Unwin
83 Alexander Street
Crows Nest NSW 2065
Australia
Phone: (61 2) 8425 0100
Email: info@allenandunwin.com
Web: www.allenandunwin.com

A catalogue record for this
book is available from the
National Library of Australia

ISBN 978 1 76063 316 5

Uncredited photographs courtesy of Claudia Roberts, Michelle Nairne and
Patrick Weaver

Set in 13.5/19 pt Granjon by Post Pre-press Group, Australia
Printed and bound in Australia by Griffin Press

10 9 8 7 6 5 4 3 2 1

CONTENTS

1

THE LEGACY

A chill ran down my spine as the Qatar Airways Boeing 737 descended and, through the darkness, the lights of Baghdad gradually came into sight in the distance. 'Oh no, what have I done?' I thought. 'I'm coming back to the place I escaped nearly two decades ago. The city where I came so close to being executed. I went through a succession of traumatic experiences to get out. Now, of my own free will, I'm here again. It doesn't make any sense at all!'

My return to Iraq in 2017 was an entirely unpredictable and surreal experience. I felt completely remote from the events that were unfolding, like I was watching someone else's story.

Going Back

After eighteen years, so much had changed. First and foremost, I had established my new life in Australia. And my feelings as we approached the tarmac at Baghdad International Airport reinforced the fact that these days I am passionately Australian and proudly regard Australia as my home. It's where I created my orthopaedic practice and where the closest members of my family live.

Sure, I have maintained contact with the expat Iraqi community in Sydney—mainly based in and around what is sometimes known as Little Baghdad, at Fairfield in the south-western suburbs—and I've kept a keen, often despairing, watch on events in the country where I was born. Who hasn't? Let's face it: Iraq has been in the world headlines for most of the time since I left.

But, as we approached Baghdad, it didn't occur to me that I was coming home. I felt as though I was arriving in a foreign country. I felt like an outsider.

Flight QR 442 from Doha in Qatar had been a circus from the time I queued at the boarding gates with my personal assistant, Michelle Nairne, and my physiotherapist and partner, Claudia Roberts. For a start, we began boarding the plane 90 minutes before the scheduled departure. It's normally half that time. I couldn't figure out why at first. But it gradually became clear when I saw the other passengers—the vast majority of the people queuing nine or ten deep at the gates were pilgrims from rural areas of Iraq who were returning from the annual pilgrimage to Mecca, known as Haj. Most of them seemed completely unfamiliar with air travel and what to do at an airport. The journey to and from Mecca was probably the first time many of them had been on a plane.

Muslims from regional Iraq tend to be highly traditional and deeply conservative. They were all dressed in white and every woman was wearing a headscarf. As I looked around the departure hall, I quickly realised that Claudia and Michelle were the only women who weren't covered.

'This is terrible,' I thought. 'It's not the Iraq I remember from the days when I was growing up.'

I was apprehensive and said to my travelling companions, 'You don't have to go through with this. You can fly back to Sydney from here.'

They immediately declined. In fact, both were horrified at the suggestion they should make an early return to Australia. In the previous days, we'd been to South Africa and the United Kingdom. But this was the leg of our trip they had most eagerly anticipated.

Claudia looked at the throng of pilgrims and lightheartedly suggested, 'At least they don't smell!' The observation came back to bite us. The truth was that many of the pilgrims did have bad body odour.

It's all part of the more zealous interpretation of Islamic teachings: a woman is committing a sin if a man smells her scent. As a result, they don't wear perfume. And the more religious Muslims take it to the extreme and don't use anti-perspirant, either. So, ironically, by adopting the literal view of the teachings, they smell more—completely defeating the purpose of the edict.

The staff at the boarding gates—largely foreign nationals who didn't speak much Arabic—were particularly rough with the pilgrims as they herded them onto the aircraft. While I don't share the pilgrims' religious faith, I believe they deserved to be treated and respected like any other traveller. Watching events unfold, I decided I needed to intervene and had a heated discussion with a female member of the airport staff who was being especially harsh with the pilgrims.

The experience didn't become any easier when we eventually boarded the aircraft. I was concerned for Claudia and Michelle, who were both massively conspicuous because of their uncovered heads. Claudia is also *very* tall, with long blonde hair. She'd stand out in any crowd in the Middle East.

To avoid potential conflict with any other passengers, I advised them not to talk to anyone. And, if they did have to say anything, not to reveal why we were flying to Iraq.

Of course, the inevitable happened. Within a matter of minutes, someone asked them why they were going to Iraq. Claudia panicked a little, didn't know what to say and blurted out, 'We're going on holiday!'

Going on holiday to Iraq, a nation that, over the decades, had become famous as the most dangerous place on earth? It was hardly a convincing answer. We've laughed about it many times since.

The Legacy

I edged my way along the aisle of the plane and into my seat, followed by a morbidly obese Iraqi woman who flopped herself down immediately behind me. The flight attendant checked her ticket. 'I'm sorry, but you're in the wrong seat,' he told her. 'You should be in Row 23 in the economy section.'

The woman argued back in Arabic, which the flight attendant clearly didn't understand. 'I have a ticket. I'm a big woman, and this is a big seat,' she told him.

The flight attendant continued to explain in English that all seating on the plane was allocated—the passenger couldn't just sit wherever she chose. Meantime, several other passengers also tried to grab a seat in business class, even though they'd only paid for economy. Finally, the leader of their tour group managed to restore some form of order, and the pilgrims were settled into more or less the right seats.

I was dumbfounded by the whole experience and thought, 'What is going on? Iraq used to be a leader of the developing nations. This is chaos. These people know nothing about how the world works.'

The rest of the mercifully short flight—it was less than three hours—went relatively smoothly, until the end. As we landed, the cabin crew made the usual announcement. 'Welcome to Baghdad International Airport. Passengers should remain seated until the Fasten Your Seatbelts sign has been switched off.' Even as the announcement was being made, 20 or 30 passengers leapt into the aisle, opened the overhead lockers and started wrestling their bags into the cabin.

Going Back

My feelings at that moment were a mixture of fear of the unknown—not being sure what would be waiting for me—and horror. I remember sitting on the aircraft thinking, 'These people are completely alien to me. This is going to be nothing like the Baghdad I knew.'

Over the years since I had hurriedly escaped the country—a decision that both preserved and changed my life—I'd been asked many times whether I would go back. Mostly, my response had been, 'Are you mad? I don't want to die!'

I still had strong memories of being a young doctor in Iraq. In the middle of 1999, as a 27-year-old first-year resident doctor, I was working with the team preparing for a standard day in the operating theatres on the second floor of the Saddam Hussein Medical Centre on the banks of the Tigris River in Baghdad. Completely unannounced, a squad of brutal Republican Guards arrived with three busloads of army deserters and draft dodgers. We were ordered to cancel the day's operating list. Then we were instructed to cut off one ear from each of the hapless victims.

The consultant surgeon confronted the soldiers and refused to carry out their orders. He was promptly marched into the car park by the Republican Guards. We later learned the guards had shot him in the head without delay.

While that was going on, the imposing leader of the military unit barked out the question, 'Is there anyone else who doesn't want to carry out the instruction?'

We all had a pretty good idea of the consultant surgeon's

fate. So, not surprisingly, the question was greeted with silence.

'If that's the case then start operating,' came the order.

I was faced with three choices when the Republican Guards announced their horrific agenda. I could meekly go along with them, breaking the first principle of doctors: do no harm. I could refuse—and follow the consultant surgeon to an early grave. Or I could run and hide.

I never seriously considered the first option. And I wasn't about to front up for a bullet in my brain. So, I ran—but only as far as the women's toilets attached to the operating theatres. I hoped I could hide there until the mutilating surgery was completed and the Republican Guards had left. Only then would I be able to make my escape.

I was in luck. No one saw my hasty exit from the theatre. Over the next five hours, I sat in constant terror in a corner cubicle of the female washroom. A couple of times someone pushed their way through the door and into the toilets. With my heart beating so loud that I feared my makeshift hideaway would be instantly uncovered, I sat tight and awaited my fate.

Each time someone came in, I assessed the situation from the sounds I could hear and worked out it was a solitary theatre nurse taking a bathroom break. No one lingered long enough to question why a single cubicle was constantly engaged.

Shortly after 2 p.m., a group of what I presume were theatre nurses came into the bathroom. They seemed to be scrubbing down, changing their outfits and wrapping up at the end of the day's surgery. After they left, I waited another fifteen minutes before I hesitantly emerged from my hide-out.

First, I opened the toilet door and popped my head out to check no one was in the washroom. The coast was clear. Next, I approached the entrance to the toilets, tentatively opened the door and glanced out. No sign of anyone. The theatre staff and soldiers were gone.

I changed out of my surgical scrubs and into my civilian clothes. Then I strode briskly through the hospital corridors, all the time trying to avoid attracting anyone's attention. I used the fire stairs to reach the reception area at the back of the hospital, walked past the throng of patients and through the main entrance. I was out of the hospital building, but not out of danger.

Quickly, I walked to the main road. After a couple of hundred metres, I hailed a taxi and instructed the driver to take me to an address in the prosperous suburb of Harthia, where a friend, Ali—also a doctor—lived.

When I arrived at his house, I explained to Ali what had happened and outlined the escape plan I'd hatched while I was confined in the toilet cubicle. I would head to Ramadi, where I'd studied at the University of Anbar. It's a remote area in the north-west of the country, dominated by Sunnis and extremely traditional. From my university days, I knew people who might be able to help me. Ali drove me there.

So began my journey to freedom, which included bribing police and immigration officials to provide me with a forged passport, taking a fearful bus journey across the border into Jordan and boarding a flight to Kuala Lumpur. A series of bizarre coincidences saw me taking a people smuggler's boat from Indonesia to Christmas Island off the north-west coast of Australia. Then I spent nine horrific months in Curtin Detention Centre in the north-west of Western Australia.

There, among the other indignities imposed by the authorities and, ultimately, the Australian Federal Government, I was known only by a number—982—and was subjected to constant messages on the camp loudspeakers urging myself and the other detainees to go back where we'd come from.

I was even falsely accused of inciting a break-out from the detention centre—which could have been disastrous, since a conviction would almost certainly have meant deportation back to Iraq. My fate would have been sealed.

But I was fortunate. I went on trial for the trumped-up charges in Broome Magistrates Court in front of one of the most unorthodox characters in the Western Australian judicial system, Antoine Bloemen.

Antoine is a former merchant seaman and US marine who emigrated to Australia and took up citizenship. Antoine had a compassionate and innovative approach to dispensing justice. He had heard cases against a number of refugees being held in Curtin—and had a good idea of the way the place was being run. He'd been the subject of the menacing stares of detention centre staff from the back of the courtroom while he was hearing those cases.

Going Back

It was the same when I appeared. Silent intimidation from the Curtin staff.

But it counted for nothing. The prosecution case against me quickly and comprehensively collapsed. At the end of the hearing, Antoine dismissed the charges. The verdict was greeted with cheers and applause from the packed courtroom.

It was the last case against a refugee from Curtin to go before Antoine. From then on, cases were sent to Darwin, where the powers that be believed they could engineer more successful outcomes.

——

Now, after all these years, a succession of events plus a lingering sense of duty had lured me back to the country of my birth.

I expected my return to Iraq to be a low-key affair. No fuss. No fanfare. It didn't quite work out that way. As we walked out of the door of the aircraft, we were intercepted by a group of smartly dressed men from the Prime Minister's Department, led by Mohammed al Attar.

Mohammed is a slim, good-looking, fashionably dressed, clean-shaven man with short, dark, heavily gelled hair. He is softly spoken and utterly charming and became an invaluable member of our team, particularly during the visit in August and September 2017.

He introduced himself and his colleagues. 'Welcome to your home country. We are honoured to have you here. Please follow

10

me,' he requested, avoiding the air bridge and leading us down a set of stairs to the tarmac below. 'We'll look after your bags.'

Waiting outside the airport terminal were two black Mercedes stretch limos, which took us on the two-minute drive to the special VIP reception area inside the airport compound. There we were met by more bodyguards and security officials, along with Adam Baidawi—an Australian-based journalist with an Iraqi background—who was writing stories about our trip for *The New York Times* and *GQ* magazine.

The luxurious wood-panelled room, furnished with leather chairs and sofas, had originally been created for the exclusive use of Saddam Hussein, his family and visiting dignitaries. Now, we were being afforded the same celebrity treatment. It was the ultimate contrast to the cloak-and-dagger nature of my escape from Iraq.

On the right, at the far end of the room, two ornate presidential chairs had been placed either side of the Iraqi national flag. Above the flag was the Iraqi eagle—the nation's emblem. Close to one of the doorways was a head-high, two-sectioned wooden room divider, folded towards us in the middle. There was no obvious reason why it was there—until we looked closer. In the space between the floor and the bottom of the divider we spotted a pair of polished leather shoes with suited legs rising above them. Clearly—and rather clumsily—a security officer had been placed there to listen to our conversation and report back anything suspicious. Which, of course, there wasn't. But this was a much more familiar feeling for me—a throwback to the old days of Saddam Hussein. We weren't alone, and we were under surveillance by the authorities.

After we were served glasses of fruit juice delivered on silver trays, our luggage was brought in and transferred to a couple of four-wheel drive vehicles. We were escorted into one of the two black Chevrolet Suburban SUVs. But these weren't ordinary models. They were heavily reinforced to withstand the impact of bomb explosions and sniper attacks. Among other things, they were equipped with jamming technology on the roof to prevent an improvised explosive device (IED) being remotely triggered while we were on the road. All the side windows were tinted to hide the identity of the people inside.

The front windscreen bore pockmarks and cracks. Claudia immediately asked me, 'Don't they have enough money to fix the chips and cracks on the windscreen caused by stones on the road?'

I gently explained to her, 'This is Baghdad.' The reinforced windscreen had done the job it was made for—repelling the bullets that had hit the vehicle over the previous months.

The road from Baghdad International Airport to the Green Zone—the 10-square-kilometre militarised area on the west bank of the Tigris River that houses the parliament, the main government offices and the embassies—used to be known as the most dangerous drive in the world. It had certainly earned its commonly used nickname: Death Road.

Happily, by mid-2017, it was a much safer journey—although there were reminders everywhere of the tight security that is still in place across the whole of Iraq. Driving out of the airport and onto the right-hand side of the road, we were joined on the six-lane highway by two large armed personnel carriers—each with a machine gun mounted behind the driver's cab, staffed by soldiers dressed in battle fatigues and balaclavas. One of the vehicles went ahead of the convoy, while the other slotted in behind.

Overhead signs indicated a speed limit of 140 kilometres per hour. Our drivers ignored it. On official government business, they weren't required to recognise speed limits.

Dotted along the 12-kilometre journey are four military checkpoints where heavily armed soldiers stop all vehicles, inspect them and question the drivers. Humvee vehicles in desert camouflage are stationed at some checkpoints. Others have a more ostentatious show of force by the side of the road—M1 Abrams tanks. The Americans left both sets of vehicles behind when they handed over control of Iraq at the end of 2011.

Entering the Green Zone, we travelled past the huge US Embassy compound on the right. It's surrounded by four-metre-high concrete blast walls topped with razor wire—these are a familiar sight in and around the parliamentary and government area of the city. The embassy is the largest in the world, covering 42 hectares and costing US$750 million to build. It's like a small, self-sufficient town with its own power station and water-treatment plant. At its peak, 16,000 diplomatic staff and contractors were based there—although the numbers have significantly reduced since the withdrawal of the American armed forces.

Further on to the left is the military parade ground built by Saddam Hussein's regime. The area is still in use for official functions, such as the celebrations marking the defeat of ISIS in late 2017. It's defined at each end by soaring archways formed by hands holding two huge, curved scimitars that meet in the middle.

Our initial destination was the Prime Minister's Guest House—an imposing five-star hotel on the left of the airport road, next to the British Embassy and close to the Prime Minister's Department. The Guest House stands in its own grounds, protected by solid iron gates guarded by armed soldiers. There's a sweeping driveway from the gates to the entrance. Again, everything sits behind blast walls.

The facilities are luxurious. A towering reception area leads into a covered courtyard, with six floors incorporating 58 rooms. Inside the rooms, the sheets, pillowcases, towels and bathrobes are all monogrammed with Iraq's eagle crest. As well as housing official guests, the building is used as a conference venue.

We were met there by four representatives of Al-Hashd al-Shaabi, the Popular Mobilization Units—the militia raised after the Shi'ite Grand Ayatollah of Iraq, Ali al-Husseini al-Sistani, issued a non-sectarian fatwa following Friday prayers in June 2014. Their specific aim was to halt the advance of ISIS, which had taken Mosul and other major regional cities and was closing in on Baghdad. Hashd had been instrumental in organising my trip to Baghdad.

A five-minute drive from the Prime Minister's Guest House—and still in the Green Zone—is Ibn Sina Hospital, named after a tenth-century philosopher and physician. This was where I would be staging a clinic the next day to assess amputees and others who'd suffered severe trauma injuries while repelling the ISIS invasion. The idea was to pave the way for a subsequent humanitarian mission when I would actually operate on patients.

Completely unbeknown to me, news of my visit had spread far and wide. Iraq has more than 150,000 amputees from the wars of the last 40 years, so there was no shortage of potential patients wanting to see me.

We arrived at the hospital at eight o'clock the next morning. As we walked from the SUV parked in the street outside, we quickly realised that the reception area and hospital corridors were heaving with people. Some were in wheelchairs, others walked on ageing and obsolete socket prostheses, and still more had crutches or walking sticks. It was chaotic—to the point that the hospital's director later apologised because the number of patients had grown beyond anyone's control.

Nearly all of the people in the reception area that morning were men—the bulk of them had suffered terrible injuries to their legs while fighting with Hashd. But alongside them were others from the Iraqi Army, Counter Terrorism and the Ministry of Internal Affairs, which controls the police. We were told they would all be amputees. But once it became clear that I was happy to operate on any wounds, I started seeing patients who'd suffered a variety of traumas.

The sense of expectation among these people was palpable as we squeezed through the massed crowd. Because of the strict military security and checkpoints on all roads in and out of the Green Zone, just getting to the hospital was a huge effort for them. The vast majority would have needed to organise special passes and paperwork to gain access to the area.

Their motivation was simple. They wanted to lead a normal life. They were tired of being the forgotten people who'd been left on the scrap heap because of the injuries they'd suffered.

Iraqis generally aren't kind to people with a disability. Employers shun amputees. Work and an income are hard to come by, and there's little or no government support. It's common for wives and girlfriends to walk out of a relationship with someone who's been seriously wounded.

To start with, I held a special briefing to explain the process of osseointegration to the hospital staff and I showed videos of patients walking with their new robotic legs. Surgeons, doctors, nurses, physios and administrators were all packed into the conference hall in the bowels of the building.

Around 9 a.m., we set up a clinic in a small room off the main ground-floor corridor, opposite the office of the hospital's director. It was like being in the middle of a rugby scrum. We were inundated with badly injured patients, who were trying to elbow their way to the front of the queue. The room itself was also full of doctors from the hospital. Everyone wanted to see what was going on, as many members of the medical staff had no experience of orthopaedics. There were urologists, cardio specialists and others from all manner of backgrounds.

For most of the next fifteen hours, I saw a constant flow of patients. We didn't complete the final examination until 11.30 that night. The next morning, I went back to the hospital for another clinic.

By then, word had spread across the whole country and new patients were appearing from every corner of Iraq. They'd made their own way or been driven by family or friends. Others had made gruelling journeys of five or more hours in taxis. All with one purpose—they wanted to change their lives from an existence of misery, pain and immobility to something much happier. They wanted to be respected as people who could make a normal contribution to society.

The stories they told of how they were wounded were nothing short of horrific. Trauma was caused by attacks with IEDs, rocket-propelled grenades (RPGs), artillery shells and sniper fire.

By the end of the clinic, I'd seen 90 patients. At the conclusion, journalist Adam Baidawi asked if it was the most patients I'd seen in such a short time. 'It's the most patients anyone's seen in such a short time!' I replied.

The magnitude of the task ahead of us was starting to sink in.

2

KIDS IN THE KITCHEN

I came from a privileged and wealthy background. My father, Abdul Razak al Muderis, had been the head of the Supreme Court under the monarchy and was hugely respected across Iraq. He was an intellectual and scholar who considered the world and its ways through a prism of knowledge, law and common sense rather than religion or tribal traditions. He was descended directly from the Prophet Mohammed and his family was one of nine that founded the original settlement of Baghdad.

My father was firmly committed to education and culture and had set aside 500,000 dinar—a small fortune at the time—for my schooling. It was never spent and remains held in my name in Iraq. Today, it's worth around US$425!

My mother was from a far more modest background and was much younger than my father.

It wasn't exactly an arranged marriage, but their meeting was hatched by my father's sister who held a high position in the Ministry of Education. Through her contacts, she asked whether anyone knew of an older, single woman who might be suitable for my father. My mother, who was a school principal at the time, was suggested. My father went to the school to meet her—and from there, they formed a relationship and married. When they met, my mother was 42, my father 65.

Their marriage was an unusual combination. But one that worked.

My mother, Kamila al-Turk, was born in Basra and was the third of ten children in a working-class family. Her father owned a car dealership and was the first to import General Motors vehicles to Iraq.

My mother had five sisters and four brothers. She took on the role of bringing up the six youngest children when both her parents died.

Her career took a downward turn when she was demoted for refusing to join Saddam's Ba'ath Party. She was forced to retire completely when she married my father.

My parents had completely contrasting temperaments. My father was quietly spoken, scholarly and considered. Among his other activities, he was a chess champion and would play from four in the afternoon until midnight most days. He wrote a couple of books about the art of the game. In later life, his passion for chess took its toll as he developed a curved spine from the position he would adopt hunched over his chessboard.

While my father was a very peaceful man, my mother was more flamboyant and opinionated. She was feisty and a fighter. It's from her that I inherited my competitive streak. My mother was the driving force behind our family—always busy and a perfectionist. Nothing was ever good enough for her—and I don't think she ever really saw me as a legitimate doctor!

In her later years, she suffered from arthritis in her knees and hips. At one point, she asked me whether I knew of a doctor who could fix up her knees.

I told her: 'Mum, I'm a knee surgeon. I can help you with your diagnosis at least.'

Her response was dismissive: 'No, I want someone who's a real doctor!'

— —

In Iraq, attitudes to money are completely different from those in Western countries.

As an example, on my second visit to Baghdad, one of my team talked to an Iraqi about banks.

'We don't put money in banks,' he was told. 'The government would steal it!'

Instead, if they have spare cash, Iraqis will buy property, which is seen as a safe and secure investment. Or they'll buy coins and gold. Both are easily converted if a family needs to raise funds at short notice.

My mother would collect currency and have it incorporated into jewellery. She had one necklace, which must have been a metre long, entirely made of high-value coins. And she would carry around 4 kilograms of gold in her handbag. In her later years, she didn't get out of the house much. But when she did, she would be accompanied by a couple of our domestic staff who would act as her bodyguards.

My father never drove a car. In the good times, he employed a personal driver. His regular driver joined the military during the war with Iran and didn't return. Another member of the domestic staff took on the task. My mother drove, but by the time I was thirteen she developed cataracts and her eyesight deteriorated to the extent that she couldn't safely sit behind the wheel. If another driver wasn't available, she would hand me the keys to her car and instruct me to ferry her around, despite the fact I was still some years off the legal driving age!

If I was stopped by police, she would berate them to the point of embarrassing everyone else in the vehicle. Not infrequently she would demand of the police: 'Do you know who I am?' Invariably, as soon as my mother issued the belligerent challenge, the Iraqi cops would back off.

—▪—

Going Back

I was born by caesarean section at the Al-Haydari Private Hospital in Baghdad on 25 June 1972. As the child of older parents, I was much loved and indulged. I was, frankly, spoilt. And a spoilt brat as well—as a few of my exploits will indicate.

Growing up in Iraq, my life was largely carefree and indulged. But my family's wealth didn't extend to unfettered financial generosity. My father allowed me the equivalent of the princely sum of 20 cents pocket money per day. I'll admit that was more than many Iraqi children received. But, at the time, I felt it was nowhere near enough for a self-respecting child in our strata of Baghdad society. So, from a young age, I turned my hand to money-making ventures.

When I was eight years old, I came up with a scheme centred on a snack Iraqis love to nibble on—sunflower seeds. Westerners might munch on chips or popcorn. Iraqis love cracking sunflower seeds and separating the husk in their mouth, then swallowing the internal part. Although it's hard work for not much reward, it's a treat that has been popular for centuries.

I would borrow money from my mother and ask my father's driver to take me to the nearest market. There I would buy a bag of sunflower seeds, take them home and roast them with various flavourings—making sure to produce something distinctly different from the seeds available in the shops. Once I had my stash ready to go, I'd walk around the neighbourhood and sell the seeds door to door. I used to sell quite a few to the locals.

Kids in the Kitchen

My next venture was to cash in on the sport of kite fighting, which was popular among Iraqi kids. Few people in the West have ever heard of it but there's plenty of kite fighting in the Middle East and even more in south and Southeast Asia— including Afghanistan, Bangladesh, India, Indonesia, Korea, Nepal, Pakistan, Thailand and Vietnam. It's recognised entertainment in Brazil, too. Each contestant flies a small, single-line kite with sharp attachments on the string. The winner is the kite that cuts the other's line.

It struck me as another entrepreneurial opportunity—and probably more lucrative than sunflower seeds. So, I switched my focus and started making kites out of newspaper, with a palm frond for the shaft, all held together with sticky tape.

The crucial point of difference with my kites was the way the string was made. I would collect old light bulbs, smash the glass, grind it up, mix that with glue and then coat the string with the paste. The glass on the string would easily slice through the lines of other kites. My creations became very popular with the local kids, who could see for themselves that my kites won plenty more battles than they lost. And no one ever figured out the secret!

Around the age of twelve, my money-making ventures became more scientific and sophisticated as the world of computers began to open up. Along with my cousin Ismail, I enrolled in a summer school that included a course on computer programming. I knew nothing about technology, but realising it was the direction of the future, my father bought an

LGA computer comprising a screen and hard drive attached to a keyboard and mouse. By today's standards, it was rudimentary. But it gave us an insight into computing and writing programs.

To be honest, I wasn't much good at programming. But Ismail was brilliant. He made and programmed a remote-controlled vehicle that would climb over objects. He also developed tennis and squash games we could play on the screen. My best effort using the DOS system was to create an on-screen cube that turned around. Pretty basic, I have to admit!

At the time, not many people in Iraq knew much about computer programming—so we were among an elite bunch. We were just kids, but we would exchange programs with other people exploring technology—including science academics and some senior figures from the Iraqi military.

In our spare time that summer, Ismail and I would play competitive chess and bet on who would win. The stakes were our toys. I could beat Ismail most of the time, so I ended up with nearly all of his most prized possessions. The novelty of losing his toys wore off fairly quickly for Ismail. And, about the same time, I tired of the computer course.

Instead, we decided to turn our attention to other scientific pursuits. We threw our energy into a series of experiments in makeshift laboratories that we created in various parts of my family home. The house was large and we weren't under constant supervision.

It was the same for other kids in the area. While their parents were at work or otherwise occupied, local teenagers would take the keys to the family car on the pretext of cleaning the vehicle. Which they would do. But the real purpose was rather more adventurous—they wanted to take the car for a burnout.

The street outside our house was popular among the local kids for doing burnouts. I hated it, so I decided to take matters into my own hands and discourage the practice. I bought packets of colourful balloons, filled them with water and placed them in the freezer for a couple of days. The idea was that I would drop them in the gutter at the side of the road, tempting the hoons—who would assume these were just standard air-filled balloons and wouldn't be able to resist the urge to drive over them. Regular car drivers would avoid them—but the balloons would be like a red rag to a bull for the local tearaways.

It worked a treat. Many of the teenage drivers targeted the balloons and only realised that nothing was quite as it seemed when they hit a solid object, rather than the exploding balloons they expected. Some cars suffered minor damage, but mostly the experience just gave the drivers a scare so they would think twice about returning to our street. The police were occasionally called, but by the time they arrived, the ice had melted and all they found was the remains of the balloon and a wet patch on the road. The ploy served its purpose.

In another experiment, with my cousin Saheel, I set up a radio station at home. We were ridiculously naive. There was only one radio station in Iraq—and it was strictly controlled by Saddam Hussein. He wasn't about to open the airways to anyone else, even if the rival broadcasters were only a couple of overactive kids!

We started with a Speak & Spell machine. It would speak a word and we would have to spell it on a keyboard. But that didn't keep us occupied for very long. Saheel was extremely knowledgeable about electronics, and somewhere along the line he had obtained a manual describing how to set up a radio station. Using the Speak & Spell machine, we rigged up a radio station that sent a broadcast signal for about a kilometre from my house. So, without any fanfare, we launched ourselves onto Iraq's airwaves.

We were kids. Content wasn't our strong point. So we just blabbed on about anything that came into our heads. But we were smart enough to adopt fake voices so we couldn't be too easily identified.

It didn't take long before we realised the magnitude of the dangers we'd created for ourselves. Within a very short time, we saw police cars everywhere throughout our neighbourhood. We worked out they were trying to pinpoint the source of the new radio station and that the consequences of being uncovered would be dire. We were way out of our depth, so we stopped broadcasting immediately. Then, we quickly dismantled the transmitter to destroy the evidence. The upside was that we had proved we could make a radio transmitter. But, along the way, we had scared ourselves witless!

The next scientific experiment had similarly disturbing consequences. Saheel landed on the idea of some experiments with powerful chemicals. We decided to remove the acid from car batteries, which was dangerous enough. But then we would mix it with things such as toilet bleach powder, which is highly concentrated chlorine. In effect, we were making chlorine gas—the basis for the bombs that the Syrian regime used against its own people during the civil war.

Once we'd created the concoction in the kitchen, we would put it into tomato jars with tightly fitting lids, shake them, run them over to the park opposite my home and throw them onto the grass. The result was reasonably impressive: when the jars burst open, they would release a pretty green-coloured gas. Of course, the small quantity of gas would be a distance away from us and would quickly disperse. It was all quite amusing at the time—but in our naivety, we had absolutely no idea that this stuff was potentially lethal.

Things eventually came to a sticky end. As we were in the kitchen, loading up another selection of jars, one of them exploded. There was a massive chemical reaction that we simply couldn't control. The kitchen was instantly filled with chlorine gas, which drifted through the rest of the house. We beat a hasty retreat from the kitchen and survived to tell the tale.

The impact on the house, however, was much greater. My family was forced to abandon our home for a week while professional cleaners and painters restored the kitchen to its former glory. We rented a farmhouse out of the city as the repair work was undertaken. Not unnaturally, my parents were less impressed by our scientific exploration than we had been. I was grounded for quite a while following that episode.

After calling a hasty end to my radio career, later on—in my days at senior high school and university—I was attracted to the idea of exploring the delights of television. During Saddam's regime there were just two official television channels. Neither was particularly exciting, and one was solely devoted to propaganda about the president. Its transmissions ended late in the evening. The screen would go to electronic snow, and the sound would be the sizzling interference that occurs when no signal is being broadcast. The joke in Iraq at the time was that the sound was Saddam snoring!

Like many of my friends, I was bored with the offerings of the state-run media, so I decided to set up a satellite dish to receive television broadcasts from as many other countries as possible. Of course, this was utterly illegal and punishable by extreme measures—including execution. Saddam's regime deployed helicopters to fly over Baghdad and all the other major cities to detect any illegal satellite dishes. Consequently, my venture was massively risky. I needed to figure out a way to conceal the dish without being obvious.

I plumped for the idea of building a chicken coop in the backyard, covering it with chicken feathers and hiding the satellite dish inside. I managed to buy a dish that had been smuggled into Iraq and installed it with my cousin's help.

Now, of course, this had to remain a tightly held secret among only a few of my most trusted friends. Obviously, my cousin was well aware of what was going on. But I only told a handful of my classmates at the highly regarded Baghdad College high school. Three of them, all from privileged backgrounds, would regularly come to my house.

Haider Inthar Khuther's father was the chief of police in Basra during Saddam Hussein's rule. His name reflects what was going on when he came into the world. Inthar refers to an air-raid siren. He was born during an air raid.

Haider was and is a very funny man. But he's a chameleon—he can change to suit the circumstances. He's a survivor. Originally he was a Sunni Muslim, but he became one of the rare breed of Sunnis who converted to the Shi'ite faith. Now, he says he's neither Sunni nor Shi'ite, but at times he seems to associate closely with the Shi'ite faith. Either way, it's worked for him. He's now the head of emergency services at Baghdad University Hospital—the most prestigious hospital in Iraq.

Mohammed Faiz Mussa's father was the Syrian president in exile. Uras Abdul Rahman al-Ani was from Ramadi, and his father was the president of the University of Anbar.

We were aware of the risk we were taking and, because we weren't sure how the helicopters detected illegal dishes, we decided caution was the best policy. Most of our viewing was late at night when the helicopters weren't flying.

Despite the fear of being discovered by the authorities, the venture did pay ample rewards. Far from being restricted to dull Iraqi television and Saddam's propaganda, a whole new world of programs opened up before us. We watched international channels from Israel, Turkey and Italy, as well as Germany's Deutsche Welle. And we also had the most prized asset—access to MTV. The dish was never discovered.

By the time we had graduated to medical school, the group of three—plus my friend from primary school, Mohannad Yusef—would come to my house to drink alcohol and play cards. Drinking alcohol wasn't that unusual in Iraq in those days.

I think a lot of our activities underlined the fact that we were living by our own rules. We had a lot of growing up to do, and our experiences over the coming years brought about a rapid mellowing of our approach to life.

3

THE FLAG BEARER

My introduction to Australia was far from my carefree and experimental childhood in Baghdad. Ten months of imprisonment—much of it in solitary confinement—in Curtin Detention Centre in the north-west of Western Australia was hell on earth. But finally I was recognised as a genuine refugee and was released.

In 2000, I set about establishing a medical career in my new country, and I qualified as an orthopaedic surgeon in 2008. It was a moment of supreme satisfaction after years of hard work. Australia's orthopaedic training program and exams are renowned as being among the toughest in the medical profession. But qualifying was just the start of the long, hard road.

The medical world is like the animal kingdom—only the fittest survive and thrive. When you start out as a student or resident, you're like a small, furry animal. Let's say a guinea pig. You're regarded as cute. You're pleasant, and people like you.

Then you develop and decide that you want to be an orthopaedic surgeon. You change and become something like a monkey. You're constantly trying to attract everyone's attention. You make a lot of noise and jump around so others notice you. A lot of the time you're clumsy and you don't really know what you're doing. You become a pest.

Once you earn a place on the orthopaedic training program, it's unusual for a doctor not to reach their goal. It takes a minimum of four years, and for some it can take much longer. But, sooner or later, there's every chance you'll qualify. At that point, you become a gorilla. You start to throw your weight around. No one can touch you. You have such a high opinion of yourself that you think it's okay to be rude to the nursing and hospital staff.

After that, you become a consultant. You are now like a hyena, feeding on what remains of the carcass when the animals further up the food chain have finished their meal. You pick up the scraps left by the established consultants. They're the lions. As a junior consultant, you try to do anything and everything. To start with, you don't get any theatre time—you have to wait for the older surgeons to finish before you get access. That means you're operating late at night. You get whatever support staff you can. And you do all the trauma surgery that no one else wants.

Depending on your skill level, you may remain a hyena for the rest of your career. But if you prove yourself along the way, you are transformed into a lion cub. Other medical professionals start to recognise you and refer cases your way. You become involved in more interesting cases. You might be given operating time in a small theatre at a reasonable time of day. And you even take on your choice of staff.

Then, when you grow into a fully fledged lion, you're given access to everything you want, as long as you follow the leader of the pride—the Lion King. As it is in the jungle, to become the leader you have to challenge the Lion King. But the stakes are high. If you lose, you get thrown out of the fraternity to fare on your own. If you win, you become the new Lion King.

So, where am I? To the most conservative of a very conservative and male-dominated profession, I'm an outsider. I don't want to be part of the boys' club. There are always a few people who are trying to fight me. But I have better things to do. I stick to providing the very best patient care I can and leave the politics and infighting to the others.

Within a short time of qualifying as an orthopaedic surgeon, I decided to pursue my long-term fascination with osseointegration. I had been gripped by the notion of combining humans and machines since I was twelve, when I was fired up by James Cameron's 1984 movie *The Terminator*, which starred

Arnold Schwarzenegger as a cyborg assassin. At the time, it was the stuff of fantasy. But, increasingly, technology was making it possible to replace damaged limbs with high-tech mechanical parts.

Swedish physician Professor Per-Ingvar Branemark coined the term 'osseointegration' in the early 1950s. He expanded on the work of other scientists, who had discovered that bone completely integrates with titanium. As often happens in the scientific community, initially there was widespread scepticism about Branemark's work. And, indeed, it took until 1983 for his findings to be generally acknowledged at a conference in Toronto. Dentists had been using the procedure for tooth implants since the 1960s, but it wasn't until the 1990s that surgeons started using osseointegration for the first implants on above-the-knee amputees.

Two separate approaches emerged. Both originally involved two stages, but the details differed. One system, developed by Professor Branemark, follows the same principles as dental implants. A threaded titanium rod is screwed into the bone canal—in the case of above-the-knee amputations, the femur. The implant is designed to protrude slightly, so an artificial limb can be clipped on. The drawback with this version of osseointegration is that it might be six months before the bone and the titanium rod fuse. After that, the new limb can be attached and the patient can start learning to walk again. Altogether, it can take anything up to twelve months before the patient is fully mobile—which is a long time.

The other system was pioneered by German engineer Hans Grundei. His work was taken up by orthopaedic surgeon Dr Horst Aschoff, who's based in Lübeck in northern Germany. This system involves hammering the chrome cobalt rod into place in the bone canal—a technique that allows patients to weight-bear on the amputated limb within hours. After only a few weeks, an artificial leg is clipped onto the implant, and the patient can begin walking. Recovery is generally much faster than with Branemark's approach.

In order to focus my attention on osseointegration, my Russian-born then wife Irina and I moved to Berlin. There, as well as practising as a surgeon, I studied through Charite University and was instructed in the osseointegration technique by Dr Aschoff.

I took time to examine what I thought would be the future direction of osseointegration and the potential for carrying out the operation in Australia. I was optimistic that it could be a useful addition to my practice. But my initial assessment was that it would only ever be a small sideline. Hip and knee replacements would always be the cornerstone of my work as an orthopaedic surgeon. I had absolutely no idea osseointegration would take off the way it has. And, in the early days at least, it didn't occur to me that I would be treating patients from all over the world.

Nothing like that was in my sights when I returned to Sydney after close to a year in Germany, ready to put my knowledge into practice and lead the first osseointegration operation of my career. I was equipped with a state-of-the-art understanding of the latest techniques. What I didn't have was hands-on experience in leading the operating team. And, of course, patients!

While I had been away, a handful of osseointegration operations had been performed in Melbourne. But the uptake was slow. All the same, news that procedures were being carried out had filtered through to potential patients. As had the fact that I was keen to introduce the German osseointegration technique.

Before long, I was contacted by a couple of amputees who were interested in undergoing osseointegration. The first was Steve Borton, who now lives in Margate on the Redcliffe Peninsula, north-east of Brisbane. Steve had been a career soldier, serving with the Australian Army and then joining the Rhodesian Army because there was little chance of frontline action with the Australian forces.

In June 1978, Steve, who was a lieutenant, led his troops on a two-week raid into Mozambique. Everyone was exhausted as they returned to base, and Steve—by his own admission—did what officers are taught not to do. Because the soldiers under his command were showing signs of fatigue, he moved to the front through an area that had been heavily mined. He stepped on one of the devices and was blown up. Within days, his right leg became gangrenous and was amputated, first through the knee and later above the knee.

Resolve and determination meant that Steve was reasonably successful in his use of the standard socket prosthesis, but he was having to cope with constant chafing, cuts, pain and sweating because of the effort required to walk. With his wife, Steve visited me at Macquarie University Hospital in Sydney's north-west. We discussed the operation, and he was keen to go ahead. The only problem was that he'd scheduled a motorcycle road trip down Route 66 in the United States just five months later. We decided it would be best for him to complete that journey with his socket prosthesis, then come back to see me. Someone else would have to be the first Australian to undergo the procedure.

Shortly afterwards, I was contacted by Brendan Burkett, Professor of Health and Sports Sciences at the University of the Sunshine Coast in Maroochydore, Queensland. Brendan is a fascinating person. In his youth he was a talented sportsman. He swam competitively, taking part in the Queensland State and Australian National Championships. He also played high-level rugby league and rugby union and, at the age of 21, toured New Zealand with the Queensland Country Rugby Union representative team.

He was hoping to carve out a future in league. But a year later, on 19 December 1985, his dreams were shattered when a car hit his motorbike. The driver didn't stop. Brendan's left leg was shattered by the impact—broken in thirteen places. His pelvis was fractured in three places. Ten days later, doctors amputated the damaged leg.

Clearly, Brendan couldn't play league anymore. But he still wanted to be involved in competitive sport, so he focused all his efforts on swimming. Over the years, he achieved remarkable success. In 1987, Brendan represented Australia at the Pan Pacific Para Swimming Championships, where he won a gold medal in the 100-metre butterfly.

He won a silver medal at the 1988 Seoul Paralympics, bronze at the 1992 Barcelona Games and silver at the 1994 Para Commonwealth Games in Victoria, Canada, before captaining the Australian Paralympic team in Atlanta in 1996. There he won gold in the 50-metre freestyle S9 event and silver in the 4 x 100-metre freestyle in the S7–10 category. Those performances also earned him an Order of Australia medal.

Two years later, Brendan was a member of the Australian 4 x 100-metre freestyle relay team that not only won the gold medal, but also broke the world record at the IPC Swimming World Championships in Christchurch.

Then came one of his proudest sporting moments. Brendan was chosen to carry the Australian flag at the Sydney Paralympic Games in 2000. He went on to win a silver medal in the 4 x 100-metre freestyle relay and retired from competitive swimming at the end of those Games.

Although he was achieving so much in the pool and in his profession, Brendan was experiencing many of the difficulties associated with standard artificial legs: constant chafing, blisters and occasional cuts where the prosthesis rubbed on what remained of his left leg, as well as sweating. Brendan remembers one particular incident. After going to the shops for a newspaper and coffee on a Saturday morning, as he was strolling back across the road, he spotted a car coming. He started to walk faster—only for his artificial leg to fall off in the middle of the street. At the very least, this situation was severely embarrassing; at most, it was potentially fatal.

When I first met Brendan, I realised he was the perfect candidate for osseointegration. He'd thoroughly researched the operation and, through his sporting background and his work, he had a deep understanding of the biomechanics of the human body. He'd also familiarised himself with the implications of the procedure.

Brendan had been looking for alternatives to his socket leg and, in 2004, discovered osseointegration. When he travelled to competitions in Europe with the Australian para swim team, he contacted and met osseointegration surgeons and patients in Sweden and Germany. He also read stories about the procedure in biomechanics publications.

At that stage, he couldn't track down any Australian surgeons who were performing osseointegration. He toyed with the prospect of travelling to Sweden to undergo surgery with Professor Branemark. His wife, Cathy, who's a trained nurse, urged caution.

Then, by chance, during an appointment with his prosthetist in Brisbane, Brendan picked up a brochure about osseointegration. He made a couple of phone calls to orthopaedic surgeons he knew from playing rugby and eventually tracked me down.

By the time we met, Brendan was already, in his own words, about 70 per cent committed to going ahead with the operation. And, after originally favouring the Swedish procedure, he had now switched his preference to the German system because he believed the Branemark screw-in approach would create more high-stress points in the leg. Brendan's enthusiasm to undergo surgery left the ball in my court. I was young, and it was a difficult decision.

I was frank when we spoke, telling him that I had never performed the operation but had studied and observed several procedures in Germany. I left Brendan to have a think about things and let me know his final decision.

The situation became more complicated when the initial X-rays were delivered. They revealed that Brendan's left femur was severely deformed. It had set incorrectly after the initial amputation and was twisted into the shape of a shepherd's crook. We had three options: decide it's too hard and not proceed with the operation; accept the deformity and go ahead anyway; or rectify the deformity and then start the osseointegration process.

From my point of view, there was only one option—fix the deformity, then embark on osseointegration. Brendan was unfazed, and he agreed with my recommendation. So, we went through the detailed planning. The most immediate need was to straighten the bone and attach a plate to secure it. Which we did. After about three months, we planned to remove the plate and proceed with the osseointegration.

As if carrying out my first osseointegration operation wasn't stressful enough, Brendan's case turned out to be one of the most complex of my career. But by separating the procedure into two stages, it became a more straightforward process.

Brendan arrived for the osseointegration procedure, was given the anaesthetic and was wheeled into the theatre. But as I was about to start the operation, I found an infected in-growing hair on his leg—exactly where the scar would be. I had no choice. There was a significant risk of cross infection. I debrided the area around the infection and postponed the operation.

Around a month later, Brendan returned to Macquarie University Hospital, and everything was prepared for the operation. That day, 25 November 2010, was accompanied by a significant bout of anxiety on my part. I had invited my professor from Kiel University in Germany, Dr Ludger Gerdesmeyer, to advise. Like me, he had watched osseointegration surgery but had never actually been directly involved. I'd also spoken to a prosthetist, Stefan Laux, briefing him that I was ready to go ahead with my first osseointegration operation. Cautiously, he agreed to help.

We started by setting up and implementing the osseointegration protocols used in Germany. Although we were meticulously prepared, I'd be lying if I suggested it was just another routine shift in the operating theatre. It wasn't. Like the first time for most things, the whole procedure was nerve-racking. I was a long way from Germany and Sweden—and the experts who had all the experience.

Brendan hadn't been able to wear his socket prosthesis for the intervening months—the longest period he'd spent on crutches in 25 years. He was pretty keen to get on with things.

He has since described being apprehensive but excited as he was wheeled into the operating theatre.

We completed the first of the two osseointegration operations in around three hours, using a custom-made implant from the German company ESKA. There were no complications or surprises along the way.

A month or so later, Brendan underwent a second operation to attach the fitting that would link the rod to his new robotic leg. As I reopened the wound, fluid gushed out of a bursa. I'd never seen that before, but by that point we were committed. I cleaned the wound and continued to fit the connectors. After that, it all went smoothly. Brendan remembers that as he emerged from the theatre, still drugged and dazed from the anaesthetic, he reached down, felt the new attachment and thought, 'You beauty!'

We kept Brendan in hospital for around three weeks to monitor his progress and supervise weight-bearing exercises to prepare for the new robotic leg to be attached. Within days of being fitted, Brendan started walking with his new prosthesis using the parallel bars in the small hospital gym. That moment was brilliant—a triumph for me and completely liberating for Brendan.

Being a high-level athlete, Brendan was familiar with following a strict fitness regime, and he committed to the rehab schedule we set for him. He was determined to walk out of the hospital, so he approached the task with complete focus.

He progressed from the parallel bars to walking—first with

Prince Harry visits my clinic at Macquarie University Hospital in May 2015 to find out more about osseointegration. PETER PARKS, AAP IMAGES

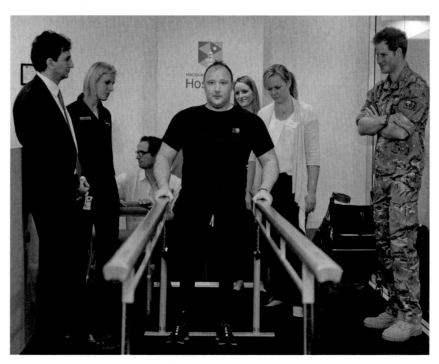

Prince Harry looks on as Lieutenant Alistair Spearing, the fourth British soldier to come to Australia for osseointegration, learns to use his new robotic legs. Alistair lost both legs above the knee serving in Afghanistan in 2011 when an IED exploded. PETER PARKS, AAP IMAGES

Perhaps the most recognisable landmark in Baghdad: the famous crossed scimitars guarding the ends of the military parade ground built by Saddam Hussein's regime.

One of the armed escort vehicles in the convoy carrying me and my team along what was once known as Death Road—the most dangerous road in the world—from Baghdad International Airport to the Green Zone. The crack across the windscreen was caused by a bullet.

Our convoy stopped at one of the military checkpoints on the road from the airport to the Prime Minister's Guest House.

The Prime Minister's Guest House, an imposing five-star hotel in Baghdad's Green Zone, where we stayed.

An Iraqi armoured vehicle guards a checkpoint at the crossing from the Green Zone into the Red Zone of Baghdad.

The Baghdad Rowing Club stands as a reminder that daily life in Baghdad was once 'normal'.

Pedestrian bridge over the Tigris River near Mutanabbi Street, close to the old quarter of the city. Barricades and armed police vehicles are strategically placed to maintain security.

Anything and everything is on sale at the chaotic Friday street market in what used to be Baghdad's bus station near the old city.

The presence of the security forces is never far away in the Red Zone—just around the corner from Mutanabbi Street.

A typical street of shops and apartments in the Red Zone, Baghdad.

A busy intersection at night in the eastern part of Baghdad.

Just beyond the functioning façade of Baghdad a damaged building remains derelict as a lingering reminder of the wars that have raged through the city.

The view along the Tigris River towards the Medical City facility (far right) where I worked before escaping Iraq with my life in 1999.

Abu Nuwas Street, lined with restaurants and bars along the banks of the Tigris, was once the busy centre of Baghdad's nightlife. Now it lies derelict and all but deserted.

Security men from the Prime Minister's Department accompany us on our sightseeing excursion to Abu Nuwas Street, a place I visited in my youth.

Anaesthetist Dr Ash Sehgal, physiotherapist Claudia Roberts and me walking down memory lane on Abu Nuwas Street in Baghdad, with our entourage following close behind.
ASH SEHGAL

Sunset over the Tigris River.

Solitary Iraqi soldiers armed with machine guns are stationed at irregular intervals along the largely disused Abu Nuwas Street. Here, one of them poses with Patrick Weaver.

A cup of tea, sir? A tea seller inside the grounds of Al Qushla, once an Ottoman-era military barracks and now home to the Baghdad Cultural Centre.

The world's largest cemetery, Wadi Al-Salam ('Valley of Peace') is located within the city of Najaf, south of Baghdad. More than five million people are believed to be buried here.

The golden dome and minarets of the Imam Ali Mosque in Najaf, widely considered to be the holiest city in Iraq to Shi'ites. More than eight million pilgrims visit the mosque each year.

Exquisite tilework decorates the outside walls of the Imam Ali Mosque. Originally constructed in 977 AD and rebuilt many times since, the bulk of the current structure dates to the year 1500.

Worshippers gather on carpets outside the Imam Ali Mosque before joining Friday prayers.

Along with the worshippers at Friday prayers, I touch the silver bars surrounding the tomb of Imam Ali ibn Abi Talib.

Inside the Imam Ali Mosque. The shrine houses the tomb of Imam Ali ibn Abi Talib, cousin of the Prophet Mohammed and the first imam (according to Shi'ite belief) and fourth caliph.

Inside the Imam Ali Mosque. From left to right: guide (with face covered); Sophie McNeill, ABC TV journalist; Michelle Nairne, my personal assistant; Simmy Masuku, theatre nurse; and Claudia Roberts, wearing the mandatory head coverings.

Taking afternoon tea with the Ayatollah of Karbala, in his reception area at the shrine of Imam Husayn. Left to right: Patrick Weaver, me, the Ayatollah and a representative of Hashd.

The magnificent internal architecture of the shrine of Imam Husayn in Karbala.

The ornate exterior of the shrine of Imam Husayn.

crutches and then with walking sticks. He left the hospital with a single walking stick, which, quite rightly, he regarded as mission accomplished.

Gradually, he weaned himself off the walking stick—at first taking a couple of independent steps in the kitchen of his home. The next day, he added one or two more steps. Over the next three weeks, he increased the distance he was covering until he could finally get rid of all the artificial aids and walk entirely on his own. These days, when he wears full-length pants, you'd be hard-pressed to know that Brendan is an amputee.

He believes osseointegration changed his life. 'For 25 years, I had a high level of quality of life,' he has since explained. 'I competed at the top level of international swimming; I was married, had kids and had a good job. But there was daily discomfort—especially with the chafing, blistering and sweating involved with wearing the socket prosthesis.

'If I had to walk anywhere, I would ask myself whether I really needed to make the journey. I would only walk when I really had to. And I'd sit down and work out the shortest way to get there.

'There's been a dramatic improvement since the osseo-integration operation. The robotic leg is very different from the socket version. The comfort factor is through the roof. There's no chafing, blistering or pain—unless you have an infection, but that rarely happens, and it's easily dealt with.

'Then there's the functional component. You have much greater control over where your foot lands. It's really like walking with your natural leg. You also have much greater feedback on the surface you're standing on. You can tell whether it's a hard surface or something like sand.

'On top of that, you have proper musculo-skeletal growth. The soft tissue in my leg and backside was withering away, and the bone on that side was osteoporotic. Three or four years after osseointegration, I developed normal muscles in my leg and I have butt muscles! The bone density in my left leg is now in the normal range and is exactly the same as my right leg. Now, I walk because I want to. Every day, I get up between 5.30 and 6.30 a.m. and go for a two- or three-kilometre walk on the beach.'

— —

Nine months later, I operated on young Sydneysider Mitch Grant. Mitch was a personal trainer in his early twenties and, like Brendan, had lost his left leg above the knee in a motor-cycle accident. He'd also damaged the ulna nerve in his right arm. A short time after undergoing osseointegration, Mitch was back at work at Good Vibes Fitness in Macquarie Park, which he owns and manages.

By December 2011, Steve Borton had returned from his motorcycling jaunt in the United States and was raring to go. Steve, who was 58 at the time, had tried a wide variety of socket prostheses and ploughed on even though they weren't ideal. 'I never complained,' he said. 'I would ride bikes, run and scuba dive. But the artificial leg was an incumbrance because of the chafing and sweating.' He was helped by his wife, a physiotherapist who provided an exercise regime to keep him fit.

He first heard of osseointegration when a Swedish medical team visited the Royal Brisbane and Women's Hospital in 2005. He listened carefully to the presentation and, at the conclusion, put his hand in the air and proclaimed, 'I'll do it!'

The visiting Swedes explained that they were operating only on people who were wheelchair bound—not amputees who were walking with socket prostheses. Steve persisted and was eventually told that because there was no support mechanism in Australia, he would have to travel to Sweden for the operation and would need to spend a year living there. The prospect didn't appeal to him.

The best part of six years later, I was able to perform the osseointegration procedure on Steve. Since the operation, Steve—who, you've probably guessed, is a larger-than-life char-acter—hasn't looked back. 'This is the best thing since canned beer,' he said. 'I've never had any problems from start to finish.

'There's really no comparison. This is a thousand times better. The most distinctive difference is that I can feel my new foot before it touches the ground. With socket legs, you never know where your foot is until it lands on the surface.

'Two-legged creatures have no idea how important it is to know where your feet are without having to look for them while you're walking. It's the difference between walking normally and struggling. And you can sense the surface you're walking on—whether it's a hard surface, grass or sand.

'I'm a big guy, and I've always been pretty active. When I used the socket leg, I would get cuts on the back of my leg. It would be rubbed raw much of the time. It was awful. Some days, I would come home angry because of the pain and the profuse sweating. I would throw the leg across the room with frustration.'

Steve's now involved in martial arts as well as his other physical activities. He wakes up in his waterfront home, looks at the waves and decides whether he'll stroll to the beach for a swim that morning. 'My only regret is that I couldn't do it [the operation] 25 years earlier,' he says.

After these early operations, the media and other hospitals started to take an interest in osseointegration. However, far from being a positive breakthrough, this was where my problems started. The laws of the orthopaedic surgery jungle took over.

It's extremely difficult to break into the orthopaedic clan. Surgeons can make a lucrative living, essentially working as small-business people. They don't take kindly to new kids on the block, who they see as outsiders and a potential threat to their income.

By nature, orthopaedic surgery is an evidence-based profession. Surgeons need plenty of evidence before they'll change practices. Typically, brand-new techniques can take anything between ten and twenty years of peer-reviewed research papers before they're widely accepted. In many ways, that's a good thing. It prevents surgeons effectively experimenting on patients with unproven techniques or technology. But it can result in a reluctance to change and move with the times.

After my early osseointegration operations, I was accused by other surgeons—inaccurately, I might add—of all sorts of things. I was called a maverick and was told I was endangering patients. For the record, I wasn't and never would.

I started noticing that some colleagues would avoid talking to me. Others, many of them surgeons I considered mentors, would talk to me—but only to inform me that I was bringing the profession and the people who were associated with me into disrepute.

A couple of senior orthopaedic surgeons even took it upon themselves to carry out extensive and, frankly, bizarre investigations into my activities. And eventually had to admit that they could find no damaging evidence.

At the time, none of the allegations made any sense to me. They still don't. I really took it to heart, though. I didn't understand why these people thought that I posed a genuine threat to the safety of the public and the reputation of the profession.

I guess I was naive. The laws of the jungle of orthopaedic surgery didn't occur to me at the time. But it didn't stop me. In 2017 I completed my 500th osseointegration operation in Australia.

4

WHEN HARRY MET MUNJED

In the eighteen months after my first osseointegration operation in Sydney, I set about establishing a more formal support structure. I created a full team to assess and recommend patients: psychologists, anaesthetists, orthopaedic fellows, nurses, pain-management professionals, perioperative-care managers, physiotherapists, prosthetists, rehabilitation experts, biomedical engineers and an amputee representative.

The team examines every potential osseointegration patient. We've created strict inclusion and exclusion criteria. In Australia, for example, we rule out children, pregnant women, current smokers or people who've smoked in the last three months, diabetics, people with peripheral vascular disease, anyone receiving active chemotherapy or who has irradiated bone. And we must be convinced patients will be prepared to follow our instructions.

Word that the new procedure was available spread quickly. And it wasn't long before inquiries started coming in from potential patients in other countries.

In his home town of Nelson on New Zealand's South Island, Phill Coulson runs a company supporting people living with mental health issues. One of Phill's hobbies is restoring rare Ducati motorcycles.

In October 2010, he was taking the first ride on his latest restored motorbike when he collided with a campervan on a country lane in Nelson. He lost his right leg above the knee in the accident.

Because of an allergy to silicon, Phill was having trouble with the liners for the socket prosthesis. He started researching more suitable alternatives and soon found my mobile number. Phill called me as I was driving to another osseointegration operation.

He then flew across the Tasman to find out whether he was suitable for the procedure. He was—and in March 2012, he became my first international osseointegration patient. The surgery wasn't straightforward, and there were a number of complications. But the procedure did successfully restore Phill's mobility.

'I have a young family, and I wanted the best system in the world so I could share as much as possible with them,'

Phill says. 'We have a tennis court and a swimming pool at home. I play tennis and go swimming. I do boxing and go to the gym. I even considered climbing Mount Kilimanjaro with a friend—but, in the end, he couldn't make it.'

Phill contacted the New Zealand media and told them he was coming to Australia for osseointegration. The two operations were filmed by the TV3 current-affairs show *Campbell Live*, hosted by John Campbell. After coverage of the operations went to air, Phill was dubbed New Zealand's first Bionic Man. His motivation wasn't individual fame or fortune, though. Rather, Phill wanted to raise awareness of people with a disability and the need for the expansion of support services.

Another Kiwi, Iain McGregor, watched Phill on television and immediately wanted to undergo osseointegration. He contacted me in Sydney and, in April 2012, he came over for the first stage of his surgery.

Iain's a typically dry, unflappable farmer from the small town of Otorohanga in the King Country, not far from the North Island city of Hamilton. You may or may not have heard of Otorohanga, but it has carved out a bit of an offbeat reputation.

In the late 1980s, Mohamed Al Fayed—then owner of the Harrods department store in London—launched legal action claiming exclusive worldwide rights to the name Harrods. He wanted to force anyone who operated a retail business under the name of Harrods to drop it.

Henry Harrod owned a fish and chip shop in Palmerston North on New Zealand's North Island, and he had a shingle outside his shop saying 'Harrod's Fish and Chips'. Because of Al Fayed's legal action, it had to go. The whole of New Zealand closed ranks behind Henry, and the town of Otorohanga even went as far as officially changing its name to Harrodsville!

As a result, there was a hue and cry in the British media, which set its sights on Al Fayed and unmercifully lambasted him until he backtracked and dropped the lawsuit. At that point, Harrodsville reverted to its original identity.

These days, Otorohanga is best known as a tourist attraction for its display of 'kiwiana' in the main street, including representations of New Zealand icons such as the flightless kiwi bird, farm dogs, the All Blacks and pavlova. Although I think the average Australian might have something to say about the origins of the pavlova!

Iain's laidback approach to life very much reflects the community where he lives. This relaxed existence was shattered in February 2012. The then 48-year-old Iain set out along the nearby main road on his Harley Davidson. A fully loaded logging truck pulled out from a side road and started driving up a steep hill. As he approached from behind, Iain misjudged how slowly the truck was travelling and crashed into the back of the heavy vehicle.

He remained conscious and looked down to see the left leg of his motorcycle leathers was ripped from ankle to thigh. Shattered fragments of bone were visible through the torn leathers. From his experience with injured animals on the farm,

Iain knew what to expect. Rather than being thrown into a blind panic, he recalls thinking, 'Looks like that leg's buggered. I wonder whether I can still drive a tractor.'

Iain's left leg was amputated above the knee. He was measured up for a socket prosthesis, but it was never actually fitted. Within four months of the accident, he had a new robotic leg—my first patient to go straight from amputation to osseointegration.

He's had absolutely no medical problems with the new leg, although he did bend the implant when he slipped on a wet surface. Eighteen months later, the shaft of the implant snapped. He was on crutches for seven months—a restriction that nearly drove him crazy—before the implant was removed and replaced by a surgeon in New Zealand who'd observed his original operation.

Iain's a mechanic by trade, and is a resourceful character. He carried on with his dairy farming for around a year after losing his leg, but reluctantly gave it away when the lease on the property ran out and the contract terms changed. He turned his attention to buying and renovating houses in the area— carrying out the plumbing and electrical repairs himself and even climbing on roofs when necessary.

In 2018, Iain and his partner bought a 100-hectare farm— which at one stage had been owned by former All Blacks captain Sir Colin Meads—in nearby Te Kuiti. He runs sheep and beef cattle on the property and is president of the local Sheep Dog Trial Association.

Iain is philosophical about the accident, but makes the most of the quality of life his robotic leg provides. 'Everyone gets dealt shit,' he says matter-of-factly. 'Things happen to people all the time. It's how you deal with the shit that's important. I wear shorts most of the time, but if I have long pants on and I'm walking on a flat surface, no one knows that I have an artificial leg.

'I miss being able to jog. It would come in handy when I'm trying to catch a lamb or a calf. That's a bit of a pain. But I've bought an automatic motorcycle that helps me get around the place. Other than that, it hasn't really slowed me down. In fact, it has made me stronger.'

One patient who'd been injured in more unusual circumstances was another New Zealander, Brian Coker.

Tuesday, 22 February 2011 started out as little more than a standard working day for Brian. He'd dropped his wife, Helen, at the airport, as she was flying to Palmerston North to visit relatives. Then he'd driven into the Central Business District of Christchurch, the largest city on New Zealand's South Island, to his job as a financial planner in the Pyne Gould Corporation (PGC) building on Cambridge Terrace. He'd spent the morning at his desk on the first floor, next to a window overlooking the Avon River.

Just before one o'clock, Brian—who was only a couple of weeks away from his 53rd birthday—decided to head out into the fresh air and sunshine. He left his office and walked to the top of the sweeping staircase that led down to the foyer. On reaching the landing, he felt the building start to shake. Minor tremors weren't unusual in Christchurch, so Brian assumed these were nothing out of the ordinary. He was wrong. This was a massive earthquake that, in a matter of minutes, destroyed much of Christchurch.

Brian grabbed the balustrade to steady himself. But the shaking intensified . . . and the building started to collapse around him. Before he could escape, Brian was thrown onto his back and was covered in debris. The noise was deafening. Amid the chaos, Brian's legs were pinned under a concrete beam.

In agony, he instantly assumed most of Christchurch had been flattened by the tremor. He feared the emergency services would be overwhelmed. There would be no hope of rescue or escape.

Brian decided to bid a last farewell to his beloved family while he was still conscious and capable. He found his mobile phone in his pocket and sent a final text message to Helen. The message was frank. There had been an earthquake. He was trapped under rubble at work and didn't think he'd get out alive. Then he added the most important part. 'Never forget how much I love you.'

Next, Brian sent a text to their son, Jonathan, who was at university in Christchurch, asking whether he was okay and outlining his own circumstances. This time, for no particular reason, he mentioned exactly where he was trapped in the PGC building.

Finally, he tried to send an SMS to their daughter, Olivia, in Auckland. But by now, the mobile networks were overwhelmed, and there was no connection. He switched off the phone to preserve the battery, on the off-chance it would be needed later.

The concrete beam had pinned his legs above the knees. Brian wasn't aware of the full extent of his injuries, but he could feel blood dripping down the remains of his legs. 'The pain was excruciating,' he recalled. 'It's hard to believe the human body can endure such pain. But, at the same time, I felt reasonably calm. I think I had simply accepted the inevitability of the situation and that there was little or nothing I could do.'

Brian could hear screaming from others trapped in the debris, but in the darkness had no idea exactly where they were or what their situation was.

'I went through some wild mood swings,' he recalls. 'At some points I wished for one more huge aftershock to bring the rest of the building down on me. At others I arranged wooden panels over my head to protect me from rubble falls. Why? I have no idea. I didn't think there was even a remote chance of being rescued. Maybe there's an inherent will to survive in all of us.'

Brian drifted in and out of consciousness. He sensed he was becoming weaker as the hours passed and the blood was literally draining from his body. He made another effort to switch on his mobile phone, but by now his condition had deteriorated so much he couldn't focus on the screen.

Going Back

In Palmerston North, Helen had made contact with their son, who told her where Brian was in the collapsed building. Unbeknown to Brian, Helen dialled 111 and was connected to the National Crisis Management Centre in Wellington. She passed on the vital information about her husband's whereabouts.

Out of the blue—and more than four hours after the earthquake—a rescuer pushed his way through the rubble and made contact with Brian.

'Hello . . . what's your name?'

'Brian Coker.'

'Are you married?'

'Yes.'

'Do you have any kids?'

'Yes. Two.'

'How old are they?' The questions went on.

The rescuer left, reassuring Brian that someone else would be back to see him shortly. Soon, another emergency service officer wriggled through the debris and asked the same questions. Then a third rescuer approached Brian . . . and repeated the list of questions. It reached the point where Brian felt like saying, 'How about you talk to the last guy? He has all the information!'

Eventually, though, Brian realised that the point of the questions wasn't to confirm his identity. They were to keep him conscious and as alert as possible. One rescuer asked Brian if he played any sport. 'A bit of squash,' was the ironic reply.

Around five hours after the quake struck, Dr Bryce Curran—a Christchurch-based anaesthetist—edged his way towards Brian. He explained that he was there to help and started cutting through the legs of Brian's pants. Australian urologist Dr Lydia Johns-Putra, from Ballarat, had been attending a conference nearby. She joined them in the wreckage of the building.

Outside, the newly qualified paramedic on duty didn't usually have approval to carry ketamine, a strong anaesthetic. But before he left the base, he'd asked higher-ranking officers for special permission to be equipped with the powerful drug. He was quickly given the go-ahead. By an odd coincidence, the approval came from Brian's paramedic brother—who had no idea of the identity of the patient who would soon be in need of the anaesthetic.

After applying the ketamine, Dr Curran and Dr Johns-Putra set about their task. Nothing could prepare them for the events that were about to unfold. Rather than the standard floodlights of an operating theatre, the only sources of light inside the collapsed building were the torches held by firefighters. The surgical instruments were equally basic: a Leatherman knife—a pocketknife normally used on camping trips—and a hacksaw, which had been sourced from the Fire Brigade. To complicate matters further, major aftershocks struck the area as the delicate procedure was underway.

Remarkably, the operation to amputate one of Brian's legs was successful. His other leg was freed and he was carried outside to the care of another Australian urologist, Dr Stuart Philip from Brisbane, who was waiting with an ambulance.

Brian was rushed to Christchurch Hospital. His life was hanging in the balance. He'd lost most of his blood and, with his vital signs diminishing, a cardiac arrest was an imminent prospect. When he arrived in the Emergency Department, the medical specialists actively discussed the level of care he should be given. They decided Brian had a reasonable chance of survival—but only if his other leg was amputated. His wounds were cleaned in the operating theatre, and his condition stabilised. He needed 46 units of blood.

Within eighteen hours, he was transferred to a hospital in Hamilton. At the time, Helen was philosophical, but forthright. 'We don't care about his legs. He is alive. We will carry on,' she said.

Over the coming weeks, Brian learned that the colleague who worked next to him had died at his desk. Seventeen more people perished in the rubble of the PGC building. It was pure chance that Brian had decided to duck outside in those seconds before the earthquake struck.

Brian spent six weeks in hospital in Hamilton and another six weeks in a rehabilitation facility in the city, under the guidance of his wife, who was a nurse. They returned home to a house that had suffered minor damage in the quake.

Brian remained in a wheelchair until September 2011, when he was fitted with socket prostheses. He could walk with them, but only with difficulty—and plenty of pain. He persisted for six months, but then watched the current-affairs show covering Phill Coulson's osseointegration operation.

Brian and Helen contacted me and came to Sydney to check whether he was suitable for the procedure. He was. However, they struggled to raise all the money they needed for his operation. Hours before he was due to fly to Australia for the second operation, the finance finally came through.

A surgeon from New Zealand also came over, and I've helped develop his skills in osseointegration. He has since carried out more than a dozen of the operations across the Tasman.

Brian's surgery was a success, and he now walks each day. He chooses to use two walking sticks, largely for a sense of security. 'It's a mental issue as much as anything,' he explains. 'Rather than anything else, I want to feel safe.'

While he's in the house, Brian mainly uses a wheelchair. But when he and Helen are working in the extensive garden of their new home on a 3600-square-metre block, Brian operates on short, stubby artificial legs with no knees.

'Osseointegration has made an immeasurable difference,' he says. 'I'm convinced that without osseointegration I wouldn't have been able to walk. It's given me a life outside a wheelchair. It's reopened a whole world for me.'

In February 2015, Brian's new life included walking his daughter down the aisle for her wedding in Christchurch.

Up to this point, Steve Borton was the only former military person I'd performed osseointegration on. The others had all been civilians.

Going Back

However, amid deepening global conflicts—especially in Iraq and Afghanistan—thousands of soldiers from Western nations were being exposed to weapons and battlefield tactics that had been designed to maim as well as kill.

Truck and car bombs, individual suicide bombers and other IEDs were the weapons of choice for jihadist movements such as Al-Qaeda and various militia groups. In addition, conventional artillery shells, RPGs, mortars and bullets were inflicting horrific wounds on soldiers and civilians.

Casualty numbers were rising rapidly, especially amputees. There were more amputees than in previous decades because advances in medical treatment meant more people were surviving devastating injuries. At the time, I couldn't help reflecting on the words of the ancient Greek physician Hippocrates, who said that the only proper school for the surgeon is war.

By the end of the first decade of the 21st century, the British Army had suffered a huge death toll in Afghanistan, and thousands more soldiers with amputated limbs were being airlifted home. Above- and below-the-knee amputees would be sent to the military rehabilitation centre at Headley Court in Surrey, south of London. Some would spend as much as five years living in Headley Court for five or six weeks at a time, undergoing specialist treatment and being fitted with standard socket prostheses. The people who were there longest were above-the-knee amputees.

Over the years, the medical staff had seen many patients

struggle with traditional artificial limbs. Even though the wounded service personnel had adapted well, their mobility was often severely limited. One of the senior officers at Headley Court, Lieutenant Colonel Rhodri Phillip, began looking for fresh approaches. He came across osseointegration and started discussing the prospects with some of the soldiers there.

He'd had a bad experience with the first case of a soldier who'd undergone osseointegration carried out by a team at a hospital in the UK using a technique I'd never tried. There were severe complications and the patient had the implant removed.

It was a major setback for the project, and at the time the authorities at Headley Court were reluctant to follow through with further osseointegration operations. Rhodri decided to explore all the other approaches and heard about our success from some British civilians who'd undergone the procedure in Sydney.

Plenty of his patients were encouraged by the possibilities of osseointegration but, particularly after the unsuccessful surgery, no one wanted to be the next. At least one serviceman turned down the opportunity through fear of the unknown.

Then Rhodri started talking to Rifleman Michael Swain, who was nineteen years old when he lost both his legs above the knee after standing on an IED in a field in Afghanistan. That was in 2009, and over the next four years he had struggled to walk with socket prostheses. Despite his best efforts, Michael was virtually confined to a wheelchair. His last throw of the dice was to travel to Sydney for osseointegration. I operated on him in December 2013 at Macquarie University Hospital.

Michael's recovery was swift, and three months later, almost immediately after his second-stage surgery, he walked onto a Qantas aircraft at Sydney Airport for the flight back to the United Kingdom on his new robotic legs, using only one crutch. Once he landed at Heathrow, he was driven back to his home in Luton, north of London. As he walked up the path to the front door of his home, his then wife and young son were watching from the window.

'Look, here comes Daddy,' his wife told their son.

The youngster responded, 'That's not Daddy. Daddy can't walk!'

What his son didn't realise was that his father could walk once more. And he has done ever since. Indeed, I was privileged to go to Windsor Castle in April 2014 to watch as Michael walked unaided to meet the Queen and receive an MBE for services to charity.

Naturally enough, Michael spoke about osseointegration with other wounded soldiers at Headley Court. One of them was a young Welsh fusilier, Shaun Stocker, who, six days from the end of his tour of duty in Afghanistan, had also stood on an IED. He lost both legs above the knee. As well, he lost his left eye, he was blinded in his right eye—although he subsequently regained 30 per cent vision—and, probably worst of all for a young man, he lost both testicles.

Shaun had considered osseointegration some time earlier. But, at that time, no British service personnel had undergone the procedure. Like Steve Borton, he decided against being the guinea pig. But after talking to Michael, Shaun asked Rhodri if he, too, could to come to Sydney for the surgery.

Shaun made the journey to Australia accompanied by a Royal Air Force surgeon, Group Captain Jon Kendrew, who was researching osseointegration and wanted to observe the procedure. Shaun's operation was as successful as Michael's. Both men say it has changed their lives.

Since the operation, Shaun has had many amazing and positive experiences. On his new robotic legs, Shaun walked 100 kilometres in five separate stages and raised more than A$120,000 for his chosen charity, Blind Veterans UK. More recently he climbed the highest peak in Wales, Mount Snowdon—in dreadfully wet and windy conditions, I might add—again raising money for Blind Veterans UK.

In mid-2018, Shaun was chosen to come to Australia to record a series of the BBC television program *Without Limits* to coincide with the Invictus Games in Sydney. It's a fascinating concept: a group of people who are living with different disabilities are sent out on a challenging journey through rough terrain. The idea is to demonstrate how the group gels to collectively overcome the physical and mental challenges they face.

Shaun has also established himself as a shrewd business-person, developing a number of properties. Most remarkably, Shaun's then partner gave birth to their son, Theo, on Christmas

Day 2015, thanks to an IVF procedure developed by pioneering reproductive scientist Dr Jackson Kirkman-Brown.

Jackson had seen large numbers of young soldiers coming back from Afghanistan with terrible wounds to the groin after stepping on IEDs. Traditional efforts to harvest semen from them revolved around attempting to find any remnants of the testicles and recovering residual semen from there. In nearly all cases it was unsuccessful. Even if they could locate any semen, it had normally been cooked to oblivion by the heat of the blast.

Jackson developed an innovative technique to remove the vas deferens from the wounded serviceman within 72 hours of the injury. Because these semen-carrying ducts are inside the body, they're somewhat shielded from the immediate impact and heat of the explosion, and the semen has a greater chance of survival.

Shaun was one of the first soldiers to undergo the procedure—and it worked. He'd always wanted to have a family, and Theo's arrival brought him immense joy.

Before long, I was invited to go to the United Kingdom to operate on more wounded soldiers. The first patient I saw there was one of Shaun's close friends from his time in hospital and rehabilitation at Headley Court, an older Scottish soldier named Gary Jamieson. Gary had lost both legs above the knee and his left arm above the elbow in another IED explosion in Afghanistan.

His circumstances were similar to those of Michael and Shaun. All had struggled with socket prostheses. Gary was confined to a wheelchair and felt he had little quality of life.

So, assisted by Jon Kendrew, I carried out the first successful osseointegration operation on a British soldier in the United Kingdom.

Gary's recovery has been transformational. With his wife and children, he now runs a pub in the town where he was born. He drives his car on a daily basis and regularly heads off with mates to watch his football team, Glasgow Rangers.

By early 2017, I'd carried out ten osseointegration operations on British soldiers—nine of them double above-the-knee amputees. They've all been outstandingly successful, and the patients are walking freely.

I've also operated on a handful of former Australian soldiers. Remarkably, considering the prominent role Australia had played in the various conflicts in the Middle East, none of them had been wounded in recent military campaigns.

Peter Molloy, for instance, lost his right leg high above the knee after being wounded in the Vietnam War. The injury occurred during the peak of Australia's involvement in the conflict, with more than 7500 troops stationed in Vietnam.

On the evening of 4 July 1969, Peter was a private in the lead section of 7th Platoon C Company as they embarked on an after-dark ambush patrol in the Viet Cong stronghold of the Long Hai mountains in Phuoc Tuy Province, south of Saigon. The mission hadn't gone smoothly from the start. An armed personnel carrier had bogged in a rice paddy, and Peter's unit was held back to provide cover while assistance was summoned.

Going Back

They were under the impression they'd be remaining at the site overnight, but they were soon ordered to follow through with the original plan. As they advanced, the machine gunner closest to Peter stepped on a landmine—an M16 jumping jack device that leapt out of the ground before exploding. Ironically, it had originally been laid by the Australian forces but had been relocated by the Viet Cong. The machine gunner died instantly, and Peter suffered multiple shrapnel wounds to both legs. Soon after, a signaller stepped on another landmine. He was killed. In all, three soldiers died and nineteen others were injured that night.

The platoon medic tied tourniquets on both Peter's legs. As he carried out the first aid, he pointed out that Peter was fortunate it was dark and he couldn't see the wounds because they were so severe.

Peter was lifted onto a special sheet and dragged along the ground to a helicopter for evacuation to the nearest Australian field hospital at Vung Tau. From there he was flown to the RAAF Butterworth military base in Malaysia and then to RAAF Base Richmond in Sydney's west. He was transported by road to Ingleburn before being transferred to Concord Repatriation General Hospital.

He fought infections and underwent bone and skin grafts. But the efforts of the medical team couldn't save his right leg and after seven months surgeons amputated the leg close to the hip. Altogether, he spent two years in hospital, working through rehabilitation and learning to walk with his socket prosthesis. Back in those days, prostheses were so basic that Peter's first artificial leg was actually made of wood. He would joke with mates that if he shuffled off this mortal coil before them, they should throw the prosthesis onto a bonfire.

During that time, Peter met his future wife, who was a nurse at Concord Hospital. Initially they lived in Sydney, but after a decade there they moved to Peter's home town of Tamworth, where they spent another twenty years before relocating to the Sunshine Coast hinterland.

Peter had been an amputee for 45 years before he came to see me. In 2014, he was looking for a surgeon to replace his left knee and came along to one of my patient briefings in Brisbane. As well as talking about knee replacements, we also discussed osseointegration. Straight away, Peter and his wife decided it could be for him. He hasn't regretted the decision for a moment. 'It's made life heaps better for me,' he says. 'I put my leg on in the morning and wear it all day. I only take it off in the shower or when I go to bed.

'You can walk much longer distances. You could hardly walk anywhere with the socket because they were so uncomfortable and made you sweat. And you have a much better gait with osseointegration. It makes walking a lot more natural and easy.

'I walk around the house without any aids. Outside, I use a walking stick as a bit of added insurance. And it also means people give me a little more space. I recommended it [the operation] to a mate in Caloundra who lost his leg in a motorcycle accident. And he's had osseointegration as a result.'

Going Back

Sadly, not all the stories of soldiers who've undergone osseo-integration have a happy ending. The battlefield experience and the terrible wounds have a lasting mental as well as physical impact. Many suffer from PTS or depression and have trouble maintaining relationships or holding down steady jobs once they're back in the day-to-day world of the average civilian.

Former US Army Captain Luis Montalván shot to inter-national fame in 2011 with the publication of his book, *Until Tuesday*. As well as being his memoir, it centres on Luis's relationship with his service dog, a golden retriever named Tuesday, who he credited with helping him turn his life around.

Luis was born in Washington, DC, in 1973 and grew up in Potomac, Maryland. He came from a Cuban-American family—some of his relatives had escaped the island nation around the time of the failed US invasion at the Bay of Pigs in 1961. At the age of seventeen, he joined the US Army and went on to serve two tours of duty in Iraq—winning two Bronze Stars, a Purple Heart, the Army Commendation Medal and a Combat Action Badge.

One evening in December 2003, Luis and another soldier were on a foot patrol near the Al Waleed checkpoint on the Iraqi-Syrian border in Anbar Province. It was an area where smuggling and corruption were rife, and Luis spotted an unauthorised Iraqi truck with a trailer. The Americans approached and spoke to the driver. As Luis walked forwards, he felt a heavy push in his back. He had been stabbed and fell, hitting his head on the ground and losing consciousness.

Luis suffered a severe brain injury, fractured vertebrae and a serious knife wound. Subsequently, he had to deal with PTS and chronic pain in his right leg. He was honourably discharged from the US Army.

When Luis returned home, he moved to an apartment in the New York district of Brooklyn. There he slipped into a rapid psychological decline and started drinking heavily. Later, reflecting on that time, Luis said that the army was almost his entire life. 'That's your identity. To lose it, as well as your mobility, you question your existence.'

While in Brooklyn, Luis cut himself off from society. He had great difficulty climbing a flight of stairs and spent most of his days alone in his apartment. He started to wonder whether he would ever recover. As he sank deeper into despair, Luis received an unsolicited email pointing out that a number of not-for-profit organisations were interested in partnering service dogs with military veterans. He investigated and signed up with one of the groups.

Through the project, he was paired with a male golden retriever named Tuesday. They quickly formed a close bond and, within a short time, Tuesday was helping Luis cope with his bouts of vertigo, reminding him to take his medication and was at his side to calm him during nightmares, anxiety attacks and bouts of high blood pressure.

On top of that, Luis had to take Tuesday out of the apartment a couple of times a day. Inevitably, this brought social interactions.

Going Back

Luis remembered, 'It was a very bleak time. I almost didn't make it out of that time. But, thankfully, like manna from heaven, Tuesday came into my life. When you go through trauma, when your life is starkly altered, when it is spiralling downward, unconditional love is as bright a light as exists.

'Before Tuesday, I caught glimpses of snipers on rooftops. Before Tuesday, I spent more than an hour in my apartment working up the courage to walk half a block to the liquor store. Tuesday is my barrier against crowds, my distraction from anxiety and my assistant in everyday tasks.'

In a story on Channel Nine's *60 Minutes* program, Luis told reporter Mark Burrows, 'Tuesday has been able to rekindle my ambitions, my dreams, my hopes, my wishes. And that's to help other people. The relationship that Tuesday and I have transcends our exterior—our skin, our fur. It's something—and I think I can speak for him in saying—that we wish for everyone.'

After the publication of his book, Luis and Tuesday gained a much higher profile, at least partly thanks to an appearance on David Letterman's television show and hundreds of media interviews across continents wherever the book was released. Luis toured the United States, raising awareness about the plight of former service personnel who were suffering PTS and promoting the value of service dogs. He also earned a Masters in journalism at New York's Columbia University.

But while his new role was satisfying and rewarding, Luis was suffering massive and increasing pain in his right leg.

It reached the point where it became intolerable. He made the decision to have the leg amputated above the knee early in 2016 and was fitted with a standard socket prosthesis. It didn't work well. His mobility was limited, and he was constantly suffering chafing and pain to his leg and groin.

He decided there had to be a better solution and spent weeks researching the options. It was then that he discovered what I was doing in Australia. He contacted me and came to Sydney for surgery in October 2016. The operation worked perfectly and, within a short time, Luis was walking on his new robotic leg. He was delighted and said, 'It feels fantastic. It feels like you are regenerating your leg, because you are no longer detached from your prosthesis.'

Within a few weeks, Luis returned to New York and was reunited with his beloved dog. Everything seemed to be unfolding brilliantly. Luis was happy, he was mobile, he was busy—and he was back with Tuesday.

In early December 2016, Luis went to El Paso in Texas for an appointment. Unusually, he left Tuesday with friends when he went to stay overnight at the Indigo Hotel.

Luis was found dead in his hotel room the next morning. He had taken an overdose of barbiturates. He was 43 years old.

I was in Tel Aviv in Israel when I received a phone call from Luis's father, telling me that his son had died. It was a major shock and the last thing I expected. Luis was doing so well. He was perfect. Absolutely perfect.

He was so happy. With his progress and his recovery, he was

the star patient. And then, all of a sudden, it ended. I felt I had failed him drastically. But obviously, the biggest loss was to his family. They are the people who have to live with it more than anyone else.

I have enormous admiration and respect for Luis and people like him. He'd suffered a huge trauma that had changed him permanently. Yet he was still an inspiration to others. I truly hope Luis is in a better place.

Around the same time I was carrying out these operations on soldiers, I was also working to improve the technology and techniques of the implants and robotic legs. I would regularly meet the biomedical engineers on my team to develop and assess new designs.

We also studied ways to simplify the surgery, reducing it from a two-step process—first fitting the titanium rod, then attaching the connector to link with the robotic leg in a separate procedure—to a single operation. We achieved that, and these days all osseointegration patients are operated on only once.

—　—

Various members of the British Royal Family have played a prominent role in supporting wounded military personnel. I know from talking to some of the injured British soldiers that Prince Charles, Prince William and Prince Harry have been regular visitors to Headley Court. Queen Elizabeth II and other senior royals often present medals to current and former service personnel.

Since his time serving with the British Army in Afghanistan, Prince Harry has taken a particularly deep and genuine interest in the welfare of injured soldiers. On top of regularly attending functions and supporting charities, in 2014 he launched the Invictus Games—a multisport event for wounded, injured or sick service personnel. The first Invictus Games were staged in London. Two years later, the Games were held near Orlando in Florida. Toronto in Canada hosted the 2017 Games, and they came to Sydney in 2018.

Prince Harry's commitment to wounded soldiers goes much further than that, though. He's genuinely interested in anything and everything that can improve their lives and living conditions.

A couple of months before Prince Harry's visit to Sydney in May 2015, I was contacted by his private secretary, who explained that the prince would like to meet me and find out about the operations I was performing on British soldiers. Naturally, I was delighted to accept the opportunity. But that raised the question of Prince Harry's security, so we had to work out the most appropriate spot for our meeting. Both Macquarie University Hospital and Norwest Private Hospital at Bella Vista in Sydney's north-west were considered. After consulting Federal Government and security officials, Macquarie got the nod.

In discussions with the Australian Security Service and Macquarie University Hospital Chief Executive Carol Bryant, we decided the royal visit would focus on the Orthopaedic Ward and Clinic. There, Prince Harry would meet both patients and hospital staff. We also moved a set of parallel bars from the Physiotherapy Department into the clinic to show him osseointegration patients practising walking on their new legs.

The prince's plans remained top secret until the morning of his visit, and it wasn't until Buckingham Palace put out an official media release that the details were widely confirmed. When he arrived in a heavily guarded motorcade, Prince Harry—dressed in his desert camouflage uniform and wearing a beret—was met by Carol Bryant, Macquarie University Dean Patrick McNeil, Deputy Dean John Boyages and my then practice manager, Belinda Bosley.

I met Prince Harry in the reception area of the clinic building, but at first I don't think he realised who I was. Maybe he was expecting someone much older. Only when we were squashed in the lift with the security officials, and I explained that he could talk to any of the patients at the clinic, did the penny seem to drop. I saw a glint of recognition in his eye, and he said, 'I guess you're the guy.'

I smiled and replied, 'And I guess you're the guy, too!' We laughed and shook hands.

Inside the clinic, I introduced him to several patients, including Juliette Hildom from the United States—who'd lost one leg above the knee and the other below in a boat-propeller accident—a Canadian and a couple of New Zealanders, one of them Penny Gifkins, a mother of two from Napier who'd lost her legs below the knee as well as most of her left hand and three fingers on her right hand after she contracted the blood infection meningococcal septicaemia. Another patient to meet the prince was Iraqi Ali Al Kinany, who'd undergone osseointegration a short time before. He'd lost one leg and badly damaged the other in the Gulf War.

However, one of the main reasons for Prince Harry's visit was to meet Lieutenant Alistair Spearing, the fourth British soldier to come to Australia for osseointegration. In 2011, at the age of 27, Alistair had been serving in Afghanistan when three of his army mates were blasted by an IED. Alistair had immediately gone to their aid and was delivering emergency medical assistance when a second bomb went off. He lost both legs above the knee. I'd operated on Alistair just three weeks earlier.

Straight away, I took the prince to the clinic room, where I examined Alistair and explained the process of osseointegration. It was there that I handed him a copy of my first book, *Walking Free,* and asked him to give it to his grandmother when he returned to the United Kingdom. From there, we walked into the main clinic and Prince Harry watched as Alistair took some of his first steps using his new robotic legs between the parallel bars.

Prince Harry was amazed. He couldn't believe that Alistair was starting to walk so soon after the operation. The prince has been associated with plenty of amputees, and he's well aware of the difficulties they face with socket prostheses—especially double amputees.

We walked from the clinic to the ward, where he met more patients. Along the way, I reached into my pocket, pulled out my business card and handed it to the prince. 'That's my card,' I explained. 'If you ever need anything, don't hesitate to contact me.'

Prince Harry took it. 'Do you know, you're the first person who's ever given me their business card?' he chuckled.

I must say, like everyone who met him during the visit, I found Prince Harry utterly charming. He came across as humble, approachable and a thoroughly good person.

Oh, and for the record, Alistair's recovery was so complete that when he returned to Scotland, he set about building his own house!

5

THE HEALING FIELDS

From an early age, I was taught the importance of making a contribution to society. Along with that, the value of humanitarian and charity work was drummed into me. Consequently, one of my dreams has long been to create something that will benefit humankind well after the end of my days.

And what I've seen in my life has dramatically reinforced the need for compassion and support for people who are struggling.

By the mid-1990s, as a result of the war with Iran, the Gulf War and UN sanctions, work opportunities in Iraq were disappearing and inflation was rampant. It was particularly hard for highly qualified academics and professionals, who had once been the cornerstone of the Iraqi middle class. They found themselves unemployed and with few prospects of finding long-term, well-paid work. No longer could they afford a new car or lavish family holidays. Instead, they were struggling to keep food on the table. Many had to sell all their belongings just to maintain a meagre existence.

For others, the pressure became too great. Suicides were common among people who previously had led an affluent existence but now found themselves at the bottom of a dry gully. I know of one family where a poverty-stricken former academic bought a chicken as a special culinary treat for his starving family. He poisoned the bird before cooking it as a symbolic last supper and serving it to the whole family. They were found dead together in their home. His injured pride and sense of dignity as the head of the family led to their tragic fate. In despair, the head of the family could see no other solution.

During the Gulf War, my family escaped from Baghdad and moved to Suwayrah, about 55 kilometres south-east of the capital. Often when we walked to the nearby market area, I noticed something that at first didn't make sense. A large refrigerated truck from a local factory would pull into the middle of the market stalls, and as soon as it stopped, the back doors would be thrown open and the driver would hand out all sorts of dairy products—milk, cream, ice cream.

We wondered what the reason was.

It turned out that the factory was connected to a farm and because electricity was cut during the bombing, perishable goods couldn't be stored for any length of time. But the cows still needed to be milked. Workers were milking the cows, running the factory on generators and producing the daily goods. Then they would distribute the products for free.

It was ironic that we didn't have electricity, we didn't have running water, but we did have ice cream!

The situation helped reinforce the importance of charity in my mind.

Once we returned to Baghdad, I became involved in one of my early humanitarian projects: helping an uncle of mine who launched what he called the First American Relief Organisation (FARO).

My uncle, who was based in Saudi Arabia, would send me money, and I would buy what was most needed. I would ask friends and relatives if they knew any families across Baghdad that were literally on the breadline, then I would distribute food, clothing and money to those families. We didn't discriminate. The only criterion was that these people were struggling to make ends meet. We would also visit Kurdish families and others who had flocked to Baghdad from the south during and after the recent wars.

The work was rewarding, although on a small scale. I was helping maybe five or ten families at any given time. And it wasn't without risk. If Saddam Hussein had found out about our activities, I'm sure he would have regarded FARO as undermining his regime. That would have come with consequences.

Naturally, my role in that initiative came to an end when I escaped from Iraq in 1999. Instead, when I was finally accepted into Australia, I turned my humanitarian attention to highlighting the plight of refugees.

In 2014, I was involved in formal discussions at Federal Parliament leading to the report on refugee and asylum-seeker policy titled 'Beyond the boats: building an asylum and refugee policy for the long term'. I currently work with Amnesty International and speak extensively on their behalf about the issues facing refugees and asylum seekers. I'm also an Australian ambassador for the Red Cross, and I work with the United Nations Commission on Human Rights, promoting assistance for refugees.

I've also used my surgical skills for humanitarian pro bono work.

In 2012—four years after I qualified as an orthopaedic surgeon—I was invited to India to work with a surgical team there. I've since been back four more times, operating in locations including Bangalore, Belgaum, Goa, Hyderabad and Mumbai.

I was also part of a group of surgeons who went to China soon after the project in India.

In both countries, I concentrated on joint replacements and repairing the horrible effects of arthritis and birth deformities. But I haven't performed any osseointegration.

I'm by no means alone as an orthopaedic surgeon carrying out pro bono work overseas. I'm one of many. There are others, though, who shy away from it because of the sacrifices you need to make. While you're away and not earning money, you still have to pay for consulting rooms and staff. Your practice still needs to function effectively and meet the needs of your patients. And many of the humanitarian projects I undertake involve flying heavy surgical equipment from Sydney to the destination. On our first surgical visit to Baghdad, for example, we carried 90 kilograms of costly excess baggage. For all that, I've found the work stimulating and enormously rewarding—and, in many cases, eye-opening.

Like India and parts of China, Cambodia is another country that carries the legacy of deep poverty—plus, of course, the disastrous rule of ideological politicians. From 1975 to 1979, the brutal Pol Pot–led Khmer Rouge regime was responsible for slaughtering more than two million people. The bodies of those who were executed by the Khmer Rouge were dumped in a number of mass graves, collectively known as the Killing Fields.

Pol Pot insisted on the nation becoming self-sufficient. Large sections of the population were forced to leave the cities for rural areas so they could grow food-producing plants. The production of food as well as drugs to treat common diseases was inadequate, and thousands of people died needlessly from starvation and treatable illnesses.

On top of that, landmines had been widely used across Cambodia and this led to soaring numbers of amputees.

In 2015, I was contacted by Dr Jim Gollogly. He had founded the Children's Surgical Centre (CSC) in the Cambodian capital, Phnom Penh, in 1998 and is also the Chief Executive of ROSEcharities, which started the following year. The CSC offers free surgery for people with a disability who come from a poor background, while ROSEcharities provides, among other things, free ophthalmic and facial reconstruction surgery. The projects work with a team of international doctors and surgeons and they also train local surgeons and health workers.

Jim was in his early seventies when he contacted me. He had been born in the United Kingdom, undertook orthopaedic training in Australia and had worked in the United States before heading to Southeast Asia. Since then, his practice and opinions have been shaped by decades of front-line surgical experience in Phnom Penh. He's operated on thousands of locals, especially landmine victims and children who were born with various disfigurements.

My three-day visit to Phnom Penh in September 2015 didn't get off to the best of starts. After traversing the chaotic city, I headed to the Children's Hospital. When I introduced myself to Jim, he seemed a little disappointed. I think he expected an aged professor with many decades of experience with the scalpel.

In that awkward moment, I had a chance to take in Jim's appearance. With his thick white hair, equally white beard, ruddy complexion and red scrubs, he reminded me of Santa Claus.

Another notable aspect of his appearance was that he had bare feet. It transpired that he even operates without shoes or foot covers. Jim's unusual approach nearly ended in tears at one point, when I was in the operating theatre with him and almost dropped a hammer on his foot.

Our first task was to carry out a clinic where we saw potential patients and worked out their treatment schedules.

Word soon spread that a foreign professor was at the hospital and would be operating. Before long, we were bombarded with patients suffering significant deformities.

The vast majority of the cases were extremely complex—the sort of conditions rarely seen in more developed nations. Adults and children arrived with both upper and lower limbs seriously deformed by trauma and infections.

As if those cases weren't challenging enough, one in particular provided more graphic evidence of what we were up against.

A male patient presented with a forearm fracture that had been operated on some time before and appeared to have healed perfectly. He was coming for a standard check-up. Without hesitation, Jim booked him in for surgery. I was puzzled and politely asked him whether further surgery was really necessary. Jim responded directly, 'We need to take the plate out of his arm for someone else.'

Immediately, my mind returned to my final months as a surgeon in Iraq. During the UN embargo, surgical material was in such short supply that we had to re-use equipment removed from patients. We'd even made splints out of oxygen tubes filled with medical cement. Quite simply, as we had in Iraq, Jim's surgical team in Phnom Penh was forced to recycle medical devices because they were difficult to source in Cambodia.

Not long after, we were presented with a patient in his fifties who had a chronic infection in a fracture at the upper end of his femur. Jim inspected the injury and gave instructions for the removal of the top of the patient's femur, which would effectively clear the infection but dramatically shorten the leg and leave the patient without a hip joint. It would also irreversibly reduce the patient's mobility. It's a traditional technique known as the Girdlestone operation.

I suggested the alternative approach of operating and cleaning out the infection from the fracture to preserve the hip movement. Jim was dubious. 'You guys come from the developed world. We have to deal with what we've got.'

Another patient was a beautiful ten-year-old girl who had a major deformity in her left knee joint. It was effectively bent backwards, meaning she walked rather like a deer. Her condition was entirely preventable. She hadn't been born like that. It was the result of a bizarre, old-fashioned treatment that is still used in Cambodia and some other developing countries.

When a patient presents with a fever, doctors often grind up an aspirin, dissolve it in water and inject it into the patient's thigh. In many cases, the potential consequences of the injection are far worse than the fever itself. The problem is that the injection can cause significant muscle scarring and have a massive impact on the structure of the quadriceps. The results can be disastrous—including forcing the knee to bend the wrong way. Not surprisingly, this young girl was walking with extreme difficulty.

Jim instructed his assistant to read an article in a Chinese publication about cutting the knee-end of the femur and rotating it. In my opinion, this was an unnecessarily invasive approach that didn't address the problem—which was in the muscle rather than the bone. I suggested lengthening the muscle and allowing the child to recover with an external fixation frame. Again, Jim dismissed my idea. For the time being, under the circumstances, I bowed to his judgement.

We finished the clinic and then saw seven or eight amputees. They were rice farmers who had to work to feed their families. They'd each lost a leg by stepping on a landmine left over from the Pol Pot era. One of them had fractured his other leg and had a cast on it. None of these patients had any prostheses.

I started talking to them and asked the local doctor to translate for me. Naturally, the patients wanted to know about the risks of osseointegration. I explained the possibility of infection and the fact that they could lose the rest of the leg. Jim interrupted the explanation. 'Why are you scaring them? They won't want to have the surgery.'

I responded, 'They should be in a position to give their informed consent.'

Obviously, we had fundamentally different approaches. After our discussions, only four of the patients—three men and one woman—decided to go ahead with osseointegration.

The next problem we faced was the lack of prosthetic legs. We could do the osseointegration operation and fit the titanium rods, which I'd brought over with me. But the patients wouldn't have any legs to walk on.

Next door to the hospital, there was a prosthetic workshop established by US actress Angelina Jolie. When I entered the workshop, to my surprise there were three student prosthetists from the Ballarat campus of Federation University Australia working there on rotation, manufacturing artificial feet and socket prostheses.

I asked them, 'Do you have any knees?' The question was answered with the shaking of heads.

My heart sank. I started to lose hope that we could successfully complete the operations.

'So what can we do?' I asked.

We pondered possible solutions—none of which seemed terribly promising. But then I discovered they had door hinges and aluminium tubes, plus a plentiful supply of polyurethane.

I gave the young prosthetists a connector—the device that links the titanium rod to the artificial leg. They wrapped the polyurethane around it and, between us, we manufactured a knee from the door hinges and the aluminium tubing. A couple of hours of improvisation and imagination and, hey presto, we had four functional artificial legs.

I briefed Jim on the development, and we arranged for the operations to start the next morning. The operating theatre was a single room with four tables—very similar to the theatres depicted in the movie and television series *MASH*. It was something out of the 1950s and the Korean War era, except that it was in a building rather than a tent.

We carried out our first osseointegration operation using a spinal anaesthetic, so the patient was awake throughout. I'd brought a range of implants with me from Australia, but because Cambodians are shorter than Australians in general and their bone canals are narrow, I could only use the smallest implants. The others were redundant.

Jim started operating on the patient he had lined up for the Girdlestone operation. I walked in and asked him, 'Can I scrub in?' He nodded approval. Once I'd completed my preparations, I tentatively asked, 'Can I try a slightly different approach?' Jim agreed. Essentially, I carried out the operation I had proposed earlier. Rather than removing the top of the femur, I fixed the fracture and cleaned out the infection. That was a turning point in our relationship. I had managed to gain Jim's trust by showing him what I could do.

The next patient was the young girl with the knee that was bending backwards. Jim's assistants had started the operation, but I persuaded them to try my approach. We extended the girl's quadricep and put her in an external fixation frame. She would have to wear that for six weeks.

From there, we took on several complex cases. We saw a young Buddhist monk, around fourteen or fifteen years old, who'd fractured his left arm. Someone had put him in a cast with his arm extended, which meant his healed arm couldn't flex at the elbow. As a result, he couldn't put his hands together in the standard praying position.

He was a delightful, gentle young man. We operated on the elbow, corrected the bone and restored full movement in his arm. That operation was one of the highlights of my time in Cambodia. He was so grateful that he could once again bend his elbow and pray properly. Often, it's the little things that make the difference.

We completed some really complicated surgery in Phnom Penh, and I think we substantially improved the quality of life for the people we operated on.

But would I go back to Cambodia? I have serious reservations.

The cost of the project didn't worry me. But I was concerned about other issues I faced. For example, when we visited a prosthetics centre, the guy who was running it immediately asked, 'Why are you here? What's in it for you?'

I told him, 'We're running a pilot program. There are 50,000 amputees in Cambodia, Vietnam and Laos, and we think osseointegration can make a big difference to their lives.' I explained that I could provide free of charge the older-style prostheses, which had been donated by our existing Australian patients after upgrading to newer models. All I needed from him was help with the fitting and follow-up of patients. I didn't think it was a massive ask, considering he was a public servant in a rehabilitation clinic.

He couldn't digest what I was saying, even though it's not

uncommon for Australian and international patients to buy used prostheses. Because the prostheses are external fittings, they don't carry any specific risk of cross infection. He told me that he couldn't accept any used parts—they would have to be brand-new legs. It made me suspicious about what would happen to any new legs I provided. It was a big disappointment.

Despite these issues, I'm still in contact with Jim and his registrar. They keep me up to date with the progress of the patients we operated on. They all seem to be doing well.

Even though Jim and I sometimes adopt different approaches, I have great respect for him and the work he's doing. He has extensive firsthand knowledge of the local circumstances and what he believes are the most effective surgical options. Jim could have taken the easy road and worked in a leading Western country, using the latest technology, earning a generous income and living a comfortable lifestyle. Instead, he chooses to live and work in Cambodia—and he is making a genuine difference to lives there.

Just as my early osseointegration operations sparked an adverse reaction from some sections of the orthopaedic establishment in Australia, my work in Cambodia also attracted an unusual level of scrutiny.

One colleague travelled all the way to Phnom Penh, requested the records of the patients I'd operated on, read through the paperwork and asked for a series of examinations of the patients—examinations that clearly weren't standard investigations. He went on to create detailed files on all the patients.

He returned to Australia and asked me to present my results about osseointegration at an audit meeting. Then, without my consent or the consent of the patients, he proceeded to discuss the results of the individual cases.

Behaviour which I found completely unacceptable.

Subsequently, I quizzed my colleague about the osseo-integration patients in Cambodia and asked how he thought they were recovering.

'Okay, so far,' was his response.

So far? If the recovery was well underway after a few months, there's absolutely no reason to think it wouldn't continue that way.

It saddens me that some of my colleagues will go to such lengths in an attempt to discredit osseointegration. They are threatening the future of genuine humanitarian projects that are delivering tangible benefits.

6

EDGING CLOSER

In late 2008, I had returned to the Middle East for the first time nine years after escaping Saddam Hussein's regime.

I was a newly qualified orthopaedic surgeon living with my then wife Irina in Berlin, studying orthopaedics and particularly osseointegration. Winter in Berlin can be ferociously cold—and, on the spur of the moment, we decided to take a break from the bitter conditions in Germany. We wanted to sample some warmer surroundings for a few days.

Iraq was far too dangerous at the time, so, without ever harbouring a great yearning to return to the country of my birth, I arranged a holiday in neighbouring Jordan.

Going Back

The Jordanian capital, Amman—a city of about four million people with some spectacular Roman remains—had been my first destination after crossing the border when I escaped from Iraq. And within a short time of arriving back there, it became clear that the changes had all been for the worst. It was obvious that the local economy had been struggling for many years.

For a long time, Iraq had been Jordan's main source of income. But after the US invasion, Iraq's trading routes and political allegiances had switched to Iran. Jordan, as one of the few safe nations in that part of the Middle East, had little choice but to survive on tourism.

We visited my cousin Laheeb. She's now living in Perth in Western Australia and has gone on to work as an electrical engineer in the mining industry. We also met up with my Islamist uncle Ahmed. Like us, he and his new wife—a doctor from Anbar Province in Iraq—were holidaying in Jordan. At the time, they were living in Riyadh in Saudi Arabia.

Uncle Ahmed was the only man my father would never discuss ideas and philosophies with. My father explained that, years earlier, Ahmed had made up his mind about everything of any significance—especially religious matters—and wouldn't even consider anyone else's opinion. There was no point in having a discussion with him—you wouldn't get anywhere.

Ahmed's new wife shared his radical religious views—and, if anything, she appeared to have hardened his line against Western nations, even though he's an American citizen.

The meeting didn't go well.

We spent the best part of two hours arguing about religious fundamentalism and violence in the region. My point was that the invasion of Iraq was led by the United States, which had then effectively occupied the nation. As a result, I felt the only solution would be for an American withdrawal and the arrival of international forces to create stability and buffer the influence of Iran and Saudi Arabia.

While Ahmed made some attempt to lighten the conversation, his wife became extremely agitated. She was fully covered with the exception of her face and spent a good deal of her time criticising Irina for the way she was dressed. Irina's originally from Russia, and wasn't used to having any restrictions on her clothing. At the same time, there was nothing outrageous about her outfit. Sure, she was wearing a top that was unbuttoned around the neck, and she wasn't wearing a head covering. But, to Western eyes, this was far from provocative.

To spite us, Ahmed's wife put on the full burqa just as we were about to take a family photo. Ahmed then suggested that Irina should button up her top before the photo.

'Look at my wife,' he said. 'She's beautiful.'

I responded, 'You think your wife looks beautiful? How can you tell when she's all covered up in black? I don't ask you to uncover your wife. That's up to her. Similarly, I can't tell my wife to button up her top. That's her choice.'

Needless to say, the photo was never taken. After such a

tense encounter, I was left with no alternative but to cut all ties with Uncle Ahmed. I haven't been in touch with him since.

In addition to the family tension, I ran into trouble with the Jordanian police as we drove to the Dead Sea. The rental car I was driving was stopped twice, and each time I was given a speeding fine. But at least the Jordanian police were thoroughly pleasant as they dished out the punishment.

Happily, there was a positive side to the journey. I was able to dip my toes back in the waters of the Middle East—in this case, in the Dead Sea, which borders Jordan on its eastern shores and Israel to the west. The Jordanian side of the Dead Sea is by far the more attractive.

If it's possible, the Dead Sea—which is actually a salt lake and is 400 metres below sea level—is getting 'deader' by the minute! The Israelis have built huge irrigation networks on the Jordan River to divert the flow of water running into the salty lake. The lack of fresh water has served to further intensify the salt levels. Its salt content is now almost ten times greater than the ocean, which means you can't sink. Pick your feet up off the bottom and you'll float.

Bathing in the Dead Sea is a unique experience. As you walk in, you feel like fish are nibbling at your feet and lower legs. In reality, there are no fish in the Dead Sea because of the salt levels. The sensation is simply the sheer concentration of salt interacting with the pores in your skin. You certainly wouldn't want to get the water in your eyes. And there's even advice to avoid shaving for a couple of days before taking a dip because of the danger of skin irritation.

Not far away is the ancient city of Petra, located in a desert valley that runs from the Dead Sea to the Gulf of Aqaba in the south. The city dates back as far as the fourth century BC and is now the most visited tourist attraction in Jordan. The architectural remains at Petra—some carved into the rose-coloured rock of the hillside where the city was built—are truly remarkable and amazingly well preserved, at least partly because of the desert climate.

Petra owed its early prosperity to its position on one of the major intercontinental trade routes. The people of the city were skilled in their management of the rugged and challenging desert environment and had developed advanced techniques including capturing and storing rainwater and dry-land farming. The Romans took over the city in the first century AD and, subsequently, Petra's significance declined as trade was transferred from land to newly opened sea routes.

An earthquake in the fourth century caused significant damage and, by the eighth century, Petra had been abandoned. The city was rediscovered in 1812 by Swiss explorer Johann Ludwig Burckhardt.

Petra was at the centre of a successful uprising against the Ottoman Empire in 1917, organised by famed British military officer T.E. Lawrence—also known as Lawrence of Arabia. The Bedouin women of the region played a crucial role in the fighting.

The city is now on UNESCO's World Heritage List, and in 2007 it was included among the New Seven Wonders of the World.

Just getting into Petra—which was famously featured in the movie *Indiana Jones and the Last Crusade*—is an adventure in itself. The entrance is through a 1.2-kilometre long, five-metre wide gorge called the Siq, with cliffs soaring hundreds of metres above on both sides. At the end of the walk is an elaborate mausoleum, designed by Greek architects in the first century and known as Al Khazneh—literally the Treasury. It was given that name by local tribesmen who believed that robbers had hidden their riches inside. Further on is a Roman colosseum, a cemetery dug into the rock face and a spectacular monastery.

Altogether, visiting Petra was an amazing experience and helped make the Jordanian jaunt thoroughly worthwhile.

A few years went by before I had any further direct contact with the Middle East. This time, a friend who's a dentist in the United Arab Emirates (UAE) gave me a call.

'The Beirut Arab International Festival has nominated you for an award. An organiser will contact you,' she told me.

All of which sounded as though it could be interesting.

In due course, someone who said he was one of the festival's organisers did, indeed, call and confirm that I'd been nominated along with Iraqi architect Dame Zaha Hadid, who by that stage was based in the United Kingdom. Zaha was the first woman to win the Royal Institute of British Architects' Royal Gold Medal. She designed the aquatic centre for the

London Olympics and had been commissioned to design buildings around the world, including structures in Hong Kong, Germany and Azerbaijan. Sadly, she died of a heart attack in the United States in 2016.

Everything seemed legitimate, and the contact at the festival assured me he would ring back with more details. He did just that. But the additional details weren't exactly what I'd expected.

'You need to pay US$100,000,' he informed me.

My response was simple. 'What?'

'That's the way it works if you want to get the award,' the caller explained in a matter-of-fact tone.

In a state of shock, I asked, 'Why would I pay you any money?'

The answer came quickly. 'Well, we'll get the media here. It's a great opportunity to raise your profile.'

I wanted no part of the corruption and bribery and immediately ended the conversation. Since that moment, I have avoided further contact with the festival organisation.

When I did eventually go to Lebanon, it was at the request of the Lebanese Army. They had asked me to operate on two Christian soldiers who'd each lost a leg above the knee during the destructive month-long war that had followed the kidnapping of two Israeli soldiers in a border raid in 2006. The Lebanese servicemen had been stationed on anti-aircraft guns when they were hit by an Israeli air strike. Despite being Christians, they'd been fighting alongside the largely Shi'ite, pro-Iran group Hezbollah, which is committed to wiping out

Israel and is considered a terrorist organisation by the United States. Clearly, compromises can be made in times of war.

I carried out pro bono osseointegration operations on both the soldiers, and the plan was that I would return to lead further clinics and surgery. But, like much of the Middle East, Lebanon is disorganised and the military has never followed up to plan a schedule.

In addition, many of the military and government leaders seem to be more focused on their own survival than conditions for their soldiers. That point was emphasised for me when I was invited to visit the head of the Lebanese Army, who wanted to thank me for carrying out the surgery.

I went to his headquarters, which—not unnaturally in a country with such a volatile history as Lebanon—was surrounded by heavy security. I was ushered into his office and he made a point of locking the door behind me. The head of the Lebanese Army was so paranoid about his personal safety that he had to lock the door whenever he was in there. More than that, he'd arranged a security system that meant he was the only person who could unlock the door to his office.

The whole system seemed utterly bizarre to me. What would happen if he was taken ill while he was in his office? No one could gain access from outside to treat him! For someone who presumably specialises in strategic thinking, this strategy seemed badly flawed.

— —

In its heyday under French occupation, Beirut was known as the Riviera of the Middle East. It had a thriving port and was popular with wealthy tourists. That was brought to an end by the civil war of the late 1970s, which was followed by widespread destruction caused by the Lebanon War involving Israel and Syria in the 1980s. Those conflicts have left enormous scars.

The city has a population of between one and two million people. It is extremely crowded and the traffic jams are massive. You can see that plenty of wealth has been injected into Beirut by expat Lebanese trying to restore some of the grandeur of the capital. But development is chaotic and many buildings remain badly damaged after the wars. For example, I stayed in a Christian suburb in the oldest five-star hotel in the city, the Phoenicia. In contrast to the relative comfort of the hotel, a high-rise building next door was still derelict.

Not unlike Iraq, the recent political history of Lebanon is a reflection of the many attempts by outside influences to effectively control the nation.

One of the most important political and commercial influences has been the Hariri family, which is backed by the Saudis.

Billionaire Rafik Hariri was prime minister of Lebanon from 1992 to 1998 and again from 2000 to 2004. Four months after leaving office, on 14 February 2005, he was assassinated at the age of 60. As his motorcade was being driven past the St George Hotel in Beirut, a 1000-kilogram bomb was detonated in a nearby truck. The occupying Syrian forces were immediately suspected of the atrocity—although four Hezbollah supporters were later charged with the murder and were tried in their absence.

The people of Lebanon are notoriously divided. The Christians and Sunnis live pretty much side-by-side in the north of Beirut, while the Shi'ites largely occupy the south of the city. You can sense the tension between the Sunnis and Christian Lebanese on one side and the Shi'ites and Hezbollah on the other.

Despite that, after Hariri's assassination, a wide range of groups joined together to voice their anger against the occupying Syrian Army. Subsequent rallies and demonstrations became known as the Cedar Revolution. On 14 March 2005, as many as one million people gathered together to protest against the Damascus-based regime. A month later, Syria withdrew its soldiers from Lebanon.

Rafik Hariri had been the driving force behind the redevelopment of much of Beirut's city centre after setting up real estate company Solidere in 1994. His second son, Saad Hariri, also entered politics and was prime minister from 2009 to 2011 and again from 2016. In 2017, he was involved in one of the most bizarre political sagas of recent years—again influenced by an outside regime.

On 4 November, he travelled to Saudi Arabia to meet senior government representatives and, completely out of the blue, announced his resignation on Saudi television, saying he believed his life was in imminent danger. Subsequent media reports suggest Hariri had been lured to Saudi Arabia on false pretences. The real reason, sources claim, was to persuade the prime minister to take a tougher line against Hezbollah. It's even been reported that violence was used to force Hariri to follow the Saudi administration's instructions. French President Emmanuel Macron is believed to have intervened and the Lebanese leader was flown to France, where the two met to resolve the situation. Within days, Hariri was back in Beirut, announcing that he had put his resignation on hold. He finally withdrew his resignation in early December 2017. No plausible official explanation for the strange episode has ever been given.

On reflection, I have to say that I'm not keen to return to Beirut or, for that matter, Lebanon. There are so many poor people there who need help, but the amount of corruption you encounter is disheartening. There is also a great deal of obvious paranoia at the official and political level about the Israelis.

I went to Lebanon twice in 2016, and both times the first question I was asked by the immigration officers was, 'Have you been to Israel?'

In fact, I had. Twice. But because the Israeli authorities don't stamp your passport, there was no evidence of my previous travels. I didn't directly answer the question, simply responding, 'I'm an Arab. Do you think they'd let me into Israel?' Each time, my interrogator nodded knowingly and moved on without pursuing the line of questioning.

Not surprisingly, it's even more difficult for an Arab like me to enter Israel.

Going Back

For my first visit, I'd been invited to deliver two papers at the Israeli Orthopaedic Association Conference, which was being held at the King David Hotel in Tel Aviv.

Just the act of getting from Australia to Israel is complicated. After leaving Sydney, I flew to Dubai. But because of the UAE's opposition to the existence of Israel, there are no direct flights to Tel Aviv. Instead, I had to fly to Amman in Jordan, then board a ridiculously short flight—probably no more than twenty minutes—from Amman to Tel Aviv.

As I discovered soon after landing, security and immigration controls going into Israel are among the tightest in the world. There's a huge downward ramp to enter the arrival hall, which ends with Israeli and other passport holders being separated into queues. Security cameras are everywhere, and on the right is a blocked-off room that looks like a waiting area. I glanced over and inside were dozens of people who appeared to be Palestinian.

I decided to join one of the immigration queues behind the most Jewish-looking person I could find, because I thought it might make entry into Israel easier. It wasn't difficult to spot him: an ultra-Orthodox Jew wearing a black hat over ringlets in his hair, with the religious scarf, the *tzitzit*, and strings hanging from his belt. He seemed to be travelling on a US passport.

He reached the front of the queue and started speaking to the immigration officer, a woman who looked as though she could still be in her teens. Clearly, she wasn't going to allow him in—at least not without further verification. Inevitably, an argument followed. The officer was laying down the law to the Orthodox Jew, but he wasn't having any of that and screamed at her. His protests only served to worsen his plight. He was sent to the blocked-off room to await his fate with the Palestinians.

Of course, it didn't bode well for me. By now, the officer was angry and agitated. There was every chance she'd take her frustrations out on me. I walked to her post, handed her my passport and tried to defuse the situation with a cheery, 'Good afternoon.'

The immigration officer was unmoved and inspected my passport, which included details of my birthplace.

The conversation didn't last long. 'Baghdad, Iraq?' she inquired.

'Yes,' I responded.

'Go to the corner room.'

I knew there was no point in arguing and simply followed her instruction. Funnily enough, I felt quite at home in the corner room. Everyone else looked just like me: Arab. Apart from the Orthodox Jew, of course, who stood out like a sore thumb.

After about twenty minutes, a middle-aged woman wearing civilian clothes and carrying my passport entered the room. She called my name in a perfect Iraqi accent. I was escorted into a nearby office, with dated decor. She nestled behind her desk, avoided making eye contact and started typing my details on the old computer keyboard in front of her. I was left standing on the other side of the desk. I had a folder in my hand with the invitation from the Israeli minister of health and the conference organiser, my business card and the synopsis of my talk.

After flicking through the pages of my passport, the immigration officer finally broke her silence. 'Do you mind if I ask you a question?' she inquired.

'Please do,' I replied.

'What are you doing here?'

'Thank you, I'm pleased you asked that question.' With that, I handed her my business card and folder and explained, 'I'm an orthopaedic surgeon and I'm here to speak at a conference. I'm here to teach your surgeons how to give robotic legs to your injured soldiers.'

She looked through the papers in the folder and asked, 'Is there anyone in Israel who will verify this?'

'Yes, of course. My surgical Fellow, Guy Raz, is waiting for me. Here's his phone number. Please feel free to call him.'

Her reply came quickly. 'We will!'

She made the phone call and, after a two- or three-minute conversation in Hebrew, looked at me and pressed the button on her desk. Another woman promptly arrived. The immigration officer looked at the new arrival and said, 'Didn't I tell you not all Iraqis are idiots!' She then turned to me and asked, 'How long are you planning to stay?'

'One night . . . and I'd like to see Jerusalem.'

'Enjoy your stay,' she said, handing over my passport.

As I pressed on through the immigration process, a visa was slipped into my passport. There was no permanent stamp. The

Israelis know full well a stamp in your passport that shows you've visited their country will prevent you travelling to a host of other destinations.

So, what did I make of Israel? It's a land of contrasts—from the successful co-existence of Jews and Arabs in the coastal area of Jaffa to the smouldering tension of Jerusalem. From the modern, clean, peaceful and pleasant city of Tel Aviv to the open discrimination and hostility of Jerusalem.

In Tel Aviv—parts of it also known as Little Russia because of the large numbers of Russian migrants and tourists there—street signs reflect the multicultural nature of the population. Hebrew is at the top, English is in the middle and Arabic is below. In contrast, Jerusalem was one of the most disquieting cities I've ever visited. Everyone in Jerusalem seemed to be on edge. Instead of the three languages showing on street signs, in Jerusalem the Arabic lettering had been scratched out and covered with Hebrew or English stickers. On one sign, the Arabic lettering had been covered by a sticker saying, 'You are Arabs—you are trying to rape my sister.' It didn't make any sense whatsoever and was purely a gratuitous insult.

The Arab and Jewish areas of the old city of Jerusalem are completely different as well. The Arab section is dirty and over-crowded. All the market traders sell the same souvenirs: Arab crosses, Jewish religious items and Christian artefacts. The Jewish area is much bigger, cleaner and obviously more wealthy. There you'll find only Jewish souvenirs. Ultra-Orthodox Jews openly walk through the Palestinian areas of the city. The

Palestinians aren't afforded the same level of freedom in the Jewish quarter.

At one point, I watched as an Arab driver tried to reverse his vehicle along a street. Immediately, an armed plain-clothes security officer intervened and told him he wasn't allowed to reverse in that area. The confrontation quickly escalated from there as the driver screamed abuse at the security guard. Within seconds, the whole incident became even more ugly— around ten security guards surrounded the driver.

As an outsider, the whole situation seemed extremely dangerous, and I said to my Israeli surgical colleague, Guy, 'Let's get out of here.'

He was much less fazed by the turn of events. 'Don't worry,' he reassured me. 'This happens all the time.'

Jerusalem is a different world.

This was graphically illustrated during my second visit, when I was accompanied by Sydney-based anaesthetist and friend Dr Mark Bukofzer—a South African Jew with Australian and New Zealand citizenship. Mark was excited to be in Israel and assumed the role of our tourist guide through Jerusalem. In freezing and wet conditions, he took us to the Museum of David and the site of the crucifixion. We went into the Church of the Holy Sepulchre and saw the stone where it's believed Christ's body was laid after he was cut down from the cross, as well as Christ's tomb.

Despite being one of the holiest places for Christians, there's nothing grandiose about its presentation. It's larger than an average Christian church, but still a far cry from the huge Islamic shrines in the Middle East. All the same, it attracts an equal level of devotion and dedication from worshippers, many of them clearly overcome with emotion, sobbing and kissing the floor.

Mark's reaction to being in Jerusalem was an interesting snapshot of the thinking of the Jewish people. He was extremely anxious when we walked through the Arab area of the city, saying how unsafe he felt. At one point, he saw two Orthodox Jews walking through the streets and suggested he should help them out. In his estimation, they were obviously lost and were prime candidates to be molested. On top of that, he refused to buy anything from the local traders. As soon as we reached the perceived safety of the Jewish quarter, he felt more comfortable entering shops and set about buying all the necessary items for his son's bar mitzvah.

One of the holiest places in Jerusalem for Jewish people is the Wailing or Western Wall—Al Buraq Wall to Muslims. It's one of four retaining walls that were built around the Temple Mount. And, these days, it's the closest place to the site of the second temple where Jews can worship. Men and women are separated at the wall, praying and reading from their religious books.

I visited the area on my first visit, accompanied by Guy. It's at the very heart of the clashes between Jews and Muslims, because the Al Aqsa mosque was built on the site of the temple after it was taken over by Muslim invaders around the seventh century.

Going Back

The guide for the tour was a Jewish woman with a strong American accent who was clearly passionate about her faith and its history. She recounted a series of historical events associated with the temple site—and, at times, talked about Muslims building a mosque on top of the temple. But, strangely to my mind, she made no mention of Christ or Christianity. If an event happened before Christ's lifetime, she would refer to 'before the current era'. Anything that happened subsequently was described as 'during the current era'. I guess it was her way of establishing that Jews don't believe in the legitimacy of Christ.

At one point, the guide identified a giant stone slab— maybe 15 metres long—which she said had been moved there as one of the miracles of Solomon. As we reached the end of a series of narrow corridors, we saw a woman reading from the Torah, the book of Jewish religious teachings. She asked for two people to help her light the candles associated with her prayers.

Guy and I volunteered, even though I have no religion and, while Guy is certainly Jewish, he's far from a zealot. So, three people with completely different views on religion managed to collaborate without anyone being harmed. In its own small way, it proved cooperation and mutual respect—even in this disputed land—is possible. Happily, not all interactions between Arabs and Jews are fuelled by anger and hatred.

— —

In Haifa, I visited an Israeli hospital that was treating 1500 Syrians—soldiers, militants from various factions and civilians—who had been wounded in the fighting against ISIS. They'd all been transported through Syria by their families, friends or colleagues and dropped at the Israeli border, in the hope they'd be accepted as genuine casualties and would be cared for by the health services. The Israelis rose to the challenge. They collected the wounded, transported them to nearby hospitals and fixed them up—before sending them back to their own country.

Sadly, there was no hint of the same generosity of spirit when I visited the West Bank—the disputed land to the west of the Jordan River, which is widely regarded as Occupied Palestinian Territory. The Israelis had captured the West Bank from Jordan during the Six-Day War in 1967 and, as a result of the peace treaty between Israel and Egypt in 1982, the Israeli Defence Ministry took administrative control.

Since the Oslo Accords were signed in 1993, 60 per cent of the West Bank has been under Israeli control, and 28 per cent has been under joint Israeli and Palestinian military control, with the Palestinians in charge of civil matters. The Palestinian National Authority in its own right controls 12 per cent of the West Bank. With the imbalance of power in the sector, it's not surprising that there are regular outbreaks of unrest.

During my first trip to Israel, I wanted to arrange a clinic at the hospital in Ramallah, which is around 10 kilometres north of Jerusalem and serves as the administrative capital of the Palestinian National Authority. I realised that I couldn't simply saunter into the West Bank on my own, so I contacted the International Red Cross to find out whether they could organise the trip. They helpfully arranged a car and driver to take me there the next day, which happened to be the Sabbath.

I was picked up by a taxi—with a Palestinian driver who actually lived in Tel Aviv—at the hotel at 7 a.m., fully expecting there would be a long and bureaucratic wait at the Israeli checkpoint that guards the passage into the West Bank. I had mentally prepared myself to be queuing there for hours.

The reality was completely different. When we arrived at the checkpoint, the boom gate was down and there were no obvious signs of anyone in attendance. The driver honked the horn in an attempt to grab someone's attention. To no avail.

So, after a few minutes, he simply slipped the cab into gear and drove on to the next checkpoint. This time it was a little more rigorous. The gate was down, and one Israeli soldier was on duty. He watched as we drove up and stopped, then pressed a button to open the gate without emerging from his guardhouse.

The moment we crossed the border, the vista changed— and, as in Jerusalem, the distinction between the areas occupied by Israelis and Palestinians was plain to see. If the houses were modern, tidy and clean, they were Israeli. If the homes were haphazard, untidy and run-down, they were Palestinian. The conditions I found at the Palestinian hospital reflected the same lack of resources and planning. The hospital was ill-equipped and obviously the funding was completely inadequate.

Abortion is illegal in the West Bank and there's little or no antenatal screening. You ask the parents whether there was any screening during the pregnancy—some say 'no', others say 'yes'. I wondered about the follow-up treatment for those who had been lucky enough to undergo antenatal examinations, because most of the patients I saw were suffering from congenital deformities including club feet and hip displacements.

We went about planning their treatment. But, because of the lack of resources and organisational structure, I'm not sure whether any of those plans were put into action. I left with a sense of uncertainty about the contribution I had made.

On the way back, I asked the cab driver what he thought about the current situation in Israel. 'People are sick of fighting,' he said. 'I take Israeli friends to Ramallah. But I have to disguise them as Arabs while they're in the car so members of Hamas don't kidnap them.'

It seems the will of the people and the actions of the military and politicians on both sides are way out of alignment.

7

I SPY

Many people will be aware of the appalling case of Australian journalist Peter Greste, who was arrested in Cairo on 29 December 2013 and charged with assisting a terrorist organisation. Peter was in the city on assignment with two colleagues from Al Jazeera English, Mohamed Fadel Fahmy and Baher Mohamed. Nearly six months later, they were found guilty after a thoroughly questionable trial and were sentenced to seven years in gaol.

The following January, the Egyptian authorities caved in to the global outrage and announced that the three journalists would be going to a retrial. Within a month, Peter was deported to Cyprus, but the two others remained in prison for a further eleven days.

Peter isn't the only Australian to be arrested on completely spurious charges in the Egyptian capital. It also happened to me and two of my associates when I visited Cairo in late November 2016 to deliver the keynote address at the annual conference of the Egyptian Orthopaedic Association.

I'll put my cards on the table right now: Cairo isn't one of my favourite places. It's dusty and absolutely chaotic. Parts of the city look like a construction site, because there are many half-finished buildings that were obviously abandoned when the money ran out. I disliked every moment I was in the city.

I was there with my partner and colleague Claudia and my surgical Fellow Solon Rosenblatt, from the University of California, San Francisco. Solon's an interesting character. He's Jewish, but he was born in Ankara while his father was serving as a US diplomat in the Turkish capital. He's also firmly committed to the continued existence of Israel, and he served with the Israeli Army in the Yom Kippur War— fighting against Egypt and Syria. So there was always going to be the potential for some tension in Egypt.

I had a sense of foreboding from the moment we landed at Cairo International Airport. There was no air bridge. Instead, we had to board one of the two massively overcrowded buses that had been allocated to take the planeload of passengers across the tarmac.

As I waited for Solon and Claudia inside the terminal,

I became aware that two huge queues were forming—one for immigration clearance, and the other at a foreign exchange desk. We were met by a driver who'd been sent by the conference organisers. Somehow, he'd managed to cross the passport checking area and was waiting for us when we arrived at the terminal.

The driver knew the standard procedures and told us to first join the queue heading to the foreign exchange desk. The instruction was that we should pay the cashier and he would hand over a visa. I'd never heard of buying a visa at a foreign exchange desk in the airport before.

After we'd been to the foreign exchange desk, I approached a female customs officer at her station. She appeared to be in her mid- to late thirties. There were a couple of stripes on the arm of her uniform. As she flicked through my passport, in broken English she demanded aggressively, 'What are you doing here?'

In English, I answered that I was there to speak at a conference. It was clear that she didn't understand what I was saying, and again she roared, 'Why do you come here?'

Our driver had been standing between the officer and me, leaning with an elbow on a bench. At this point, he intervened and responded in Arabic, saying, 'Let him pass.' Reluctantly, our female inquisitor stamped out passports and allowed us through. But as a final act of disdain, instead of handing us our passports, she roughly hurled them back in our general direction, leaving us to gather them up and restore some semblance of order to our documents. It was an even more hostile reception than many travellers—particularly Muslims and Arabs—receive at American airports!

As we emerged from the terminal, we were bombarded by cab drivers desperately trying to lure us into their cars. In the end, our driver navigated us through the hassling cabbies and drove to the InterContinental hotel where the orthopaedic conference was being held.

At reception, we were told that the hotel could provide a Mercedes and a driver to take us on a sightseeing tour of Cairo. It was around four o'clock in the afternoon, and things were about to go seriously awry.

Different rules apply to the vehicles and the roads in Cairo. From the outset, I was convinced that Egyptian cars aren't fitted with brakes—instead, the drivers use the horn to alert everyone else to get out of their way!

The main road into the city is marked for three lanes of traffic in each direction. But Cairo's drivers completely ignore the markings. Instead of three lanes of traffic on either side of the road, there are six! I asked our driver what was the point of the road markings. 'They're just for decoration,' he responded.

We came across only two sets of traffic lights all the time we were in the city. Both were red when we approached them—so, not unnaturally, the driver stopped. This sparked outrage from other motorists. As we slowed to a halt, a cacophony of horns started blaring, demanding our driver should accelerate through the lights.

Going Back

Before long, we drove past a beautifully decorated palace. We stopped the car and climbed out to take photos, as almost any tourist would. Then we spotted an ornate Coptic church the size of a small mosque. Despite its beauty, we weren't inclined to take photographs.

The sightseeing expedition went rapidly downhill from there. As we drove across a bridge over the River Nile, we saw the spectacular St Mark's Coptic Cathedral, about 4 kilometres to our left. It's the centre of the Coptic Christian faith and is attached to the Church of St Peter and St Paul.

I tried to take a photo on my phone while Claudia, in the back, went to take a picture on her new Nikon camera. As she aimed the lens, a beaten-up white Hyundai sped past. The car's passenger—ominously dressed in a black jumper and black pants—leaned out of the window and started yelling in Arabic, 'Pull over, pull over—you're not allowed to take photographs.'

Our driver—a short man in a white shirt and blue tie, with his gut hanging over the top of his grey suit pants—and I weren't about to follow the instruction. Who knows what we would have been letting ourselves in for? But the man in black was so assertive and insistent that we did eventually follow the Hyundai and steer onto an exit from the bridge.

The passenger from the Hyundai—who we quickly realised was actually wearing a police uniform—clambered out and came to the driver's door. 'Give me your driver's licence,' he gruffly ordered. Our driver obliged.

Then the man in black walked around to the front passenger side of our car, where Solon was sitting. He knocked on the window and insisted it should be wound down. 'Give me your passport,' he instructed. Solon complied—and the man walked away with the document in his back pocket.

Now, this would have been uncomfortable for any of us. For Solon, however, it was particularly intimidating because of his military record back in 1967, when Israel launched air strikes on Egyptian military bases and sent tanks and troops rolling across the Gaza Strip and Sinai Peninsula.

The passenger from the Hyundai then approached the back window where Claudia was sitting. She was so terrified by the events that she froze and wouldn't open the window when he barked the order at her. I had to lean over and lower the window. 'Where are you from?' he asked aggressively.

'Australia.'

'I want to see your passports.'

'We don't have them. They're back at the hotel,' I responded.

'Give me the camera,' he instructed, looking in Claudia's direction.

She handed it to him without hesitation and he walked away to his vehicle. Maybe the camera was the prize he was after, we speculated. If that was the case, it would be a cheap price to pay.

The immediate problem, though, was that the Hyundai passenger was still holding our driver's licence and Solon's passport, which was sticking out of the back pocket of the policeman's pants.

Quickly, as the cop moved to walk from our car towards the police vehicle, with admirable sleight of hand, Solon picked his pocket, snatching the passport.

The policeman climbed back into the passenger seat of the Hyundai, then the car sped away. Our driver followed, ducking and weaving through the teeming traffic in hot pursuit.

I'd been holding the other two passports in my jacket pocket and, as we were driving, handed them to Claudia and said, 'Hide these.'

After about five minutes, the white car screeched into what looked like a junkyard beneath the bridge. The surroundings appeared threatening. The yard was a patch of dirt around 50 metres square, with a shed in one corner. Around the yard, about 30 men—every one of them rough and physically intimidating—were lurking.

Once we'd come to a halt, the driver and I climbed out of the car. We were ushered into the shed. Solon got out separately.

Claudia, who by now was alone in our car, was terrified and locked all the doors to protect herself. The rough guys who'd been hanging around in the yard moved towards the Mercedes, slowly crowding around the vehicle with their eyes fixed on Claudia. She felt her safety was hanging by a thread and also was convinced the driver and I were about to be bashed within the confines of the shed.

Fortunately, the only assault we faced was verbal. We were berated and informed that what we thought was a junkyard was actually a police station!

Inside, to my surprise, there were rooms with desks and chairs. I managed to find the Hyundai passenger, who turned out to be a police lieutenant, standing in front of a colonel.

The lieutenant was pointing to the camera and, in Arabic, explaining to the colonel that we were taking photos. I intervened and asked the colonel, 'Can I have the driver's licence and the camera back?'

'In five minutes,' he informed me.

The colonel gave the lieutenant a series of instructions and the junior officer left the room. The driver and I followed in his wake.

The lieutenant then informed us we were about to be transferred to a much bigger police station.

'But why?' I asked.

'You're not allowed to take photographs of the Coptic church,' came the response. To this day, considering we were a few kilometres from the building, I still find this puzzling. For the life of me, I have no idea why photos of the church were forbidden.

After clambering back into the Mercedes, we were ordered to follow the Hyundai. We complied. But as we drove to our new destination, I asked Claudia to search for the phone number of the Australian High Commission in Cairo. I called the number and, with a sense of relief, managed to talk to an Australian official. The conversation didn't unfold as I expected—and it reflected the awful state of the police and justice system in Egypt.

I explained to the Australian woman on the phone that we had been arrested in Cairo.

'What did you do?' she asked.

'We were trying to take a photo of a Coptic church.'

'Well, that was pretty stupid. Don't you know you're not supposed to take photos in Cairo?'

'Okay, but what should we do? We need your help.'

'The best thing you can do is pay them off,' I was told.

'Are you serious?'

'Call us back if you're still being held at the police station in 24 hours.'

We followed the Hyundai to the imposing Shoubra Police Station—a massive facility on the east side of the Nile, which has become one of the symbols of police brutality in Egypt. It's protected by a 10-metre high wall. There are towers on the four corners, each staffed by a police officer armed with a powerful machine gun.

The Hyundai and our Mercedes pulled up at the huge black gates that form the front entrance. Our driver climbed out— and, as he did, another black Mercedes with a driver dressed in the same uniform arrived. The second Mercedes driver—who had been sent by the hotel—also got out to check what was going on.

Claudia saw this as a potential escape route. 'I want to go back to the hotel with the other driver,' she said, probably more in hope than expectation. To be honest, by this point, none of us was going anywhere unless instructed by our captors.

Claudia's Plan B was a little more desperate. She had no idea what was going on and shouted, 'Lock the doors.' Her uncertainty was soon swept away. A large, heavily armed man dressed in a khaki uniform approached our car. I pointed to his firearm and asked Claudia, 'Do you know what that is?'

'A gun?' she responded.

'That's not just a gun,' I pointed out. 'It's an AK47. It doesn't just kill one person; it'll kill 50 or 60 at a time! I wouldn't bother locking the car—if he wants to kill us, he'll just blast us through the doors. A life in this part of the world is worth no more than the price of the bullets.

'Oh—and it might help if you could stop shaking!'

That wasn't going to happen. Claudia's teeth were chattering with sheer terror. 'I can't,' she blurted out.

By now, Solon had followed the driver out of the car to discuss events with the police officers. This wasn't likely to achieve much, because Solon doesn't speak Arabic. But I guess it made him feel as though he might have some influence on our fate.

The driver returned, and I inquired, 'Can Claudia go back to the hotel in the other car?' I had to ask the question, but didn't expect a positive response.

'No,' the driver announced emphatically. 'No one can leave. We have to drive into the police compound.'

I stayed in the car with Claudia while a bunch of policemen in dirty clothes dragged their AK47s with the nozzles on the ground and circled our Mercedes.

The black gates opened, and we drove in as instructed. Our driver steered the car to the right and parked. By this stage, we'd already been detained for around two hours, without having any idea how long the ordeal was going to last. The uncertainty was particularly frightening.

We tumbled out of the car, walked further to the right and entered the ground floor of the police offices. Inside, it was impossibly gloomy and dirty. But the cells in front of us were clearly visible. Glancing at my companions, I could tell we all had a deep sense of fear that we might end up in those very same cells.

We turned right and right again, bringing us to a dreary staircase that reminded me of the stories of Charles Dickens during the dark ages of the London slums, with small brown tiles on the steps and walls. We climbed the stairs and, with tension rising, walked down a long corridor, accompanied by three policemen in the same black outfits as the passenger in the Hyundai. One sported three stars on his shoulders while the other had one star and two bars. Clearly, these were more senior officers.

At the end of the corridor, we walked into an office dominated by a huge dark brown desk and two dark brown Chesterfield sofas pressed against the walls, facing the desk. Alongside, two occasional chairs were facing each other. There was a window on the left-hand side.

One unusual aspect of the office was that there were no computers. It confirmed the rumours I had heard that

Egyptians are paranoid about Israel hacking into their technology. Their answer? Don't use computers!

The decision worked in our favour. A quick check of Solon's online presence would have unveiled his Facebook page, which boldly displayed an image of Solon sitting on a captured Egyptian surface-to-air missile in the Sinai Desert during the October War in 1973. He was fighting with the Israeli Army—a fact which would have placed in even more serious strife.

Sitting behind the desk was a police officer: a lieutenant colonel. Five other police officers were in the room with him. To the right of the lieutenant colonel's desk were three grey old-style telephones—with his mobile phone alongside. The phones were ringing constantly, and the senior policeman was forever barking instructions in Arabic into one of the mouthpieces. Solon and I chose to stand.

When the phones finally fell silent, the lieutenant colonel rose to his feet—revealing that his formal shoes had been left beneath the desk. He was wearing a pair of black Nike slide thongs. With socks. Not the most flattering fashion statement.

He walked around to the front of his desk. I addressed him straight away, telling him that the officer who'd arrested us was an idiot. My fear was that we'd been reported to National Security. That could mean we'd follow the same path as Peter Greste—being held in gaol until the Australian authorities were informed, and then becoming the subject of protracted diplomatic negotiations, largely designed as a show of strength by the Egyptian Government. We would have been particularly valuable captives—especially if the officers had found out that Solon's an Israeli citizen and I'm in the RAAF Reserve.

But finally, things started to turn in our favour. Almost immediately, the lieutenant colonel began shouting at the arresting officer, telling him he was a fool. The other police joined in, reinforcing his junior status and incompetence. I was pacing up and down, venting my frustrations at our treatment.

I then pointed to Claudia and exclaimed, 'This woman is sitting on your sofa shaking. She's done nothing wrong. How can you threaten perfectly innocent people like this?' The lieutenant colonel tried to placate me and urged me to sit down.

At that point, a general walked in. The lieutenant colonel stood aside and ushered his superior officer into the chair behind the desk.

The general started talking to the other officer in Arabic, saying, 'We should try to sort this out here and now rather than transferring it to the National Security Headquarters,' he urged.

I intervened, introduced myself and explained why we were visiting Cairo, and asked the general to help us.

Solon adopted a different approach, attempting to defuse the situation by putting his arm around the general's shoulder and saying reassuringly, 'Let's sort this out over a coffee.'

I wasn't entirely sure whether the softly-softly approach would be successful. But the police seemed to understand the word coffee and summoned an attendant who, in a matter of minutes, produced a tray of small cups of short, intense Turkish coffee.

There was a moment of distraction when the general picked up one of the phones on the desk. Claudia asked me in a faint and exhausted voice, 'Can you tell me what's going on?'

I explained what I'd overheard from the conversations in Arabic between the police officials. 'The guy who stopped us called National Security and told them we were spies,' I told Claudia and Solon. 'But now, everything seems to be okay. All the other people appear to be on our side. They're trying to release us. But they have to get clearance from National Security.'

The general ordered the arresting lieutenant, the passenger in the Hyundai, to leave. The junior officer saluted and walked out of the room with his head bowed. After a dressing-down by the general and the other officers, he'd been sent home for failing to follow the standard reporting process. Instead of referring the case to his commanding officer, he'd jumped the gun and straight away reported the incident to National Security.

The police then called our hotel to check our credentials and establish that we were legitimate delegates at the conference. The conference organiser delivered the confirmation over the phone and arranged for a representative of the Ministry of Health to speak to the general face to face. Which was fine and dandy—except that it meant we had to be cooped up in the grim surroundings of the police station for another hour or more.

Eventually, the Ministry of Health official arrived, wearing a brown suit—everything that day seemed to be one shade of brown or another. He announced, 'This must be a mix-up. This is a professor from Australia who's a keynote speaker at our conference.'

In the meantime, there had been several phone calls with what seems to be the duty officer at the National Security Headquarters and they were awaiting the decision about our fate from their chain of command. We ended up staying in the police station for two more hours before we received the final phone call from National Security Headquarters. The general passed the message to me that we were cleared to go. But first the paperwork must be finalised. That was a big relief.

The general started dictating to a junior officer who was writing a statement on a pad of lined paper, outlining events and saying, 'We searched their person. We searched their cameras. And found no evidence that they were spies.'

They hadn't carried out any of those inspections, of course. So, essentially, the police faked it! I had to sign the statement. But to make sure there could be no evidence against us, I signed with my mother's name.

During the proceedings, the police had given Claudia a carton of ridiculously sweet apple juice, which she had avoided drinking. Now, they started laughing and joking and said to her, 'You have to drink the juice or we won't let you go!' It was a price she was happy to pay. Before we left, Claudia's camera was returned.

To be honest, I think the factor that had protected us was that I'd be invited to the conference by the Egyptian Ministry of Health. The head of the department might well have played a part in achieving our release.

By the time we were freed, it was around 8.30 p.m. and dark. But, despite the dramas, we resumed our sightseeing excursion. I asked the driver to avoid Tahrir Square—which had been the centre of the mass demonstrations during the Arab Spring of 2011.

Obviously, he didn't listen. Fifteen minutes later, we ended up there!

As well as giving us a summary of the significance of the demonstrations, the driver also made a point of gratuitously informing us: 'This is the place where the CBS journalist Lara Logan was sexually assaulted.'

On a much more pleasant note, we also went to the River Nile, where we walked along a couple of boats.

During the sightseeing tour, my phone rang and, after a brief conversation, I told the others, 'We have to go back.'

Claudia immediately thought the worst. 'What, to the police station?'

'No,' I reassured her. 'To the hotel!'

When we arrived, we received a huge welcome from the hotel and conference officials—along with a massive bunch of flowers for Claudia.

Going Back

I believe we were the victims of the innate suspicion of foreigners, who are broadly regarded by the Egyptian authorities as spies or potential spies. The mood of insecurity followed the fragmentation of Egyptian politics that started with the Arab Spring uprisings.

After massive street demonstrations lasting eighteen days, long-time dictator Hosni Mubarak was forced to step down and cede power to the Supreme Council of the Armed Forces. Elections were held and won by the Islamist Muslim Brotherhood, which installed Mohamed Morsi as president in mid-2012.

Morsi followed his beliefs and attempted to introduce an Islamic constitution—as well as trying to write into law unparalleled presidential powers. The country again dissolved into mass protests and general turmoil. To resolve the crisis, the Egyptian military staged a coup in mid-2013 and installed army chief Abdel Fattah el-Sisi as the country's leader. The following year, el-Sisi resigned from the military and was elected as Egypt's president, apparently with the support of 97 per cent of voters.

The day after the 'spying' incident, I was due to address the conference—but even that didn't run smoothly. We had decided to visit the pyramids on the morning of my talk, which was a reasonable enough proposition as they're not far out of the city. We were driven there in around 45 minutes.

We reached the pyramids to be greeted—not unexpectedly—by a throng of tour guides and dozens of kids trying to sell us cheap souvenirs.

I Spy

As happens in these places, on the tour inside the pyramid, we were deluged with signs saying 'No Cameras'. The observation sounded ironically familiar by this stage! But the guide was less vigilant than the Cairo police—the instruction was overlooked after the payment of a small gratuity.

The journey back to the conference centre wasn't as straightforward as the journey to the pyramids—it took no less than four hours! It was just a sea of cars all the way. The massive traffic snarl was so bad that, a couple of kilometres from the conference venue, we abandoned the vehicle and walked the rest of the journey.

We were way behind schedule, and there was no opportunity to get changed. So I walked up to the microphone in front of a packed audience dressed in the T-shirt and blazer I'd been wearing for the casual visit to the pyramids. It was not an auspicious start. More misadventures were to come, though. When I was welcomed to the stage by the chair of the session, he introduced me as 'Munjed the spy'!

Halfway through my talk, the Egyptian minister of health and his entourage walked in. As soon as he was spotted, the audience stood and applauded, completely drowning out my address. I had no alternative—I simply had to stop while the minister took his place on the stage.

This wasn't a quick process. The minister wasn't about to cut short his moment of glory, and he milked the occasion for all it was worth. He ambled through the audience, greeting friends and acquaintances along the way. Then he slowly strolled onto the stage, walked behind me as I stood speechless at the microphone and joined the panel members sitting to one side. He made a point of kissing each of them in turn. Only when he took his seat did the applause die down, allowing me to resume my talk.

I'd never experienced anything like that before—or, for that matter, since. On reflection, if the minister had indeed played a part in securing our release from custody then I don't resent his moment of glory.

The postscript to our brush with Egypt's security forces came three weeks later, in December 2016. During Sunday mass, a suicide bomber detonated a 12-kilogram IED in the Church of St Peter and St Paul, next to the Coptic cathedral that we'd been photographing. A total of 25 people died in the bombing, mainly women and children. Another 49 were wounded.

The attack was roundly condemned by the Grand Mufti of Egypt—the country's most senior official of Islamic law—along with Coptic church leaders, Roman Catholic Pope Francis and even the militant Islamic group Harakat Sawa'd Misr, also known as the Hasam Movement and regarded by some countries, including Egypt, as a terrorist organisation. Hundreds of Coptic Christians and Muslims joined together in protest outside the church, chanting slogans against the perpetrators of the slaughter.

8

BACK TO BAGHDAD

Returning to Iraq wasn't on my radar. But, like many events in my life, chance played a major role. Just on dusk one evening in February 2017, I was driving through the historic area of The Rocks in Sydney with a couple of colleagues when an unexpected phone call came through. There was no indication of the caller's number, but I answered anyway.

The mystery voice on the other end of the phone was speaking in Arabic with a strong Iraqi accent, and I heard the question, 'Is that Munjed?' Beyond that, everything was overwhelmed by technological crackle and interference. The reception was terrible.

I kept shouting, 'Who is this? Who is this?'

Eventually, the line cleared and the caller introduced himself. 'I'm the Iraqi ambassador in Switzerland,' he explained. 'I used to be the Iraqi ambassador in Australia, and I'm familiar with the work you're doing there. Can I ask you a question?'

'Yes, of course,' I responded.

'Would you be prepared to take a call from the prime minister of Iraq?' The question made me sit up straight in my seat. It's not a regular occurrence that the prime minister of a foreign country asks for permission to speak to me!

'Certainly, I would. I'd be happy to talk to him,' I answered.

Around half an hour later, as my colleague and I were sitting in The Bridge Room restaurant on Bridge Street, my phone rang again. It wasn't the Iraqi prime minister but Hussinane Al-Shakh from the prime minister's office. After exchanging pleasantries, he outlined the proposal. 'We have thousands of people in Iraq who've been badly wounded in the fighting against ISIS,' he explained. 'A lot of them are amputees. We are wondering whether you could come to Iraq to help these people by operating on them.' Then he added, 'Of course, we're happy to pay you.'

I quickly rejected that part of the plan. 'There's no need to pay me. And yes, I'd certainly be interested,' I told him.

The proposition caught me completely by surprise. The prospect of going back to Iraq filled me with curiosity and anxiety in roughly equal proportions. I joked at the time that this was the Iraqi Government's way of getting me back into the country so they could punish me for escaping all those years earlier.

Even though I had agreed in principle to return to Iraq, I had no idea how the whole project could be organised. 'Someone from the hospital will contact you and let you know the general situation, as well as the sort of numbers you could expect to be dealing with,' Hussinane explained.

My first contact with the Ibn Sina Hospital in Baghdad's Green Zone came from its director, Dr Yasser al-Timmimi, and two surgeons who operate there. They called a few times, initially discussing the general parameters of the project. We then talked more about my trip during regular phone calls and emails over the next few weeks. The Iraqis were absolutely desperate for me to go. They were saying, 'Just come over and we'll work it out when you get here.'

That wasn't precise enough for me. Such a venture needs careful and detailed planning to make the most of the opportunity. If no one knows exactly what's going on, precious time that could be used for treating patients is almost certainly wasted amid the confusion and, inevitably, misunderstandings.

The Iraqis proposed March for my first visit. But the notice was far too short and, besides, I had other long-standing commitments. Finally, we agreed that I would go to Baghdad for three days in May.

Completely coincidentally, after we'd set the schedule, another Iraqi called me. 'I'm organising TEDxBaghdad,' he told me. 'The event is being held in May, and I'm wondering whether you would be prepared to be one of the speakers.' The stars had aligned.

'I'd be delighted to—and it so happens that I'll be in Baghdad in May anyway,' I informed him.

That first clinic at Ibn Sina Hospital was like nothing I'd ever experienced. For a start, the level of security at the hospital is way above anything you would experience in civilian Australia. It was the equivalent of walking into a military base.

The entrance to the building is carefully secured. On a daily basis, the front gates remain closed and locked. Access from the four-lane roadway is by a narrow passage that runs through a guardhouse staffed 24/7 by soldiers dressed in camouflage battle fatigues and armed with machine guns.

The hospital itself has a special status. It belongs to the Iraqi Ministry of Health and is under the direct control of the minister, who at the time was a woman named Dr Adila Hammoud. The minister's husband is an orthopaedic surgeon—and also happens to be the hospital's deputy director.

Ibn Sina was built by four Iraqi doctors and opened in 1964. Since then, it has very much reflected the history of the country. Only months after it was completed, Ibn Sina was purchased by Saddam Hussein's regime for a knockdown price and was used to treat Saddam, his family, friends and leading members of the ruling Ba'ath Party. It was where one of Saddam's sons, Uday, was operated on after being wounded in an assassination attempt in the 1990s.

Ibn Sina was taken over by the US armed forces after Saddam was deposed in 2003. It became one of the main trauma hospitals during the worst of the anarchy that followed. At its peak, the hospital was treating around 300 trauma patients each month. The United States handed the keys of the hospital back to the Iraqi Government in 2009.

It's still regarded as one of the best government medical facilities in Iraq. That being said, measured against the hospitals where I operate in Australia, it is extremely basic and shows its age. The corridors are painted regulation cream and pastel colours, and the dark-stained timber doors haven't been updated since the place was built.

On the ground floor, a single corridor runs from the reception area at the front, past the administration offices on both sides to the X-ray, physiotherapy and pharmacy rooms. At the back, a doorway leads into a yard and car park. Administrators and medical staff on the ground floor sit behind old, heavy wooden desks. Any additional furniture appears to date back to the 1960s as well.

Some of the facilities in the public area on the ground floor would be condemned in Australian hospitals. Take the toilets, for example, which are shared between the staff and the public. Let's put this politely—the bathrooms at Ibn Sina Hospital aren't going to win any awards!

The male toilets, located a few metres on the left as you walk into the hospital from the reception area, leave plenty to be desired. There are two urinals and two cubicles with standard squat facilities. Rather than flushing cisterns, the cubicles are each fitted with a hose attached to the wall. It's not a system that works efficiently—often you'll find the bathroom floor wet.

Further along the corridor on the left is the women's bathroom with two cubicles that are fitted with Western-style toilet bowls and flushing cisterns. But the flushing mechanism often doesn't work. And there's usually water on the floor of this bathroom as well. Plus there is never any toilet paper.

The wards are on the first floor. At the back of the hospital, public patients are packed into dormitories with as many as six or seven people in each room. Some of the patients lie on beds that have bare mattresses covered with a blanket. Other patients have no blankets or are lying on the floor. Private patients are at the front in single rooms. But the beds and bedding are the same. Someone suggested that the accommodation is designed to encourage patients to leave hospital as soon as possible. The beds don't look at all comfortable!

The surgical theatres are on the second floor. They're not state-of-the-art facilities, but, for all their limitations, I've operated in worse conditions in other developing nations.

I can imagine the frantic scenes that must have unfolded at the hospital as Iraq was engulfed in some of the major wars of the last 40 years. To be honest, it was like a war zone when we arrived.

Hundreds of people were jostling in the reception area and had spilled over into the ground-floor corridor of the hospital. A few lucky ones had managed to snare a seat in reception. But most were standing—in many cases for hours—or sitting in wheelchairs trying to force their way to the front of the queue.

Most had made an enormous effort to come to the hospital. On the first day of the clinic, they were predominantly locals from Baghdad. While they didn't have to travel great distances, the journey would have been arduous. The vast majority lived in the Red Zone—the rest of Baghdad that lies outside the heavily protected central area of the Green Zone. They needed special permits to cross the border between the two zones, and it may well have taken hours to be processed at the military checkpoints. Not one of them complained.

They were all reaching out for help and desperately hoping to put an end to the years of pain and suffering they had been enduring. They wanted the chance—the last chance, as many of them saw it—to return to a virtually normal life. Grown men, hard as nails after fighting ISIS—among them tough para-military volunteers, enlisted soldiers, crack counterterrorism troops and federal police officers who'd been horrifically wounded in the vicious battles—were in tears, pleading with anyone who'd listen to be included on my surgical list.

The range of injuries we saw was shocking. Initially, I was told all the patients would be amputees wanting to undergo osseointegration. But I made it clear I could also treat others who'd suffered a major trauma. In the end, many of those I saw during that first clinic had lost limbs or parts of limbs. Others were suffering from debilitating infections following one or more operations that had often been undertaken in neighbouring Iran.

Some of the stories of how they were wounded were beyond anyone's imagination. One former soldier was injured after an ISIS car bomb exploded. He immediately ran towards the scene to rescue as many people as he could. He pulled a young child from the debris, clasped the boy to his chest and raced away from the scene. As he left the carnage behind and believed he'd carried the child to safety, another vehicle exploded in front of him. Unwittingly, the boy acted as a shield that protected the soldier's torso from the second blast. Tragically, the child was decapitated. The soldier lost most of his right arm, which had been exposed as he carried the child.

Another patient had spotted a suicide bomber in a crowd and decided that the only course of action was to tackle him to the ground. As he made the grab, the terrorist detonated his deadly device, killing himself and inflicting terrible injuries on his captor, who lost both of his legs.

Then there was the middle-aged man who had lost one leg and was having severe difficulty with the other. He could walk short distances with crutches but found it extremely uncomfortable to sit down. Despite the pain and discomfort, he still worked in a pastry shop every morning. Another patient had lost both his arms but still insisted on working each day.

The strength of character these people displayed was nothing short of remarkable. I know the Iraqi people, so it wasn't a great surprise to me. But my colleagues Claudia and Michelle were overwhelmed by what they saw. They were deeply shocked by the horrific stories of how these people had been injured—and, in equal proportion, amazed that our patients could detail their experiences without even a hint of anger or self-pity.

The horde of patients jostling for a prime spot in the clinic room, the hospital corridor and the reception area was so vast that we had to introduce a numbering system to create some form of order. My job was looking after the patients, and Claudia managed the note taking. Others, including the hospital staff, were involved in crowd control.

On the first day of the clinic, Claudia tried to follow standard Australian procedures—taking detailed notes on each patient. This was a huge task, because every patient's story had to be translated from Arabic into English. For the first 45 people we saw, Claudia wrote full one-page reports. It took her hours. Then it dawned on her that the reports would be going nowhere. The hospital didn't require them, and no one would read them.

After that, she streamlined the system. It became a much quicker exchange. Name . . . date of birth . . . which part of the military they served with (counterterrorism, army, Hashd, police or civilian) . . . smoker or non-smoker . . . nature of the injury . . . treatment plan . . . phone number.

Another handbrake on the work of the clinic was the constant interruptions from surgeons, university professors and the media—all of them wanting to find out about the visitor from Australia and what he could do for these patients. Once again, in the face of questioning by medical professionals and the media, not a word of complaint was uttered by the patients.

As well as the awful injuries we witnessed, there were other major issues that made surgery in Iraq a complicated process. The general awareness of a healthy lifestyle is nowhere nearly as advanced as in developed nations. Diabetes is a significant problem, largely because of unhealthy diets. Hepatitis is also widespread.

The biggest threat of all, however, is smoking. It seems that almost all Iraqi men smoke, generally cigarettes. And Iraqis aren't casual smokers. Many of them can get through up to three packets a day. That's 60 cigarettes!

Then there are the shisha pipes—the freestanding, traditional, often ornate hookah pipes used to smoke flavoured tobacco through a water basin. They're still part of the social ritual and are readily available in restaurants as well as in many Iraqi homes.

In developed nations, I won't operate on patients unless they're non-smokers or have quit for at least three months. But if I applied the same rule in Iraq, I'd have a theatre list in single figures!

In between seeing patients at the clinic, I was invited to meet the then prime minister, Haider al-Abadi, and the minister of health, Dr Adila Hammoud, in the nearby palace that now houses the Prime Minister's Department. Like most of the grand buildings in the Green Zone, it had been built for Saddam Hussein. I was driven there with my three colleagues—Claudia, Michelle and journalist Adam Baidawi— in a heavily armoured SUV.

The palace stands in its own well-manicured grounds, and the interior reflects Saddam's wild spending on palaces and monuments to himself. There's no shortage of marble or chandeliers.

Funnily enough, I remembered being here once before, when I was a kid. I was in the audience for some kind of ceremony featuring Saddam front and centre. Back then, I didn't get to spend any extended one-on-one time with the nation's leader!

I spoke to Prime Minister al-Abadi for around half an hour, largely in English. Initially, I got the impression that he thought my visit was little more than a commercial enterprise. But his eyes lit up when I opened my laptop and showed him videos of osseointegration patients walking on their new legs.

The prime minister, whose original area of expertise was engineering, wanted to know more. I began to explain the source of my fascination with the technique. I asked, 'Have you seen *The Terminator*?'

No response.

'What about *RoboCop*? Have you seen *RoboCop*?'

He had.

'It's just like that,' I told him.

By the time we returned to the hospital, word of our presence had obviously spread. The crowd of patients at Ibn Sina had swelled even more!

As well as my work at the hospital and the meeting with the prime minister, I delivered two talks during that first visit to Baghdad. On the second evening, we travelled out of the Green Zone to a Lebanese club, where I spoke to a room full of local orthopaedic surgeons. Security tightened noticeably as we went through the checkpoint into the Red Zone. The driver kept one hand on the siren to make it loud and clear to anyone and everyone that his vehicle had right of way.

The moment we arrived we were surrounded by bodyguards carrying machine guns. They maintained the tight cordon around us as they escorted us into the club. It was even worse afterwards. As soon as I finished the presentation, we were stampeded by surgeons wanting to talk to me. This sparked the arrival of even more security.

My TEDxBaghdad talk—an independently organised conference to promote Iraqi innovation, connect talented Iraqis and contribute to the reconstruction of Baghdad as a capital of Middle Eastern culture—the next day was at the Al Rasheed Hotel, a five-star establishment on the border of the Green Zone and the Red Zone. It has long been regarded as one of the most luxurious accommodation options in Baghdad and has been at the centre of a number of famous incidents.

During the war with Iran in the 1980s, Saddam Hussein organised a major conference of the Non-Aligned Movement—a group of states that are not formally aligned with or against any major power bloc—at the Al Rasheed. It was designed to be a show of force by the dictator. The Iranians weren't about to take that lying down.

The Iranian Air Force launched huge bombing raids on

Baghdad, hitting military targets across the city. The attacks culminated in the pilot of an Iranian fighter plane, which had been hit by anti-aircraft fire, opting for a suicide attack rather than ejecting. He lined up the Al Rasheed Hotel and flew straight into the building. The impact was huge and caused serious damage. The raids and the pilot's actions served their purpose. The Non-Aligned Movement conference was switched to New Delhi.

After the First Gulf War, a mosaic depicting President George W. Bush looking shocked was installed on the floor of the hotel's lobby. It meant that everyone who went through the area would walk on the image of the US leader—showing him the soles of their feet. In Arab terms, that's just about the ultimate insult. The Al Rasheed became a US military centre after the invasion of Iraq in 2003, and American soldiers smashed the mosaic.

Later that year, the hotel came under rocket attack when US Deputy Secretary of Defence Paul Wolfowitz was staying there. He wasn't injured, but one high-ranking US officer was killed, and a government official was wounded. Subsequently, the hotel has undergone various refurbishments, the most recent in 2011.

I was no stranger to the Al Rasheed Hotel, and I knew exactly what to expect when I was preparing for the TEDxBaghdad talk. Two decades earlier, the hotel had played a significant role in my life in Baghdad. The Grand Ballroom—an ornate auditorium with a capacity of around 1000 people, which features columns down both sides—was the venue for the reception after my first wedding.

9

IN THE LINE OF FIRE

The plan for my second visit to Baghdad, in August 2017, was to operate on as many patients as possible in ten days. But, even as we were checking in the 90 kilograms of excess baggage—surgical tools, equipment and implants—at Sydney Airport, the whole venture remained surrounded by uncertainty.

Initially, the people who were campaigning most enthusiastically for me to go to Baghdad were the surgeons who wanted to learn about osseointegration and other advanced operating techniques. But at one stage, the powers that be told me I wouldn't be allowed to operate in Iraq. It took some delicate diplomacy and careful negotiation, but we eventually cleared that hurdle.

The prime purpose of this visit—dictated by the Iraqi Government—was to operate on fighters from the military, paramilitary, counterterrorism and police who'd been severely wounded in the battle to drive ISIS terrorists out of their country. They'd suffered huge numbers of casualties since the summer of 2014, when ISIS launched a lightning attack from its nominated capital of Raqqa in Syria.

Everyone who has taken an interest in the Middle East over the years is aware of the horrors ISIS has inflicted on the region. Not only did they adopt some of the most brutal tactics ever seen but they also celebrated their complete disdain for anyone who wasn't part of their horrific war machine. The videos of beheadings and other atrocities they posted on social media remain notorious and among the most disturbing images of the early 21st century.

What isn't as well known is just how close ISIS came to storming all the way to Baghdad. The writing was on the wall in December 2013 when, shortly after the authorities closed a protest camp outside the city, Sunni rebels—initially under the banner of Al-Qaeda in Iraq—took control of Fallujah, just 75 kilometres from Baghdad.

To give you some idea of how close ISIS was to taking the Iraqi capital, let's put the capture of Fallujah into Australian terms. It's the equivalent of ISIS being 10 kilometres south of Goulburn and headed for Canberra. For Sydneysiders, it's like having ISIS controlling Gosford, Wollongong or the lower Blue Mountains. In Melbourne, ISIS would be approaching Geelong from the west. In Brisbane, terrorists would have taken the Gold Coast. In Adelaide, Murray Bridge would have been overrun, and the murderous Sunni forces would be advancing on the South Australian capital. In Perth, ISIS would have taken Mandurah or Morangup.

In June 2014, making the most of the growing political and social unrest in Iraq, a relatively small and vastly outnumbered ISIS unit launched a carefully coordinated offensive and quickly forced the demoralised Iraqi Army into retreat. Panic spread among the regular Iraqi soldiers and, within days, Mosul—Iraq's second-largest city, 400 kilometres north of Baghdad—fell to the invaders. Nineveh Province, to the east of Mosul, was overrun soon after, as Iraqi soldiers deserted en masse in the face of the onslaught. Iraqi resistance collapsed.

Tikrit, 140 kilometres north of the capital and the place where Saddam Hussein was born, also came under ISIS control that month. It was the site of one of the greatest atrocities committed by the jihadists. At least 1500 air-force cadets based in the city were executed. None of them was armed.

At the height of its success, ISIS had conquered one-third of the landmass of Iraq. It went on to declare a new caliphate—which literally means succession, and follows the Islamic tradition that began with the death of the Prophet Mohammed in 632 AD. The Sunni successors to Mohammed became known as the caliph.

Abu Bakr al-Baghdadi—who claimed he was directly descended from the prophet—was named as the leader of

ISIS, taking on the title of Caliph Ibrahim. He was born near Samarra, 125 kilometres north of Baghdad, in 1971 and was named Ibrahim Awwad Ibrahim Ali Muhammad al-Badri al-Samarrai.

After graduating from school, he was disqualified from joining the army because of bad eyesight. He went on to university, where he studied religion and was regarded as largely insignificant. He kept to himself during those years, but was known to openly oppose violence—in complete contrast to his later activities.

He came to prominence after rising through the ranks of Al-Qaeda in Iraq—which, at the time, was also known as the Islamic State of Iraq—and was named as its head in 2010. The terrorist group expanded into Syria on the back of the uprising against President Bashar al-Assad in 2013 and rebranded itself as the Islamic State of Iraq and the Levant.

Before long, it had raised an active army—many of them Sunni dissidents who'd previously been soldiers with the Iraqi Army but had become disillusioned after the Americans disbanded the military following the fall of Saddam Hussein. The well-equipped fighting force was backed by significant funds from taxes ISIS imposed in the areas it controlled and the sale of oil from the regions it had captured.

The situation in Iraq became so parlous that, during Friday prayers on 13 June 2014, the Grand Ayatollah of Iraq, Ali al-Husseini al-Sistani, issued a fatwa against ISIS. In effect, it was a declaration of war against the Sunni extremists and a call for all able-bodied Iraqis to join the fight against ISIS. Tens of thousands of volunteers responded and created Al-Hashd al-Shaabi—the Popular Mobilization Units, otherwise known as the paramilitary.

Hashd includes a wide variety of completely disparate militia that had been previously fighting for their own interests. It's predominantly Shi'ite, but incorporates around 40 different groups—from Sunni tribesmen to Christians and Yazidis, a Kurdish religious minority. At its peak, Hashd could claim up to 65,000 soldiers.

Behind the scenes, the guiding hand supporting Hashd was Iraq's overwhelmingly Shi'ite neighbour, Iran—which was supplying weapons and ammunition, and worked closely with the paramilitary. Hashd's involvement in land battles was crucial to the success of the fight against ISIS and, along with air strikes by US planes and other Allied aircraft, they halted and then drove back the Sunni fighters. But in achieving their goal, thousands of the paramilitary—along with regular army soldiers, counterterrorism fighters and police—had suffered terrible injuries.

The Iraqi Government—mostly for pragmatic reasons, but also for humanitarian motives—was committed to providing the best possible health care for the war wounded.

This is where I fitted in. But it wasn't as straightforward as that. For a start, I needed to know where the funding for my mission was coming from. Although I offered my surgical skills for free, there were still expenses to be covered. Various medical-device companies had provided surgical equipment and implants at cost price.

I started talking to the paramilitary about picking up the tab for the surgical equipment needed to operate on their wounded fighters. Initially, I was told there was no chance. This would have brought the project to an end before it had even started. Finally, after many long and arduous discussions, the paramilitary agreed to foot the bill for their wounded fighters.

However, at the start of our second visit to Baghdad, we still didn't have formal approval for the operations to go ahead. I had a choice: put the project on hold while the politicking continued, or back my judgement that the issues would be resolved. I decided to take a chance. I went ahead with the first scheduled operations.

By the end of our first day of surgery, I still hadn't been given the official go-ahead. Even into day two, the uncertainty remained. That afternoon, the hospital authorities called a halt to our activities. The theatre list was suspended. We couldn't do anything, and unrest and tension quickly started to build among the patients and staff.

Then, an individual who was clearly a high-ranking official arrived at the hospital escorted by a small army of paramilitary soldiers. He came straight into the operating theatre.

I had no idea who he was, so I politely posed the question, 'May I ask, who are you?'

'I'm a humble citizen,' he responded.

It was clear he was much more significant than he was

149

letting on, so I decided to seek his help to get the surgical lists back on track.

'I've come here to operate on counterterrorist and army soldiers, paramilitary fighters and police officers who've suffered terrible wounds protecting Iraq from ISIS,' I told him. 'I've already started operating on them, but I still don't have permission to carry out these operations.'

After a brief pause, the important person, who I subsequently found out was the deputy head of Hashd, Abu Mahdi al-Muhandis, said, 'You do now'.

'From who?' I asked.

'From me,' he responded. 'Give me five minutes.'

He pulled a small mobile phone worth no more than US$20 out of his pocket, dialled it and issued an instruction to someone on the other end: 'I need my patients to be treated and procedures to start.' He hung up, left the theatre complex with his entourage and strode to the office of the hospital director, Dr Yasser al-Timmimi.

Half an hour later, I was summoned to Dr al-Timmimi's office, where I found him sitting in front of his desk looking like a timid mouse. The same man who one hour earlier had been barking orders at me was now desperately trying to earn the favour of the paramilitary deputy leader.

Al-Muhandis turned to me and announced, 'You're good to go'.

The relief was massive. Until now, I'd been working clandestinely—knowing that I could be ordered to stop at a moment's notice. Now, it was official. We could get on with the work we'd come here to complete.

On my first visit to Ibn Sina Hospital, I saw a variety of patients from all four areas of the Iraqi fighting force. But because Hashd was bankrolling the mission, when it came to my second trip, the majority of the patients were from the paramilitary.

The desperation of the patients and their families had been clear to see as soon as we arrived in August 2017. We based ourselves in a meeting room just 10 metres from the reception area and on the right of the ground-floor corridor. The throng of patients and their families spilled over from the reception area into the corridor, where they would linger—trying to corner me or my colleagues and exert pressure to gain a place at the top of the surgery list. Unfortunately, there wasn't much I could do. The operating schedule was organised by the team at the hospital.

Through the government, Hashd and the hospital administration, I had been given the target of operating on 48 military personnel. But I also campaigned for civilians to be included. Hundreds of them had made the trek to Baghdad in the hope of undergoing osseointegration. Time and again, though, I was firmly told that no civilians could be considered until the military quota had been achieved. Until then, I would not be given permission to operate on any civilians—even though a number of them were prime candidates for very complex surgery, including osseointegration.

It became clear that a decision on civilian operations would have to be referred to the prime minister.

Along with my young American colleague, Matt Weldon—who'd been working with me in Sydney as a resident for the previous five weeks—I faced a variety of challenges when we operated in Baghdad during that scorching summer of 2017. Matt, who hails from Houston in Texas, is an interesting character who always operates wearing his favourite cowboy boots! He'd never before experienced the clinical conundrums we came across in Baghdad.

The first, of course, was the condition of the patients. Their injuries were some of the most complex any of us had ever seen. The devastation inflicted by bullets, IEDs, rockets, shells and mortars was far worse than anything we routinely see in Australia. Added to this was the fact that many of these patients had previously undergone surgical procedures that we wouldn't regard as ideal. And, often, infection had set in, damaging tissue and bones.

Then there were the conditions in the hospital. Some equipment and surgical fixtures and fittings that are the norm in Australia simply weren't available. And although the doctors and physiotherapists mostly appeared knowledgeable, eager to learn, well prepared and enthusiastic, some of the nurses didn't seem to be familiar with the latest procedures. For a handful, even basic hygiene and sterilisation methods were either a mystery or an unnecessary detail—replaced with a shrug of the shoulders when standards slipped.

Then there were the cultural and language difficulties. I speak fluent Arabic, so it was okay for me. But other surgeons and staff who came with me weren't in the same position. Plenty of details seemed to be literally lost in translation for patients as well as some of the medical staff.

For example, one of the patients who was scheduled for afternoon surgery was instructed in the morning not to eat anything before his operation. I understand that at lunchtime, Sophie McNeill—who was covering our visit for ABC TV's *Foreign Correspondent* program—saw the patient disappearing into a cupboard with a plate of food. When he was challenged, the patient simply said, 'I know I'm supposed to be fasting. I'm taking the plate of food into the cupboard so no one can see me eating. It'll be okay if no one sees me. They won't know I've eaten anything!' Fortunately for the patient and the operating team—both of them facing a potential disaster in the theatre if the patient had food in his stomach—the beans were spilled. His operation was delayed for 24 hours.

Our days at the hospital started around eight o'clock each morning. We continued operating, with only a brief break for lunch and dinner on the run, until the operating list had been completed. The earliest we finished in the theatres was 11.30 p.m., and on many days it wasn't until after 1 a.m. that the final patient was wheeled back to the ward. We took only one Friday off, because it's the Muslim holy day. Most hospital staff members weren't available, leaving us with only minimal support.

Many of the military men I operated on had been through hell in the months and years before I met them. In the end, around 50 per cent of the patients I recommended for osseo-integration decided not to have the operation. Fear of the unknown, I guess.

Every single one of the patients we treated had a story to tell—many of them reflecting key aspects of life in Iraq.

THE DANCING MAN: HAITHEM JABBAR RAHEEL

The first person in Iraq to walk on a new robotic leg after undergoing osseointegration was 29-year-old Haithem—a short, slim man with a shock of dark hair, a beard, eyes that constantly smiled and a broad, cheeky grin. His relentlessly cheerful attitude was a tribute to his resilience, particularly considering his ordeal of the previous three years.

Despite the history of bitter and bloody conflicts between Iraq and Iran, by the second decade of the 21st century, large numbers of wounded Iraqi soldiers were being sent to Iran for treatment. Haithem, who's single and from Kirkuk—about 250 kilometres north of Baghdad—was one of them.

He'd suffered terrible injuries fighting with the para-military against ISIS in the autumn of 2014 near the town of Baiji, 200 kilometres north of the capital. Like so many of the wounded Iraqis, he stood on an IED while on patrol. His right leg was blown off above the knee.

Haithem lay wounded on the ground for around half an hour, receiving rudimentary medical care, before being rushed to hospital in an ambulance. He remained in hospital for the next year, being pumped full of antibiotics to ward off the life-threatening danger of infection, before being transferred to a medical facility in the Iranian capital, Tehran. For the first six months there, he was confined to a wheelchair. Eventually, he was fitted with a socket prosthesis—but he never mastered walking with it. In the end, he gave up and, in mid-2016, went back to the certainty of his wheelchair.

Haithem's X-rays clearly indicated that osseointegration would work well. He enthusiastically accepted the idea and underwent surgery the next day. No more than 24 hours later, he was discharged from hospital with only paracetamol—he was one of the lucky few to get paracetamol—and a big grin, declaring, 'I feel as though a new life is opening up for me.'

The next chapter in that new life began when we returned in December 2017 and Haithem was fitted with his robotic leg. He took to it quickly, and within a day he was walking short distances using a frame, under the supervision of Romanian prosthetist Bogdan Dimitriu, who we flew to Baghdad especially to work with our patients.

By day two, Haithem was walking with the aid of two crutches along the ground-floor corridor close to the physiotherapy department. Bogdan was adjusting the fitting of his new leg so it would force Haithem to develop the strength of different muscles—a crucial part of helping him walk virtually normally.

Haithem was discharged from hospital and scheduled to return one month later for further checks and potential alterations to the robotic leg. His prospects are outstanding. 'I am so happy,' he says. 'It feels very comfortable. I have wanted to walk for so long. It won't be long before I make you dance with me! I will dance first, then think about what else afterwards!'

What does the future hold for Haithem? Well, there's every chance he'll be able to dance again. It all depends on him. I know that before the operation he declared he's from the paramilitary and intends to return to their ranks once he's able to walk again. I want him to concentrate on his dancing.

A FATHER AND SON: ALI BASIM JABBAR SHAREEF

People with a physical disability face a tough life in Iraq. There's no anti-discrimination policy, and there are few social-support networks. Instead, the future holds the prospect of prolonged unemployment, financial hardship and constant struggle—even open hostility in public places.

Ali, who's stockily built with dark hair and a pencil-thin beard running down the centre of his chin, was wounded in the fight against ISIS in 2014, also at Baiji. 'We were surrounded by ISIS for two days, and we'd used nearly all our bullets and grenades,' he remembers. 'I was injured when they attacked us with guns and seven car bombs.'

Looking back, he had been fortunate to survive the battle-field. More than 70 of his fellow paramilitary fighters were killed that day. He was shot in the lower right leg, suffering severe damage to the arteries and nerves. After a week in hospital, doctors delivered the news that his leg would have to be amputated below the knee. 'If we don't amputate it today, gangrene might set in tomorrow and you could die,' they told him.

'From that point of view, it was the best choice,' he reflects. 'I thank God I only lost one leg.'

At the time, he was married with a four-year-old son, Hussein. Soon after he was injured, things changed. Ali's wife left him and their child. He became a single father with little means of support, other than his parents. Hussein found it difficult to come to terms with his dad's injuries. 'Early on, he refused to come near me,' Ali recalls. 'Slowly, slowly, he understood and accepted it.

'This is what happens in Iraq. This is quite common. Disabled people don't have rights. They don't look after you. They treat you like garbage in the street.'

Ali, who lives with his parents and Hussein on the northern outskirts of Baghdad, was the first patient to undergo osseo-integration in Iraq. The next morning, his father and son visited him in the ward. He showed them his leg and celebrated with them, teasing Hussein with the words, 'I'm the first person who's had this surgery in Iraq. Maybe I will be a famous man!

'This is one of my best mornings. I will not forget this morning. It will change my life for the better.'

When we returned four months later, Ali was the second Iraqi to be fitted with his new leg. That day, he walked out of the hospital using one crutch, hand in hand with Hussein, saying, 'I have a good relationship with my son. But I hope this will help him look at me in a new kind of way. I want to be able to do all the things we used to do together before I was wounded. I want to take him to the zoo and on lots of outings. Spend time together.'

TWO NEW LIVES: AHMED ABD ALRAHMAN YOSIF

Happily, not every wounded Iraqi soldier experiences the collapse of his family and personal life. Ahmed was engaged to his cousin, Safa, when he was horribly injured near Fallujah in May 2015.

She never wavered in her support for him, and they were married in 2016. In August 2017, two days before I operated on him, their first son was born. Ahmed was in hospital at the time and still hadn't seen his son when he underwent surgery to amputate his right leg above the knee and clean the infection from his badly damaged right shoulder. These were only some of the injuries he had suffered. He had also lost most of the fingers on his right hand and is blind in his right eye.

His injuries were sustained when, along with his paramilitary colleague Uday, Ahmed approached a factory entrance. An IED erupted, instantly killing Uday. 'I didn't hear anything,' Ahmed recalls. 'It felt as though someone had pushed me from a long way off. I couldn't see anything with my right eye and had blurred vision in my left eye. I still do. But I remember noticing blood and parts of my right hand and fingers falling off.'

Ahmed lay bleeding profusely from his wounds for half an hour, calling for help, while the rest of the patrol checked the surrounding area for more bombs. Once the all clear was given, he was lifted into an ambulance and lost consciousness on the way to hospital in Fallujah, before being transferred to Baghdad.

Ahmed was completely disorientated for the next couple of months. 'I didn't know where I was or who I was,' he says. Over the next two years, he underwent more than 40 operations in Iraq and Iran. But he was never free of pain or infection.

In December 2017, I inserted a rod in his right leg, ready to attach a new robotic leg on our next visit. Later, I performed what's known as reverse shoulder replacement surgery on his right arm. It's called that because, instead of the normal configuration of a ball on the top of the arm and a socket on the shoulder itself, the operation places a socket on the top of the arm and a ball on the shoulder. It's a relatively new technique that isn't widely used. But it works well and is becoming more popular.

Five months later, I performed osseointegration on his right wrist, inserting a rod as the base for a prosthesis that will allow him to grip items, even though it won't look like a normal hand. Two reconstructive surgeons from London's Royal Free Hospital—Dr Norbert Kang and Dr Alex Woollard—also travelled to Baghdad at the same time as part of my team and operated on Ahmed.

After the osseointegration and shoulder surgery, Ahmed could feel hopeful about his future. 'My wife and I have been waiting for this operation for four months—so we're very happy. But I'll be even happier when my shoulder has recovered,' he explains. 'Previously, I couldn't move much because my leg was very uncomfortable. Now, it's more comfortable. And it will be wonderful when I can get more movement in my shoulder. It will make my life easier. This is one of the few good things that has happened to me since I was injured. It will help me find a new life.'

After the shoulder surgery, Ahmed's main complaint was that he was bored staying in hospital. He's now walking smoothly and confidently on his new leg and has a broad smile on his face. He's come a long way in a short time.

'I MAKE BOMBS, NOT CAKES': MOHAMMED HUSSEIN ABD ASADA

Plenty of people in Iraq don't know their birth date—especially older people and families from remote areas. Traditionally, there was no registration of births in regional parts. The records simply weren't kept.

Instead, a convention emerged that Iraqis who didn't know their exact birthday adopted 1 July as the day they came into the world, rather like 1 August being the birth date ascribed to all racehorses in Australia. You'd be amazed, even now, by how many Iraqis will tell you 1 July when they're asked for their date of birth. There's also a superstition among some Iraqis that it's unlucky to reveal your birth date. I don't know why.

When I first met Mohammed—a handsome, cheeky and

wiry 25-year-old taxi driver, who's married with two children—he either didn't know or wasn't willing to reveal his birthday. Routinely, we ask all patients for their date of birth. Baghdad-based Mohammed wasn't impressed. 'I don't care about celebrating birthdays,' he responded.

'Isn't there a day when you have a birthday cake?'

'I make bombs, not cakes,' he replied, with a defiant grin. In truth, his comment probably wasn't far from the mark.

Mohammed had been serving with the paramilitary to the west of Mosul in late 2016 when a shell exploded a few metres away from him. One of his fellow patrol members was killed in the blast. Mohammed turned his left side towards the impact to protect himself.

He suffered shrapnel wounds to his left eye, left arm and left leg, and was unconscious when he was taken to hospital in Mosul. He emerged from the coma only after he'd been transferred to Baghdad. Regaining consciousness brought home the grim reality of his injuries. 'I was in a dark place. I didn't want to talk to anyone,' he recounts.

Over time, he started to recover. The shrapnel was removed from his eye. 'I was good looking again,' he quips. But there were still significant problems with the rest of his recovery. Mohammed's left leg was badly infected, and our first job was to debride the wound, removing dead or damaged tissue to allow the healthy tissue to survive and thrive.

On my second visit, we addressed the injuries to his left arm—he still couldn't fully extend his elbow. In this case, the solution was an elbow replacement. But, with no implants on hand, it meant ordering one from overseas.

We operated on Mohammed in December 2017, implanting a new elbow. The operation should eventually restore full movement of the arm, which will help him return to the workforce. 'Taxi driving is about all I can do,' Mohammed explains. 'I wasn't fully educated. I only went through the first two years of primary school. I didn't work at it. I didn't do anything. I wasn't any good at school. I just stayed home. Since then, I don't feel my life has been terribly fulfilling.'

So what about his life would he change? Mohammed looks confused and confronted. There's a long pause. 'That's the first time anyone has asked me that. I'm shocked by the question.' He pauses again. 'I guess I wish I was born outside Iraq. It has been my wish for a few years. Because of the politics and the security issues.'

THE MAN FROM THE MARSHES: JWAD PACHAY JABER

In Western nations, adult illiteracy is relatively rare. In Australia, compulsory education to Year 10 means most adults can read and write. There are, of course, significant pockets where that's not the case—especially in remote Indigenous communities. In addition, some migrant groups cling on to their culture and language rather than learning to read and write English.

It's different in Iraq. Even now, plenty of kids barely go to school. Either they get bored or they're more important to their family as a source of income. In Iraq, 20 per cent of the population is illiterate. UNESCO figures from 2015 indicate that around 86 per cent of Iraqi men are literate, but less than 74 per cent of women.

When I met Jwad in September 2017, he was 37 years old and couldn't read or write. He was originally from the wetlands close to the Iranian border in the south-east of Iraq, and was one of the Marsh Arabs who were absolutely despised by Saddam Hussein. Of all the ethnic and cultural groups in Iraq, they suffered more than most under his regime.

The Marsh Arabs were poor, ill-educated people. They eked out a living raising water buffalo, some sheep and cattle, or growing rice, barley, wheat and millet. By the 1990s, the marshes also had become the most important source of fish in Iraq.

The Marsh Arabs lived in small reed huts either at the side of a waterway or on artificially created reed islands. Their lifestyle reflected their ancient origins. Some were nomadic, following the seasons to provide the best feed for their animals. Many of their social traditions were based on the customs of the desert tribes. Altogether, it was a bleak and sparse existence.

Jwad didn't have a great start in life. Both of his parents were blind, and he had completed only the first year of primary school by the time of the First Gulf War. During and after the Shi'ite uprising in the region in 1991, Saddam ordered the waters of the Tigris and Euphrates rivers to be diverted from the marshes. This was carried out for two reasons: to cut off food supplies to the Marsh Arabs, and to eliminate hiding places for dissident soldiers.

The marshes were turned into virtual deserts. Saddam's troops attacked marsh villages, burning down houses and, according to some reports, poisoning water supplies. The population of 500,000 Marsh Arabs in the 1950s shrank to around 20,000. Many fled to refugee camps in Iraq or over the nearby border into Iran.

Along with the majority of their people, Jwad and his family—his parents, six brothers and two sisters—were forced to escape and took refuge on a conventional farm at nearby Al-Ahwar. They survived on a diet of milk, bread and yoghurt, but Saddam's soldiers would routinely steal their supplies.

To help his family's circumstances, Jwad carried bags for people who were shopping and, occasionally, drove cabs. 'I hated Saddam so much,' Jwad says. 'All the bad things that happened to me—leaving school, no education—that's all down to him. I've had a very hard, bad life because he didn't want my family to live where we were.'

Ironically, when he turned eighteen, Jwad was conscripted into Saddam's army—the same force that had driven his family from the marshes. He lasted only eighteen months in the military before he escaped, hiding in a van carrying fruit and vegetables to Baghdad.

To evade detection, he obtained forged documents, changing his first name to Abdullah. Being a fugitive was terrifying. 'I was arrested several times,' he remembers. 'I had a fake ID, and sometimes I had to give the guards at the checkpoints money to let me go through.' He couldn't return home, and eventually he found work on a fishing boat on the Shatt al-Arab waterway between Iraq and Kuwait.

Following the call in 2014 by the Grand Ayatollah of Iraq, Ali al-Husseini al-Sistani, for all Iraqi men to fight against ISIS, he joined the paramilitary. Around seven months into the fighting, near Samarra, 125 kilometres north of Baghdad, he stumbled across a group of soldiers clambering into an Iraqi military ute equipped with a machine gun on the rear tray, which was used primarily to attack helicopters. He assumed they were Iraqi soldiers, but quickly realised his mistake when the ISIS fighters who'd seized the vehicle opened fire. Jwad took bullets in the front and back of his left arm. Shrapnel from a grenade struck him in the back.

He remained conscious and remembers seeing muscles protruding from the wounds and fragments of his bone scattered on the ground around him. He also felt excruciating pain. A paramilitary colleague bundled him into a car and drove him to the nearest hospital, where they once again ran into ISIS. Jihadists had surrounded the facility, and unleashed round after round as the car approached.

Jwad's colleague turned the vehicle around and sped out of range. Before long, they stopped a truck carrying a consignment of chickens destined for the hospital. Jwad climbed in with the chickens. In the tense moment as the truck approached the hospital, the ISIS terrorists paused. Then they waved it through.

Once his condition had been stabilised, Jwad was transferred to hospitals in Baghdad and Basra—and then Iran.

With his medical problems still unresolved, he borrowed money to travel to India for surgery. It didn't go well. He contracted an infection that required another three months of treatment.

Jwad had been through a lot by the time I saw him. His arm was still carrying significant damage from the bullet wounds. Matt Weldon operated and shortened his arm before attaching an Ilizarov frame that would help lengthen the arm in the subsequent months.

The marshlands that were once Jwad's home have also made a recovery. After Saddam was overthrown, the remaining marsh inhabitants broke down the artificial dykes and allowed water back into the wetlands. The water only covers around half the area that once made up the marshes, and the relatively small number of people who have returned to their old way of life face major problems with basics such as clean drinking water and effective sewerage. But it's a start for them.

ONE FOOT IN THE GRAVE: MOHAMMED SALAH SALMAN

There's a belief among some Middle Eastern religions and communities that the whole of a person's body must be buried in one place. Of course, this poses a challenge for patients who've had part of a limb amputated.

When I first saw 35-year-old Mohammed in August 2017, he told me that he had been a vegetable farmer with a smallholding near Basra. He had regularly taken his produce to the city's markets, providing an adequate living for his wife and four children—three young boys and a daughter.

His life changed in 2014, with the Grand Ayatollah of Iraq's declaration of a fatwa against ISIS. Supported by his wife, Mohammed joined the paramilitary forces serving in Saladin Province, south-west of the terrorist stronghold of Mosul. He served as a driver and, over the next two years, saw many friends killed and wounded.

His own tour of duty came to a shuddering end in April 2017 when an IED exploded in the street directly under his car. Mohammed took the full brunt of the blast, which badly damaged both feet and the lower parts of his legs. Two others in the vehicle suffered only minor sprains and small fractures.

Mohammed regained consciousness when he was being treated in a field hospital. He was then transferred to Baghdad, where he underwent four hours of surgery. Less than a week later, he was moved back to Basra.

It was clear as soon as I looked at Mohammed's X-rays that the previous surgery hadn't been completely successful. His left leg could be saved with a further operation, but the bone in his right ankle was already dead. The lower part of the leg would have to be amputated before an osseointegration operation.

Mohammed was philosophical about the blast and the prospects for his future. 'It happened,' he mused. 'It's a common thing. I had been involved in three previous explosions when I wasn't injured. If the explosion had been 50 metres away, we wouldn't have been wounded. Now, I think I'm in good hands. I feel comfortable with it.'

Even so, he decided not to tell his wife about the operation before it was carried out. 'She would only worry,' he declared matter-of-factly.

The surgery went smoothly, but there was a twist. Mohammed insisted that we keep his amputated foot and lower leg in a plastic bag after it had been removed. It was placed to one side of the operating theatre as we completed the procedure and was nearly overlooked by the theatre orderlies as Mohammed was wheeled into the recovery area. After being alerted to the omission, the orderlies returned to the theatre to recover the severed leg, which was placed overnight in a hospital refrigerator.

Mohammed was discharged the next day and was driven, with the amputated lower leg in its plastic bag, to Najaf, Iraq's most holy city, to bury it in a grave in the world's largest cemetery, Wadi Al-Salam. The journey took more than two hours and was completed in the height of the Iraqi summer, when daytime temperatures regularly soar to 48 degrees Celsius!

Let's just say I was pleased to be back in the relative comfort of the operating theatre at Ibn Sina Hospital rather than in the cab with Mohammed and his amputated lower leg

All the same, the ritual was very much a part of Mohammed's religious beliefs. When he eventually dies, the rest of his body will be buried in the same grave—reunited with the amputated foot.

Mohammed made an excellent recovery and was fitted with his new leg in December 2017. Within a short time, he was walking freely and was delighted with the outcome. 'It has been very good—much better than before, absolutely.'

'THERE IS NO LOVE STORY': ABBAS JASIM HUMOOD

Even in the early part of the 21st century, arranged marriages are common in the Middle East. If they're not directly organised by the families of the couple involved, there's often considerable pressure from parents for particular relationships to form.

Abbas is 25 years old and lives in Najaf. He signed on as a soldier in the Iraqi Army just after his 21st birthday. Two years later, he was severely wounded in an advance against ISIS through the centre of Anbar Province in the west of Iraq. He lost his right arm above the elbow and suffered shrapnel wounds to his chest, lower abdomen and face.

Despite his injuries, Abbas married his twenty-year-old cousin, Hawraa, in 2016. 'There is no love story,' he explains. 'My family knew her, I didn't. They suggested she would be a suitable wife. So I met her and asked her to marry me.' Now they have a son, Mahdi, who was born in October 2017.

Abbas is content and says his wife is, too. 'My wife has a similar personality to me,' he says. 'I want a woman to be a housewife. All her time is for her family. She's not a student and she doesn't work. She's happy doing that.'

Abbas remembers every vivid detail of the day he was injured. He was the machine gunner on the back of an army ute advancing through the streets when an ISIS rocket struck his right arm, slicing it off in an instant. 'I didn't see the rocket coming,' he says. 'There are no words to describe how I felt when I saw I had lost my arm. I thought I was going to die.'

The impact knocked him off the ute and onto the road. Immediately he saw that he was losing an enormous amount of blood, and he knew he needed urgent medical assistance. He scrambled to his feet and started sprinting towards the medical centre at the nearest military post. Abbas ran for around five minutes before his legs weakened and collapsed beneath him because of the massive blood loss.

No one else on the ute suffered substantial injuries, and they soon caught up with Abbas as he lay on the road. His colleagues dragged him onto the vehicle and raced to the closest hospital, where doctors debrided the tissue surrounding his wounds and sutured his arm.

Days later in a Baghdad hospital, infection set in and he underwent further procedures to clean and dress the wound before being transferred to a hospital in Najaf. Within five days, he was sent home to his parents, five brothers and two sisters.

Abbas remains in the army, but he is only required to turn up for a couple of days a month to collect his salary. 'I do nothing,' he says. 'I just show myself at the army base. They told me to do that. But they won't ever find me anything to do. The rest of the time I just spend at home with my family. I'm very proud of my son. He looks just like me. But there's nothing else to do.'

He hopes that will change when he's learned to master his new arm. 'I think the future looks good for me,' he predicts. 'When I have my new arm, I will go back to the military and see if there's a job I can do there.'

'I FEEL GOD HAS GIVEN ME A SECOND LIFE': FITYAN HUSSEIN ALI

Baghdad was one of the most dangerous places on earth in 2009. Thousands of people were being killed. Every day there were bombings, shooting and kidnappings. People were being thrown from rooftops by various terrorist groups and street gangs that ruled the Iraqi capital.

Fityan is married with two young children—a ten-year-old daughter and a nine-year-old son—and was a major in the Iraqi police force in those dark days. Even he admits that the authorities were incapable of keeping up with the whirlwind of violence engulfing the Iraqi capital at the time. 'It was terrifying to be in Baghdad,' he remembers. 'Everyone was frightened. The police couldn't keep control. Even the American soldiers couldn't stop the killing.'

Around 7 p.m. on 18 March 2009, Fityan was driving home after work with his daughter, headed along the main road through the northern Baghdad suburb of Al Shaab. Without warning, an explosion erupted under the driver's side of the vehicle, sending the car skywards before it crashed back to the ground. To this day, Fityan doesn't know whether the bomb was on the road or attached beneath the car.

Going Back

He checked on his daughter. She was uninjured. He looked down at his left leg and knew it was badly damaged, but he still had control of his right leg. He wrestled with the driver's side door, which had been jammed shut in the explosion. Using all his power, he forced it open and stepped out. But his left leg couldn't support his weight, so he tumbled onto the road. 'I was in severe pain. I thought I was dying,' he recalls. In fact, his left leg was suffering complex injuries, including compound fractures, extensive tissue loss and vascular damage.

Police colleagues drove him to hospital. Within hours, his left leg had been amputated above the knee. Amid fears of gangrene setting in, his right leg was amputated below the knee nine days later. The next year was a long battle to achieve a level of mobility. He acquired two socket prostheses, which allowed him to walk with crutches.

Fityan underwent further surgery on his left leg in Germany in 2014, which allowed him to wear a more modern Genium X3 prosthetic leg. It's fitted with a robotic microprocessor knee, a significant advance. This meant he could throw away the crutches and walk with just one stick. After undergoing osseointegration, Fityan—who was 46 at the time—was aiming to dispose of the walking stick as well.

He's been promoted to the rank of general and expects to continue advancing his career and his family life after he's learned to walk on his new legs.

'I accept what happened to me,' he says. 'I feel God has given me a second life. God willing, I will be like a normal person.

It will change my life, the way people look at me. My family has been very supportive, and I believe every day will be better.'

——

These are just some of the military cases I've dealt with in Iraq. There are thousands more like these. Most of the fighters I operated on in Iraq were members of the paramilitary, but that doesn't mean I'm particularly supportive of Hashd. I don't support any organisation that relies, at least in part, on violence and counts among its numbers religious fanatics and street gangs. And I don't sympathise with the paramilitary's strong association with Iran. The fact is I've operated on a large proportion of their fighters because Hashd is by far the most efficient of the defence forces in accessing my humanitarian project. Hashd arranges for its wounded fighters to come to the hospital, often with X-rays, allowing them rapid access to my clinics.

It also helps that one of the senior doctors at Ibn Sina is the brother of Hashd's medical director.

My role in forming the surgical lists is limited. Usually, it's the hospital staff who dictate the order of patients, although I have more influence on the civilian cases I take on.

As I'm sure you can imagine, my work there is particularly rewarding. It's hard for me to explain the joy I feel. Many of these patients were wheelchair-bound. Now, they're recovering much of their previous mobility.

Despite—or because of—the ordeals they'd been through, our patients are remarkably resilient. In Australia or the United States, it's not unheard of for patients who've undergone osseointegration or other complex trauma operations to complain about the pain 24 hours after surgery. In Iraq, the patients take far fewer painkillers—mostly nothing stronger than paracetamol. And no one in Iraq moans or whinges. I guess it's because they're used to a tough way of life.

An example of this Iraqi fortitude came to light when one of my osseointegration patients phoned my mobile a few weeks after being fitted with his new leg. 'Dr Munjed, can you tell me what's wrong? My leg is bleeding a little bit.'

'Is there any pain?' I asked.

'No. No pain. But there's a little bit of blood where the leg's attached.'

'What have you been doing?' I inquired.

'I've just come back to Baghdad from a pilgrimage to Najaf.' The city is the focus of an annual pilgrimage by Shi'ite faithful—a journey of about 150 kilometres from Baghdad.

'How did you get to Najaf?'

'I walked,' he told me—to my absolute horror.

'And you used your crutches, didn't you?'

'Crutches, Dr Munjed? I threw those away as soon as I walked out of the hospital.'

The good news is that as long as there's no pain, he's fine. But I did recommend that he curb his enthusiasm for long-distance walking!

10

THE CIVILIANS

The official Iraqi point of view was that my team was in Baghdad in the scorching summer of 2017 to operate on military and security personnel who'd been injured in the fight to repel ISIS from its borders. Nothing more, nothing less.

I had a broader agenda. The affiliations of patients and the causes of their injuries don't matter to me. Whatever their circumstances, they deserve the best medical treatment available. Quite simply, I wanted to extend the humanitarian mission to operate on civilians as well.

Almost as soon as we arrived at Ibn Sina Hospital, I started negotiating with the authorities to include civilians on the surgery list. But I needed to tread an extremely delicate path. I couldn't overstate my case for fear of alienating the authorities.

As far as I was concerned, once I'd reached the target number of 48 operations on soldiers who'd been wounded in Iraq's most recent conflict, I would be free to extend my horizons to civilians. But I wasn't in a position to plough on without the tick of approval from the powers that be. On top of that, I didn't have control over my theatre list. It was largely created for me by the hospital's senior staff members, who had a specific briefing to concentrate on military, police and government patients.

The hospital's director Dr Yasser al-Timmimi specifically— and emphatically, I might add—instructed me not to operate on anyone who wasn't from the military. He eventually barked at me, 'There will be no operations on civilians!'

To be honest, I couldn't see the sense in the edict and was determined to talk around whoever it took to change the order. My purpose was to help as many Iraqis as possible—I wouldn't be able to achieve that if I was constantly arguing with the authorities. Still, whenever the chance arose, I talked to hospital and government officials, pointing out that once we'd completed the allotted number of operations on injured soldiers, we'd fulfilled our part of the bargain. Surely that would open the way for civilians.

One of the strongest advocates for the civilian operations was Mohammed al Attar from the Prime Minister's Department. Mohammed had met us at Baghdad International Airport when we arrived for our first visit to Iraq, and he had been our link with the department since then. He'd done a magnificent job, providing for all our needs. From his time with us, Mohammed could see the desperate need for civilians to be included in the surgical list.

He was constantly lobbying his colleagues in the Prime Minister's Department to give me the go-ahead. He even drafted a letter for the prime minister, approving the civilian operations. But the movement of the Iraqi bureaucracy was painfully slow.

Time was ticking by—we were due to leave Baghdad on Tuesday, 29 August. As our days in Iraq were drawing to a close, civilian patients and their families were becoming more anxious by the hour, fearing they would miss out on surgery. The uncertainty was agonising for them. For us, too.

Relatives of patients would lurk in the hospital corridors, badgering my colleagues and, whenever I emerged from the theatre area, me! Local surgeons, hospital staff and even senior government officials also were cornered. The tears—sometimes wailing—and begging of the relatives were constant and deeply moving. Sadly, for most of the time, I could only empathise and tell them the decision was out of my hands.

Finally, on Sunday, 27 August, the lobbying paid off. The hospital's director gave me the official go-ahead to operate on civilians. I'm not exactly sure who made the decision, but I think it was the result of the intense pressure on the offices of the prime minister and minister of health.

Going Back

When the news came through, I was asked whether I was excited by the development. I replied, 'No. I'm pleased, but not excited. There have been too many delays and too much bureaucracy for me to be excited. But I'm pleased.'

— —

Among the many moving stories of the civilian patients I've operated on in Baghdad, two have particularly stood out for the teams I've taken to Iraq.

They involve a young woman and a young man, little more than kids when they suffered terrible injuries that threatened to send their lives spiralling into depression and disaster. Both of these young people were supported at the hospital by their mothers, who tirelessly campaigned for their children to have the operations they so desperately needed.

TEARS FROM HEAVEN: AMANI NASSER JABER

I first saw Amani at Ibn Sina Hospital in Baghdad in August 2017 after the Iraqi authorities had approved operations on civilians. Amani's is a story that has touched people across the world. Since she lost her legs at the age of ten in 2009, she's experienced the depths of despair but has recovered to become a champion para-athlete. Altogether, she's won three gold medals in competitions across Asia. Still, she would have given away all her medals in a heartbeat to be able to walk again.

As her athletic performances indicate, Amani is fiercely determined. 'I won't allow anyone to push me in my wheelchair,' she says. 'I have to do it for myself.'

Soon after meeting Amani, I asked her, 'What's your number-one wish?'

'I want to walk,' she told me.

Her mother added, 'If Amani can walk, it will be an achievement for all the people of Iraq.'

The barrier to me operating on her in August had been the cost of the titanium rods and her new robotic legs. With no health insurance scheme or state subsidy to cover the bills, her family simply couldn't afford the equipment. I decided to delay operating until our next visit four months later, hoping this would give them the opportunity to raise the necessary funds. There were tears of disappointment, of course. But I reassured Amani that the surgery would go ahead at some point.

When we returned in December, Amani was one of the first patients I saw. Neither Amani nor her mother had any idea how that consultation would unfold. To be honest, neither did I!

The crunch came quickly. If the operation was to go ahead, how would the implants and robotic legs be paid for? Amani's mother sadly told me her family still didn't have the money. On the spot, I made a snap decision. 'Don't worry. I don't care whether you can raise the money, I'm going to operate on you in the next two weeks. If it's necessary, I'll pay for the implants myself,' I told them. I felt it would be worth every last cent to give Amani the chance to make the most of her life. Again, there were floods of tears—but this time, they were tears of happiness.

Amani comes from the city of Nasariyah, which sits on the Euphrates River a little more than 350 kilometres south-east of Baghdad.

One evening when she was ten years old, a mortar shell struck a car in the street outside her family home. It erupted in a huge fireball. The strong shock waves caused by the explosion dislodged a kerosene heater that had been warming Amani's house. It tumbled onto Amani, inflicting terrible burns to her lower legs and other parts of her body.

The day after the accident, Amani slipped into a coma. A well-connected relative arranged for a military helicopter to fly her to a US Army hospital, where she remained unconscious for three months. After a further six months, doctors saw that her wounds had become gangrenous. The following day, Amani underwent a double below-the-knee amputation.

Details of Amani's condition were kept from her mother, who's a primary school teacher. The reason? It wasn't the first family tragedy she'd suffered. Some years earlier, an older daughter had died after being shot in the stomach during a US attack. She was also ten years old.

Following Amani's operation, the family finally encouraged her mother to visit her young daughter in hospital. But they still hadn't explained the extent of Amani's injuries. When Amani's mother saw her, she became hysterical. Amani tried to get out of bed to comfort her. But without the lower part of her legs, Amani fell to the floor.

For the first time, both Amani and her mother were confronted by the awful reality of her injuries. Amani was devastated and slipped deep into depression. 'I felt incomplete,' she explains. 'I knew what had gone would never come back. I lost the will to live, the will to talk and to eat. I withdrew into myself. Whenever I saw any family or friends, I felt I hated them.'

Her mother also reflects on that time. 'She was devastated. When she came home after those nine months in hospital, it was very difficult. But after about a year, I felt more in control of her situation.

'The second year, I saw Amani being very depressed. I knew I had to do something to improve the situation. So, I enrolled her in a group with women in a similar position who were learning to cook and swim. During her time at the women's group, a coach took Amani aside and trained her for one month in the wheelchair javelin. At the age of thirteen, she won the first competition she entered.'

That victory helped to build up Amani's self-esteem. 'It was a big boost,' her mother recalls. 'She felt good after that. At last, she understood what it meant to be happy again.'

In her mid-teens, Amani became the wheelchair javelin age-group champion of Iraq and went on to win the Asia Para Games javelin title, establishing herself as a national identity along the way.

Eventually, Amani went back to her education—taking on the challenge of studying the first years of high school with a group of considerably younger kids. She found it tough, but was determined to push through the difficulties. 'I don't feel completely comfortable at school, but I love studying,' she explains. 'There's a problem with some of the other girls and teachers who don't accept my situation too easily. In the south of Iraq, a female training in sport isn't really accepted. The pressure is on that I really should stay at home and do nothing.'

Her mother elaborates. 'I've even received a threatening letter. But I care so much for Amani that I want her to do everything she can in life. In Iraq, it's actually a very brave stand.'

The next step was for Amani to explore all the possibilities of walking again. Prompted by the director of an Iraqi feature film about her life, she went online and discovered osseo-integration. And once she saw videos of other patients walking freely she was in no doubt. 'To watch the videos gives me hope,' Amani says. 'When I saw them, I felt it was me who was walking again, not just the people in the videos.'

I operated on Amani on the morning of Wednesday, 20 December 2017. The four hours of surgery were complex. After I had amputated both her legs above the knee—which would give her the best chance of walking again—I inserted the titanium rods. The canals in the bones of Amani's legs were extremely narrow, and during the operation her left femur fractured. I repaired it there and then, but it meant her recovery would take a little longer.

The fact that she hadn't walked for almost half her life was also a significant complication. In her case, it's not a question of learning to walk again—it's a question of just learning to walk. At the time of the operation, I estimated it would take anything up to two years before she walked unaided. But she will.

As Amani was wheeled back into her room after the operation, her mother leaned over and kissed her on the left cheek. Then she dissolved into tears—this time, tears of joy and relief.

When I saw Amani again in April 2018, her legs had healed and she was ready to begin weight-bearing ahead of being fitted with her new legs. As I sat with her on her hospital bed, Amani told me she had something for me. Leaning forward, she placed one of her gold medals around my neck. She was bestowing on me a precious possession from her past to thank me for giving her the most precious gift for her future—the ability to walk again.

There will be more tears from Amani and her mum when she does finally walk with her new legs. One of my colleagues reflected that, as Amani takes those first steps, they'll be tears from heaven.

A MOTHER'S LOVE: GHADBAN SUBHI MAHMOOD

One of the most familiar sights in Ibn Sina Hospital in August and December 2017 was a short, middle-aged woman wearing a black *abaya*—the loose-fitting, full-length robe that is symbolic of piety—and a sombre brown, patterned headscarf. Her desperation bordered on obsession.

Going Back

From daybreak until the early hours of the following morning, she would haunt the hospital corridors with a mournful expression. Like a ghost, she would appear from nowhere, pleading with members of the visiting surgical team to operate on her son. She often sobbed openly, and frequently wailed. She would passionately present her case in Arabic to anyone who would listen, regardless of whether they understood what she was saying or could do anything to promote her son's cause.

The woman was Amira Najeeb Saleeh, the then 52-year-old mother of Ghadban Subhi Mahmood, who'd lost both his legs when a mortar shell exploded in front of him on 26 February 2017. No parent wants to see their child suffer, and Amira's commitment to her son was both unshakable and admirable. 'My life has ended,' she said at one point. 'I just do everything for my son.'

Time and again, I explained that I couldn't operate on Ghadban until the necessary permission came through. Regardless, she begged again.

On that last Sunday of my August trip to Baghdad, we could finally deliver the good news to Ghadban and his mother. I asked one of the Iraqi surgeons to tell them what they'd been waiting to hear.

It was an emotional time. Everything they had saved and campaigned for was going to come true. Amira beamed, raised her hands to the heavens and repeated, 'Happy, happy, happy!'

Ghadban's family had been close to the centre of some of the worst excesses of ISIS, as they were living in eastern Mosul—Iraq's second-largest city and the jewel in the caliphate crown after the ISIS advance into Iraq in the summer of 2014. The original settlement of Mosul was established on the west bank of the Tigris River and later spread to the east bank—that area was the site of the ancient Assyrian city of Nineveh, which is mentioned in the Bible's Old Testament.

Mosul expanded rapidly in the early years of the 21st century and, at one stage, its population soared to around 1.8 million. As ISIS fighters swept across Iraq, they attacked and swiftly captured Mosul. Hundreds of thousands of refugees fled, and the population of the city shrank to around 600,000 people. Ghadban's family had remained in the city only because they were too poor to move.

Tragically, as well as slaughtering thousands of Iraqi Army soldiers and civilians, ISIS went on a rampage that destroyed priceless buildings. Some of them dated back more than several thousand years and were reputed to contain the tombs of Old Testament identities such as Jonah. They also set fire to the university library, burning treasured and irreplaceable books and artefacts. In addition, it was from inside the historic Great Mosque of al-Nuri in Mosul that ISIS leader Abu Bakr al-Baghdadi declared the establishment of the new caliphate.

With ISIS controlling the city, Ghadban's family spent most of the time in their house. 'We felt sad. We felt as though we were prisoners in our own home,' Ghadban explains.

The Iraqi counterattack didn't materialise until the autumn of 2016, but when the offensive finally came, it was decisive. Allied planes bombed ISIS from the air, while Iraqi counter-terrorism forces, regular army, paramilitary and police led the ground assault. While the terrorist group retreated from other regional cities it had captured, Mosul remained one of the last jihadist strongholds. However, by mid-2017, the last few hundred defenders of the caliphate were fighting a desperate rearguard action in the narrow streets and alleyways of the old city on the western banks of the Tigris, using civilians as human shields to cover their escape.

Of those civilians who remained in Mosul, around 150,000 were trapped in the city's west, facing shortages of food and water and living in desperate conditions. Close to the end of the battle for Mosul, increasingly desperate ISIS fighters were reported by the United Nations to have killed more than 150 fleeing Iraqis—including women and children—close to an ice-cream factory in the city. Then, in an act of mindless defiance before they abandoned the city and retreated to their final stronghold of Raqqa in Syria, ISIS destroyed the very mosque where the Islamic State had been proclaimed.

Ghadban was 22 years of age when I met him, the oldest of three children and the family's only son. His sisters were aged nineteen and thirteen.

Around nine o'clock in the morning on 26 February, Ghadban had walked out of the front door of the family home on his way to school—and straight into the path of a mortar shell that exploded in the street immediately ahead of him. This tall, solidly built young man took the full blast on the lower part of his legs.

Amira rushed out of the house and immediately applied first aid, quite possibly saving her son's life. She has stayed at his side ever since, taking every opportunity to passionately advocate for him.

Ghadban was rushed in a neighbour's car to the nearest American hospital. He spent five days there, undergoing surgery to amputate both legs—the right leg above the knee, and the left below the knee. He was then transferred to the hospital in Erbil, the capital of the Kurdish region of Iraq, where he remained for the next two months.

As he recovered, Ghadban tried to walk with socket prostheses, but he couldn't master them. As a result, he was confined to a wheelchair. Still, the family was determined Ghadban would walk again, and they researched every possible surgical alternative. Finally, through Iraqi friends in Australia, they were alerted to the potential of osseointegration.

Ghadban emailed me, and I suggested that he should come to Baghdad when I was there in August. Once she knew I was going to Iraq, Amira set about raising the A$80,000–$100,000 for her son's operation and his new robotic legs. She sold her house, car and the little gold she possessed; she cashed in the back pay she was owed from her job as a teacher—schools had been suspended in Mosul after ISIS had taken control— and borrowed money from family and friends. She was also in touch with an overseas charity that was offering financial assistance.

Then the two of them embarked on a nine-hour taxi journey from Mosul to the Ibn Sina Hospital in Baghdad. They had to contend with traffic jams and long stops at military checkpoints along the way.

I operated on Ghadban the day after I'd been given the go-ahead to treat civilian patients. He came into the operating theatre late on the Monday evening, the day before we were leaving Baghdad. It was an instant of sheer joy for Ghadban and his mother. 'I'm very excited. I've spent three months waiting for this moment,' Ghadban said in the minutes before he was wheeled into the theatre. 'I've spent those three months exercising so I was ready for this day.'

Amira couldn't keep the smile from her face. 'It's like his life will change considerably when he can walk again and lead his life as a normal person,' she beamed. 'It's a dream come true.'

The operation went smoothly and his news legs were fitted when we returned in December.

Everything went well for the first few hours. Ghadban started moving enthusiastically and felt particularly comfortable on his left leg. He told me that it felt like the limb he'd been born with. He could feel the surface he was walking on through his artificial feet and legs.

It took Ghadban a little more time to get used to the longer artificial right leg. But he was progressing well when he left the hospital at the end of his first day of walking. Unfortunately, on the second day, he lost his balance as he was trying to stand from his wheelchair. Subsequent X-rays revealed that he'd fractured the head of his right femur. I operated straight away to repair the damage. It was a setback, and he needed to keep his weight off the fractured leg for three months. After that, he began walking again using the parallel bars to take the early steps.

Of course, this young man who suffered such horrific injuries dreams about more than simply walking again. Before he was wounded, Ghadban wanted to join the military—to become an officer in the Iraqi Army. Clearly that aim was shattered at the same time as his legs. Now, he wants nothing more than to live like a normal person. 'I don't want people to think of me as disabled,' he says. 'I hate this wheelchair. When I stand and walk, I want to complete my studies and hang out with my friends.'

Losing his legs has also cost him an important relationship in his young life. Before he was injured, Ghadban had been planning to marry his fiancée. But as soon as he was injured, her family broke off the relationship, believing a disabled man wouldn't be able to provide a stable lifestyle for his wife and family.

Despite that, Ghadban kept in touch with his girlfriend, hoping that once he could walk, her family would relent. Sadly, it didn't happen. In November 2017, she told him her family didn't want her talking to him any longer. Even with his new legs, they didn't believe he would be able to provide her with a normal life. She would always have to support him. It was an emotional chapter for him, but every cloud has a silver lining.

Along with his mum, Ghadban came to Baghdad for a check-up in August 2018. They were no longer the desperate mother and son I had first seen a year earlier. Their lives have been transformed. Ghadban is walking smoothly and naturally, with just a single crutch. In time, he may be able to get rid of that. On the other hand, he may find that he wants to keep it because of the sense of security it provides.

Ghadban has finished school with excellent results in his final exams and will be going on to university. But the biggest change is that he's confident and smiling. Constantly.

And his mum? The woman who used to be dressed all in black with a dark headscarf as she haunted the corridors of Ibn Sina Hospital now wears a head covering of bright green and red, with flashes of gold and black. After those tense days of sobbing and pleading for her son to undergo osseointegration, it's now almost impossible to wipe the smile off her face. She's truly happy, happy, happy.

'LIKE A BIRD SET FREE FROM A CAGE': MOHAMMED KHAREEM

The brutality of life in Iraq after the Second Gulf War is hard to imagine for anyone who didn't live through it. Mohammed saw it from close quarters. In 2007, terrorists kidnapped his father, a university cleaner. To this day, his family has no idea why. He wasn't an important figure and wasn't wealthy. There was no likelihood of a large ransom payout.

For four long weeks, no one knew his fate. Then came the awful news—his body had been discovered in a Baghdad street. His head and arms had been hacked off. No one has ever been convicted of his murder.

Mohammed, who was born in 1985, joined the Iraqi police force and was serving in Mosul in 2011. He was fighting ISIS terrorists in the street when an IED detonated, smashing his right leg. The injuries were so serious, he realised straight away that it would need to be amputated. The operation was carried out one week later, leaving only a short stump.

Mohammed struggled for a year afterwards.

'I hated feeling that I needed the help of other people to do things,' he explains. 'It affected me so much. My work. Even my family and friends. I thought no one would accept me or want to marry me.'

Happily, his worries were unfounded. In 2014, Mohammed married his cousin, Lina, and they now have two young sons.

Living at home with his wife, mother and brothers, he was afraid that he was letting down his children. 'My hardest moment was when my eighteen-month-old son dragged my crutches over to me and asked me to pick him up and carry him. I couldn't do it. I went to my room crying,' he remembers, choking back tears.

Even though he was wounded during the fighting against ISIS, he came to me as a private civilian patient during our second visit to Baghdad in the Iraqi summer of 2017. He was absolutely determined to undergo osseointegration. In pursuit of that goal, Mohammed sold his house and his wife's gold jewellery to help pay for his new robotic leg. But he doesn't regret the sacrifices.

Mohammed can't wait for the day when he can walk and carry his children. 'That would be one of the best things,' he says. 'I only went to school until I was ten, and I made money by carrying bags at the airport and train station and driving taxis. I will do anything to get work and earn money for my family.'

Mohammed's osseointegration went smoothly, and he was fitted with his new leg in December 2017. It'll be a lengthy rehabilitation for him to learn to walk because his amputation is so high. But he understands the process and is determined to go through it, literally step by step. 'It will feel so good. I will be like a bird set free from a cage,' he smiles.

Mohammed took his new leg home with him the evening after it was fitted. Of course, his family demanded a demonstration. His oldest son helped him fit the leg before Mohammed walked two or three steps in front of the gathered audience. They were only a few small steps for a man, but a giant leap for Mohammed's whole family.

'It was a wonderful moment. The whole family shed tears of happiness,' Mohammed explains. 'I couldn't believe my dream had come true. I'm very relieved, but I'm particularly happy for my son. He used to bring me one shoe. Now he brings me two shoes.'

'I DON'T WANT TO BE A BURDEN ON MY COMMUNITY': AETHAM ABDUL HUSSEIN MOHAMMED

A badly injured person's desire to walk again is a normal human emotion. But in Aetham's case, there were other motivations as well. He felt a responsibility to society to make a useful contribution.

After being released from hospital following the amputation of his right leg close to the hip and his right arm below the elbow, he spent three months at home, sitting in a wheelchair and rarely plucking up the courage to emerge into the wider world. 'I was very sad, but I was thinking about how I would continue with my life,' he explains. 'I don't want to be a burden on my community.'

Aetham—who's tall, sports a moustache and lives in Babylon, about 125 kilometres south of Baghdad—joined the Iraqi police force in 2002 at the age of 25. He was wounded while fighting ISIS in a field in rural Anbar Province on 19 August 2016, when a small missile landed a few metres away from him. His body armour protected his torso and saved his life. But one of the twelve people fighting alongside him was killed.

'It was horrific. My uniform caught fire and the whole of my right side was in flames,' he remembers. 'I rolled in the sand to put out the flames. I saw my wounds and my blood. I felt like I was going to die.

'There were some rocks and small trees nearby, but, because of my injuries, I couldn't move to take shelter. I was waiting for someone to come and rescue me—or for ISIS to kill me. I thought a sniper could take a pot shot at me at any moment.'

There was a lengthy exchange of gunfire, and Aetham was left lying in the open for half an hour or more before paramilitary soldiers and police came to rescue the wounded. Aetham was rolled onto a blanket and dragged through the dirt and dust to a forward station. It took another six hours to transfer him to a field hospital for emergency treatment. Soon after, in a Baghdad hospital, surgeons amputated his right leg and his right arm.

He faced fresh challenges when he was given a dated socket prosthesis in December 2016. 'To start with, it was very difficult to walk,' he explains. 'But gradually, somehow I got used to walking with it.'

Within a month, he was given an artificial arm, which stretched his horizons. 'Before I had the artificial arm, I was very shy about leaving the house,' he says. 'I was worried about the way people looked at me. But afterwards, I began to build up my confidence.'

His confidence received another boost when, during our second visit to Baghdad, I operated on him as a civilian patient and inserted a titanium rod in his right femur, ready to attach a new robotic leg. His reaction, before he returned home to his eleven-year-old son and twelve-day-old daughter, was favourable. 'I'm optimistic my life will be changed in a very dramatic way,' he says.

I saw Aetham again during my fifth visit to Baghdad in August 2018. He was walking well on his new leg and was so enthusiastic about his improved lifestyle that he persuaded me to perform further osseointegration surgery on his right forearm.

'IF MY CONDITION STAYS LIKE THIS, I HAVE NO FUTURE': YASSER NABEEL

Osseointegration isn't the only surgery we've carried out to help civilians in Iraq. My colleague and friend Dr Kevin Tetsworth—an American-born, Brisbane-based orthopaedic surgeon who joined us in Iraq in December 2017 and again in April and August 2018—operated on seventeen-year-old Yasser Nabeel from Najaf, about 150 kilometres south of Baghdad.

The teenager is the oldest of six children—he has three sisters, and his two youngest siblings are boys. Yasser was born with two club feet, which severely restricted his ability to walk—to the extent that he regarded 50 metres as a long journey. Clearly, that's a huge limit on the lifestyle of a ninth-grade schoolboy, and it has led him to have feelings of hopelessness and depression. His father says, 'My son has been very depressed about his condition. And so am I. Like any family, we wanted many things for our oldest son that we haven't been able to achieve.'

They considered selling their house to raise the US$12,000 they needed to pay for Yasser to undergo surgery with a Russian specialist. As it was, the surgeon charged them US$50 to examine Yasser and write a report about his condition and the surgical options. But even US$50 was a lot of money for them, his father points out.

Yasser's policeman father is a keen sportsman and, at the age of 42, was still playing football in a competition in Najaf. Like many young men, Yasser is also keen on sport—in his case, he plays wheelchair volleyball. And, in the two years since he'd taken up the game, he'd become part of a hugely successful team that had won, among other trophies, an Iraqi national title.

He's a strongly built young man with a wide range of friends—including some overseas mates he's made through sport. But, at his age, he was obviously becoming extremely conscious of the impact of his difficulties in getting around.

He and his family had decided the time was right to address the issue. 'I am very happy and excited to get rid of my problem,' Yasser said before his surgery. 'It's God's will. As soon as the operation is over, I want to continue my life like normal people.

'If my condition stays like this, I have no future. I wouldn't be able to work. I am optimistic that the operation will change that. I would like to be a taxi driver.'

Kevin and I examined the X-rays of Yasser's lower legs and came up with a course of action—a procedure known as an Ilizarov frame. Kevin operated on Yasser's feet and attached the frames, which allowed gradual adjustment of the joints over the coming months to change the angle of the feet. After that time, his feet will sit flat on the ground.

The morning after the operation, Yasser and his father had high hopes for the future. Yasser's father said, 'I am hoping for the best. I hope my son will be able to walk the same as the other kids. Like any father, I would be happy if that happens. Our whole family is excited about this. It would be a great thing to watch my son play with other people.'

The prognosis is excellent. While Yasser won't be able to walk completely normally or over marathon distances, he'll certainly have much greater mobility and a more normal gait. For a sports-mad teenager, it'll change his life.

'ARE YOU AN AMERICAN SPY?': ABU MAHDI AL-MUHANDIS

Abu Mahdi al-Muhandis is the deputy leader of Hashd, the Iraqi paramilitary force.

I had met and spoken to him a number of times to finalise details of the operating schedule for the wounded soldiers. In April 2018, however, he came to the hospital late one night on a civilian matter. He suffers from arthritis of the knee and wanted me to give him a pain-relieving injection. It's a completely routine procedure that I was happy to carry out.

Everything seemed remarkably straightforward until, in the early hours of the morning, I received an urgent call from the chief doctor of Hashd. 'He's in agony,' the medico stressed. 'He's in so much pain he can't sleep. What the hell did you inject him with?' Then, comparing my actions to the poisoning of Russian double agent Sergei Skripal and his daughter Yulia in the United Kingdom a month earlier, he asked, 'Are you spying for the Americans? Did you try to kill him?'

There was a sense of fun about his question, but it was underscored by a more sinister note of concern about the events that had unfolded. He instructed me to stand by for another phone call and to be ready to attend the patient's house at short notice.

The order filled me with foreboding. I suspect al-Muhandis is actually the leader of Hashd in everything but name and is an enormously powerful figure in Iraq. He is on the list of designated terrorists in the US and was sentenced to death in his absence after being convicted of masterminding the bombings of the US and French embassies in Kuwait in 1983. Definitely not someone to upset.

I slept little that night and around 5 am I woke Claudia and we went down to an early breakfast and then onto Ibn Sina. Around 7.30 am I called the paramilitary doctor I'd spoken to the previous night to catch up on the latest developments. Al-Muhandis had drifted off to sleep. I would receive another call as soon as he woke up.

Around 9 am, the call came through. 'A car is on its way to pick you up from the hospital in five minutes.'

When we arrived at the home of the paramilitary deputy leader, I was relieved to see him sitting up at a table eating breakfast.

'What's the matter?' I asked and then added a phrase Claudia uses. 'Are you a sooky-sooky la-la?'

He smiled. 'I thought you'd be taking me to hospital this morning for osseointegration,' he responded. As he was speaking, he pointed to his mid-thigh, saying, 'You can amputate at this level.'

He then invited me to join him for breakfast. But it wasn't long before the tension mounted again. We started talking about the number of paramilitary soldiers who'd lost their limbs fighting ISIS—more than 1000 amputees and several thousand more with musculo-skeletal injuries. Al-Muhandis looked at me and said, 'Your task is to treat all of these patients before the end of the year.'

Without thinking, I replied with some verses from the Koran: 'I will do my best but there are limitations on what can be done in that timeframe.'

Al-Muhandis smiled. 'So you know the Koran.'

'I memorised the Koran when I was 12 years old,' I told him, before stupidly adding, 'but then I saw the light.'

The room immediately fell silent and stayed that way for at least two minutes. It seemed an age. I thought, 'What have I done? This could be my equivalent of the Last Supper.'

The Hashd deputy leader finally spoke and changed the subject, resuming the conversation by talking about Persian rugs. I hoped that meant he'd misheard me. But of course he hadn't.

After breakfast, Al-Muhandis escorted me downstairs, held my hand and took me into a room lined with photographs of dead people. 'You mentioned seeing the light. All these people died in the name of God, striving to see the light of their faith,' he told me.

My heart sank, but I tried to ease the tension with a flippant remark. 'Are you going to kill me?' I inquired.

With a peaceful smile, he responded, 'Your time has not yet come. We still need you.' With that, he accompanied me to the waiting car and left me with the reassuring words 'I can walk better now.'

TABLES TURNED: ZHIDA AL SAADI

I hadn't seen Zhida for the best part of 30 years. But as soon as I set eyes on her in April 2018 I knew exactly who she was. Zhida, who's now in her seventies, had been one of my lecturers when I was at medical school in Baghdad.

Our interaction hadn't been extensive, and it wasn't among the finer moments of my academic career. Zhida was a lecturer in gynaecology and obstetrics. I distinctly recall attending only one of her lectures—and being thrown out of it because I'd fallen asleep!

This time, it was me who put Zhida to sleep. Well, not exactly me, but the anaesthetist who prepared her for the operating theatre, where I performed a revision hip replacement. It went well. Zhida and I later reflected on our previous meeting with a grin.

—-—

The Civilians

Our first four operating visits to Iraq in 2017 and 2018 were all frantic. We saw 90 potential patients during the fifteen hours of clinical examination in May 2017. Our first surgical trip in August involved 58 operations on 51 patients—43 of them from the paramilitary, three from the federal police and five civilians. We carried out a total of 23 osseointegrations on 21 patients—two of them bilateral amputees. In addition, there were 34 complex trauma patients and one total hip replacement. During our 17-day stay in Baghdad leading up to Christmas 2017, we carried out 190 operations including 62 osseointegrations. And in April 2018, we performed dozens more operations.

Remarkably, when we returned from our second operating mission to Baghdad, Iraq was ranked fifth in the world for the number of patients who had undergone osseointegration. Australia led the way with 476 osseointegration operations. Sweden was second, with less than half that number—230 operations. Germany and the Netherlands were equal third on 130 each. Iraq was next on 85—the only developing nation in the top five. Sadly, this reflects the number of amputees in the country as a result of the conflicts that have raged there over the last four decades.

As well as improving the lives of individuals, I hope my contributions in the Middle East can help make people less nationalistic and more passionate about forging a peaceful future across the region.

11

AN AUDIENCE WITH THE AYATOLLAH

Iraq, of course, is an overwhelmingly Muslim country. Currently, it's estimated that more than 90 per cent of the population are followers of Islam. But that certainly doesn't mean the country is unified in its faith. Beneath the surface, Iraq is divided. While Sunni Muslims make up the vast majority of the Islamic world— anything up to 90 per cent—Shi'ites are the largest group in Iraq.

Around 60–65 per cent of Iraqis are Shi'ite while between 32–37 per cent are Sunni. There is also a small but significant number of Christians and Yazidis—a religion that incorporates aspects of Islam, Christianity, Judaism and Zoroastrianism. The Yazidis believe a being known as the Peacock Angel rules the world. Because of that, they've been labelled devil worshippers and have been persecuted by ISIS.

Surprisingly, there used to be a long-established Jewish community in Baghdad—well known as traders and generally accepted into Iraqi society. In fact, in the days when Iraq was a more secular country, one of my father's best friends was a rabbi. But after World War II—and especially following the overthrow of the Iraqi monarchy in 1958—tensions rose between religious groups, and the Jews left.

The bitter rivalry between the two main Muslim sects is at the heart of many of Iraq's problems. Under Saddam Hussein, the Sunni minority controlled the government, and Ba'ath Party members—many of them Sunnis—held senior posts in the bureaucracy. However, Saddam formed alliances with anyone he thought would be useful to him—including Shi'ite groups. Despite this, when I was growing up in Iraq, no one knew or cared whether their neighbours and acquaintances were Sunni or Shi'ite.

Attitudes changed in 2003 when the Coalition forces, led by the United States, toppled Saddam and took control of the country. After the initial battles, there was little resistance to the invading force. Many Iraqi soldiers simply laid down their arms and deserted. They went home rather than continuing to fight. In the early days of the occupation, the American military paid the wages of Iraq's remaining soldiers.

The United States then created the Coalition Provisional Authority and appointed the first American administrator,

Paul Bremer. He regularly referred to ending the Sunni domination of Iraq. But he completely misunderstood the nation and its people, and his determination to remove Sunnis from positions of responsibility fostered what has become an often bloody rivalry between the two major Islamic sects.

Within a fortnight of his appointment, Bremer dismissed the existing Iraqi military and most civilian employees of Saddam's government. His idea was to end, once and for all, the influence of Saddam. But the move backfired spectacularly.

Having lost their jobs, 400,000 former soldiers plus hundreds of thousands of public servants had little or no prospect of finding long-term work. Their future looked grim. Unemployment soared to around 70 per cent of the workforce. In other words, seven out of ten Iraqis had no opportunity to work, which undermined social stability. Not surprisingly, this led to widespread rioting.

Eventually, the United States agreed to pay around 250,000 former regular soldiers between US$50 and US$150 a month. Conscripts were given a one-off payment. But few were happy with the deal.

Many former Iraqi soldiers formed or drifted into private militia groups and launched open warfare against the occupying forces. Within months, they were joined by highly motivated religious fanatics who had spotted an opportunity to increase their power and influence. The Iranian Government also identified an opening to establish a foothold among the disaffected Shi'ites.

These rebel groups soon became better equipped and organised, and they started launching guerrilla attacks on the invasion army and associated institutions. Among their most devastating rebel sorties was an attack on the United Nations headquarters in Baghdad, based in the Canal Hotel not far from the lawless area of Sadr City. The huge bomb blast killed 22 people, including Sérgio Vieira de Mello— the Brazilian Special Representative of the United Nations Secretary-General.

Clashes rapidly escalated, and the invasion force lost control of the streets of Baghdad and other major population centres. Within a few months, Iraq became known as the most dangerous country on earth.

By the time the United States finally withdrew from Iraq at the end of 2011, sectarian clashes were rife. The first Iraqi prime minister after the end of the transitional government in 2006, Nouri al-Maliki, was widely held responsible for further stoking unrest by promoting and supporting Shi'ites in most areas of the government and Iraqi society. Only under the administration of his successor, Haider al-Abadi, did the government adopt a more balanced and logical approach. Al-Abadi also promised to tackle the country's systemic corruption. But, by then, it was so entrenched that he achieved only limited success.

The failure of the two administrations to substantially improve working and living conditions for the vast majority of Iraqis, coupled with the continued corruption, was a key reason why the electoral groups associated with both former prime ministers lost ground in the national elections held in May 2018.

The rift between Shi'ite and Sunni Muslims has its roots all the way back in the early days of Islam. Shortly before he died, the Prophet Mohammed announced that his successor would be his cousin and son-in-law, Ali ibn Abi Talib. But following the prophet's death in 632 AD, a dispute developed over the leadership of the faith.

One group, which became known as the Sunnis, wanted the senior members of the Muslim community to decide who should be the political and religious leader, known as the caliph. A similar method is used by Catholics to elect a pope. The senior Muslims chose Abu Bakr, who had been a key adviser to Mohammed and was also his father-in-law.

But a smaller group wanted the mantle of imam, or leader of the faith, to be handed to Ali—as Mohammed had indicated. Their belief was that only God could choose the prophet's successor, and that by naming Ali, God had spoken through Mohammed. The split had been established.

However, after the death of three caliphs, the Sunnis turned to Ali to be their fourth caliph. His dual reign as both caliph and imam was punctuated by civil wars. Finally, in 661 AD, Ali was attacked with a poisoned sword while he was praying at the Great Mosque of Kufa, south of Baghdad. He died two days later and was interred in a secret place to prevent his grave from being desecrated by opponents.

His burial site remained unknown to most people for nearly a century, until the sixth Shia Imam, Ja'far Ibn Muhammad As-Sadiq, allowed it to be revealed that Ali's grave was in Najaf, not far from Kufa. With the announcement of Ali's burial site, Najaf became the most holy place for Shia Muslims and the most holy site in Iraq. Each year, millions make the pilgrimage to the city. Interestingly, Shi'ites believe that Adam and Noah are buried next to Ali.

Ali was succeeded by his eldest son, Hasan, who became the caliph and the second Shia Imam. However, he relinquished the title of caliph after a few months as part of a peace deal with the Sunni leader, Muawiya. Hasan was poisoned in 670 AD. In turn, his younger brother, Husayn, became the third Shia Imam.

Muawiya's death in 680 AD brought more bloody clashes. Husayn refused to pledge allegiance to Muawiya's son and nominated successor Yazid. The people of Kufa wrote to Husayn, promising to support him and asking for his help. Husayn responded by riding, with a small band of supporters, towards Kufa. The governor of Kufa was emphatically opposed to Husayn's mission and sent as many as 30,000 soldiers to block their entry to the city.

Even though his force was completely outnumbered, Husayn and his younger brother, Abbas, decided to take on their opponents. They were duly slaughtered, along with their supporters, in the Battle of Karbala. Husayn was buried in Karbala. His shrine is now the second-most holy place in Iraq.

Abbas is buried in a separate shrine close by.

Husayn's death is still commemorated each year among Shi'ites with the event known as Ashura. At that time, tens of millions of pilgrims visit Karbala. More extreme Shi'ites publicly harm themselves with knives and swords as a sign of their devotion to the third Shia Imam. It's a ritual I regard as barbaric.

The significance of the Twelve Imams—the last Imam Mohammad ibn al-Hasan was born in 869 AD and is considered to be still living in occultation, effectively an eclipse-like state when a closer object obscures the view of the imam—is one of the fundamental differences between the two Muslim sects. They are the spiritual leaders of the Shia community and, according to some Sunnis, are afforded a status of divinity that can only be held by God.

—　—

To this day, Shia religious leader Grand Ayatollah Ali al-Husseini al-Sistani holds enormous power in Iraq. Even though he was born in neighbouring Iran, the Grand Ayatollah hasn't adopted the political and religious model of that country. While religious leaders in Tehran have imposed Islamic law and hold sway over the political establishment, al-Sistani has opted for a more hands-off approach, often known as quietism, which observes a routine separation between religion and politics.

While he doesn't involve himself in day-to-day political events, he has intervened at crucial times to steer the nation towards a more settled future. In 2003, in defiance of the United States' plans to administer Iraq in the longer term, the Grand Ayatollah called for the formation of a National Assembly, a new Iraqi constitution and democratic elections. His influence forced the Americans to hasten the democratic process.

Three years later, he helped calm the rising tension after Al-Qaeda bombed a revered shrine in Samarra. And his June 2014 declaration of a fatwa against ISIS, issued after Friday prayers, was a turning point in the war against the terrorist group. It led to the formation of Hashd, the paramilitary group that played an important role in defeating the jihadists. More recently, he opposed the plan for the Kurds to secede from Iraq and set up an independent nation.

The Grand Ayatollah is a person of fascination and some mystery. He's in his late eighties and, these days, is a reclusive figure who, for health and security reasons, rarely leaves his home. He spends much of his time studying religious philosophies and teachings.

Al-Sistani was born into a family of Muslim clerics in Iran in 1930, although there's some dispute about the exact location of his birth. The Grand Ayatollah says he was born in Mashhad, in the north-east near the border with Turkmenistan. Others believe he came into the world in Sistan—in the south, close to the border with Pakistan—and moved to Mashhad as a child.

He studied religion with his father in Mashhad before moving to the world centre of Shia religious scholarship, Qom, south-west of Tehran. At the age of 21, he relocated to Najaf to further his religious studies with his predecessor as Grand Ayatollah, Abu al-Qasim al-Khoei. Al-Sistani rose to the role of Grand Ayatollah after the death of al-Khoei in 1992, and he established a reputation for being a moderate who navigated a delicate course during Saddam's reign—despite his mosque being closed by the dictator.

At various stages, the Grand Ayatollah has been challenged by more activist Shia leaders.

Out of the blue, after my first visit to Baghdad, someone in the Iraqi community in Sydney told me that the Grand Ayatollah had heard about my work and wanted to meet me. Even though I'm an atheist, it's not the sort of invitation I could turn down. It's the equivalent of being invited for a one-on-one audience with the Pope. But the details were only discussed once I was in the Iraqi capital.

Representatives of the Grand Ayatollah came into Ibn Sina Hospital, and we decided that the following Friday would be most suitable for the visit. Being the holy day, large numbers of the hospital staff would be taking the day off, reducing the support available to help us operate.

I needed permission from the Prime Minister's Department to go ahead with the journey south. After brief discussions, they gave it the thumbs up—along with an assurance that they'd also organise an armed convoy to take us there.

An Audience with the Ayatollah

The arrangement turned out to be exactly the same as the motorcade to and from the airport. We sat in two black bomb-proof Chevrolet Suburban SUVs with darkened windows to hide our identity, escorted by two utes with machine guns mounted on the rear tray, one driving ahead of us and the other behind us. Soldiers wearing menacing battle fatigues and black balaclavas manned the machine guns throughout the journey.

We left the Prime Minister's Guest House around 6.30 a.m., as the temperature was already rising towards the day's maximum of 48 degrees Celsius. The drive took around two and a half hours. We travelled out of the Green Zone and along the road towards the airport, then turned onto the main highway to the south.

The road is busy with modern cars and large trucks carrying goods from the container port on the Shatt al-Arab waterway in the south. All of them have to negotiate military checkpoints, where the vehicles are thoroughly checked to make sure they're not carrying bombs. Drivers are required to show their licences and identity documents, as well as the paperwork for the load they're carrying.

It can be a long and exhausting process. At one point on the outskirts of Baghdad, trucks and oil tankers were queued as far as the eye could see on the other side of the road heading into the capital, waiting for their turn to be inspected. The delay could have been hours.

Passenger vehicles go through a similar process, but the delays aren't as long. Soldiers in desert camouflage uniforms and police wearing dark and light blue camouflage search some cars. For others, documents are inspected and the vehicles are waved through.

As the buildings lining the road give way to more open spaces, there are some improvised shops on the side of the highway. Among them was a butcher's shop, covered only in a flimsy canvas, with whole skinned animal carcasses hanging from hooks. The sheep for sale were quite possibly marinated in dust, as well as petrol and diesel fumes!

By this stage, the landscape on either side of the road appears largely dry. Amid the scattered roadside shops between towns are small piles of rubble. The dominant colour is grey— although to people who know the Middle East, this stretch of Iraq is one of the greenest in the region.

On the way, we drove through the historic city of Babylon, which dates back more than 4000 years and was once regarded as the greatest city on earth. During the reign of Nebuchadnezzar II, it was home to both the Hanging Gardens—one of the Seven Wonders of the Ancient World—and the spectacular blue-glazed brick Ishtar Gate. A reconstruction of the gate, including some of the original bricks, is now on show at the Pergamon Museum in Berlin. A replica of the gate has been built on the site of old Babylon.

Sadly, the area around Babylon is still rated as too dangerous for visitors to inspect the glories of the old city. Instead, we stuck to the main road, which—with its four-storey brick and concrete apartment buildings above workshops and retail outlets—certainly didn't reflect the magnificence of the ancient civilisation that once thrived here.

We drove on and eventually reached the barren, flat and sandy landscape that surrounds Najaf. Because it's the holiest city in the Shi'ite faith, Najaf has been at the epicentre of many of the clashes between the Shia and Sunni Muslims. The man who went on to lead the Iranian Revolution, Ayatollah Ruhollah Khomeini, lived and taught in Najaf for fifteen years after he left his homeland during the rule of the Shah. Saddam Hussein expelled large numbers of Shia clerics—including Khomeini—following the Iranian Revolution.

In 1991, after the First Gulf War, Saddam's forces ambushed the leaders of the Shi'ite revolt inside Najaf's Imam Ali Mosque and killed nearly everyone. The mosque was closed for the next two years, and large numbers of people living in the surrounding area—many of them of Iranian descent—were deported to Iran.

Shortly after 9 a.m., we arrived in the holy city, not far from the Imam Ali Mosque. But before we could clamber out of the SUVs, the four women—Claudia, theatre nurse Simmy Masuku, my personal assistant Michelle and Sophie McNeill from ABC TV's *Foreign Correspondent* program—were required to cover their heads in the traditional hijab.

The women needed to wear two separate scarves—a white tubular piece of fabric that covered their forehead, encasing the hair, plus another piece of fabric that fitted over the head and dropped down towards the shoulders. Once they had complied with the dress regulations, we walked a few hundred metres through a street market to a hotel that overlooks the mosque.

At that stage of the hot and hazy summer morning, only a few early shoppers were lazily strolling through the wide and dusty pedestrian area leading to the mosque. Most women walking towards the mosque were dressed in black, with a black head covering—indicating their deep religious beliefs. There was more variety in the men's clothing. Some wore contemporary clothes—T-shirt and jeans—while others were in more traditional full-length robes and headscarves.

Approaching the mosque, the sound of the Koran being chanted over loudspeakers filled the air. People were carrying the coffins of family members on their shoulders towards the holy site. Traditionally, the bearers of a coffin should walk around the mosque and then take it to the nearby cemetery. In Iraq, bodies should be buried as soon as possible and almost always before sunset on the day of death.

As we waited on an upper floor of the hotel for the Grand Ayatollah's representatives, we could see both the mosque and the massive cemetery of Wadi Al-Salam, which translates as the Valley of Peace. The cemetery is the world's largest burial ground, and it occupies about 15 per cent of Najaf. It stretches as far as the eye can see and is more than 1400 years old. More than five million people are believed to be buried in the cemetery. To put it in context, Australia's biggest cemetery—Rookwood in Sydney's western suburbs—is the world's sixth-largest covering 314 hectares. It contains the remains of more than 915,000 people.

Being interred in Wadi Al-Salaam is considered a guarantee of entering paradise. Pilgrims bring the bodies of their relatives to the city, or they may take elderly or seriously ill people there to spend their last days.

Thousands of bodies from all around the world, from as far east as China and as far west as Morocco and including Australia and the US, are brought to Wadi Al-Salaam for burial. Shi'ites will spend tens of thousands of dollars to ensure their loved ones are interred here. A refugee I met in Curtin Detention Centre, who went on to edit an Arabic newspaper in Sydney, insisted on taking his mother's coffin to Najaf, a journey that cost him US$50,000. With all due respect to people's beliefs, I think there are better ways to spend that sort of money.

A couple of senior figures from the paramilitary and an officer from the Prime Minister's Department had travelled with us from Baghdad to Najaf, clearly in the hope that they would be able to come with me to meet the revered Grand Ayatollah.

The cleric's representatives, three unarmed young men who looked like almost anyone on the streets of Najaf, arrived. They were wearing black collared shirts and grey pants and sported carefully trimmed beards. Their one distinguishing feature was that they all wore identical silver rings with a colourless stone.

They introduced themselves before advising me, 'Okay, follow us.' Then they told the security guards, the representative of the Prime Minister's Department and Hashd, 'Thank you. We'll take over from here.'

That didn't go down well. The security contingent insisted that they were responsible for my safety and needed to accompany me. A stand-off developed, but the three young men from the Ayatollah's staff were insistent. 'He's under our protection now. The Ayatollah won't see any officials.'

The government and paramilitary representatives were forced to back down as a crowd gathered to witness the heated discussion.

The Grand Ayatollah's assistants led me from the hotel, through the Imam Ali shrine and, on the other side, into a souk—a traditional Iraqi market. We walked around 700 metres through narrow, crowded alleyways, and then waited for about twenty minutes before heading to Al-Rasool Street. There was a lane to the left, maybe two metres wide, which was protected by a high gate made of vertical metal bars. We were met by a cleric, who ushered me into the laneway, which was crowded with men in religious and military uniforms. The houses on either side were old and humble. Knots of power cables hung low above us.

I was guided to the Grand Ayatollah's home, which was about 50 metres along the laneway on the right-hand side. It is an extremely modest dwelling of about 100 square metres. Outside, around a dozen armed security guards wearing military-style uniforms protected the entrance.

An Audience with the Ayatollah

The front door was open, and I was escorted into a hallway, where I was met by one of al-Sistani's sons, dressed in traditional Shi'ite religious clothes—a black gown with a black turban. The black turban indicates a Shia who is descended directly from the Prophet Mohammed. Sunnis who are descended from Mohammed wear a white turban with red and green trimmings.

The Grand Ayatollah's son was around 170 centimetres in height and might have been in his sixties. He spoke to me in Arabic, with a strong Iranian accent, before leading me down the hallway to a large sitting area on the left, furnished with a group of plastic chairs and rugs on the floor.

We drank tea, and he talked for about ten minutes, mainly about politics and his thoughts on the high level of corruption in Iraq. He also explained the confrontation between the Ayatollah's assistants and my security guards back at the hotel, saying that his father had lost trust in all political parties in Iraq. In the past, he had met political leaders in private, only to find subsequent false reports of their discussions fed by the politicians to the media. As a consequence, the cleric had slapped a blanket ban on meeting bureaucrats and party officials of any affiliation.

After finishing the tea, we headed back into the hallway and to the next room on the left. Sitting under a fluorescent light was the Grand Ayatollah. He stood as I entered the room, shook my hand and blessed me.

As we sat, I explained that I'm not a religious person. 'Just to make sure, Your Excellency, that you know I'm not a follower of any religion. I'm actually an infidel,' I told him.

The Grand Ayatollah smiled and responded, 'If we are not brothers in religion then we are brothers in humanity. And I thank you for your humanity.' He spoke very softly and slowly but clearly in Arabic. Like his son, though, he had a distinct Iranian accent.

We talked about the impact of terrorism and the evils of ISIS. He was completely inclusive of Iraqis, regardless of their religious beliefs or faith, and clearly indicated that Iraq should be a country for all its people. We then discussed my patients in general terms, and he thanked me for everything I was doing. In fact, for the majority of the time I was with the Grand Ayatollah, he was thanking me for the help we were providing for the wounded militiamen and civilians.

I guess we spoke for around ten minutes, and I came away with an extremely positive impression. My first thought was that he reminded me very much of my father: quiet, considered, intellectual and highly knowledgeable. It also struck me that, although he's a cleric, his influence spreads much wider. Effectively, he is the safety valve for the nation.

As I left the meeting with the Grand Ayatollah, his son approached me once more and handed me a book and a silver ring, which was exactly the same as the ring the three young men had been wearing. 'This ring is a symbol of our gratitude for your work and I hope you enjoy reading my father's book *Intellectual Expatriates*.'

I thanked him, placed the ring on my finger and left.

I returned to the hotel to link up with the other members of my team, and we visited the Imam Ali Mosque—a huge, awe-inspiring and beautiful example of Islamic architecture and art. The external walls of the mosque are covered in turquoise mosaics, while the dome is plated with gold and flanked by two gold-covered minarets.

The original shrine was constructed in 977 AD. It was destroyed by fire a little more than 100 years later, then rebuilt; it has been rebuilt a number of times since. The main redevelopment took place in 1500. More than eight million pilgrims visit the Imam Ali Mosque each year.

Waist-high security barriers cordon off the mosque, with openings at various points for visitors to enter the compound. Iraqi Muslims are much more accommodating than those in other countries—non-believers are allowed into the shrines, unlike Saudi Arabia, where they're refused entry. Surrounding the mosque are covered walkways to protect pilgrims from the raw heat of the sun, and rosewater is sprayed into fans to help cool pilgrims in the peak of the Iraqi summer. Visitors sit on carpets as they prepare to enter the building.

Contrasting with the opulence of the mosque itself, the people making the pilgrimage to the holy city come from all walks of society. Many are extremely poor. As is often the case with religions, the poorer the people, the more devout their beliefs.

Alongside the throng of worshippers, my team and I were ushered towards the entrance to the mosque. Before setting foot in the shrine, all visitors have to take off their shoes and leave them outside. This is often challenging for the average Westerner, who immediately fears that someone will run off with their unguarded footwear. For the record, I've never heard of such a thing happening.

The interior of the mosque is packed with faithful Muslims chanting verses from their prayer books. Brightly coloured tiles and intricate decorations glitter as they are illuminated by spotlights. There are conflicting instructions about taking photographs inside. Some officials tell you it's forbidden, while others happily give you a wave to indicate that everything's allowed.

People drop to their knees to kiss the ground or the rugs covering the floor. Others touch and kiss the walls. The most holy point, of course, is the tomb of Imam Ali ibn Abi Talib. But before we could reach the tomb, the men and women were separated. Women must approach the tomb from one side, men from the other to ensure there is no close physical contact between the sexes in the scramble to touch the tomb.

The silver tomb has windows protected by silver bars and a door with a silver lock. Inside is a smaller tomb featuring ornate ironwork. Pilgrims clamour to touch and kiss the silver bars and any other part of the tomb they can reach. There's plenty of gentle pushing and shoving, as worshippers jostle for their favoured spot. The atmosphere is heady, almost hypnotic.

Getting to the silver bars was a challenge, because thousands of people had made the journey to the shrine with the same purpose—to touch the tomb. Clearly, though, we had a huge advantage over everyone else, as the Ayatollah's representatives and the guards escorted us through the crowd so I could touch the silver bars.

After spending around twenty minutes inside the mosque, we were escorted to a large room for a formal reception, which included the obligatory glasses of tea. Typically in Iraq, it's *chai noomi basra*—a delicious tea made from dried limes.

Altogether, the visit to Najaf and the shrine was both moving and fascinating.

I had also been invited to meet the Ayatollah of Karbala, who's based in the second-most holy city in Iraq. Karbala is about 80 kilometres north of Najaf and a little more than 100 kilometres south of Baghdad. The city contains the tombs of Imam Husayn and his brother, Abbas, who were killed during the Battle of Karbala. At the foot of Imam Husayn's tomb is a mass grave containing the bodies of the 72 followers who also were slaughtered during the battle. They're known as the Martyrs of Karbala.

The shrine of Imam Husayn is another absolutely beautiful example of Islamic religious architecture. The columned walls around the shrine are decorated in turquoise and light blue. The dome rises nearly 30 metres above the shrine, and there are two minarets. Like the Imam Ali Mosque in Najaf, the central dome and minarets are covered in gold. At the bottom of the dome are twelve windows.

Inside, the shrine is richly decorated and brightly illuminated. It includes nearly 70 rooms, many of them used for religious education. More than 50 million pilgrims visit Karbala each year for Ashura, commemorating the death of Imam Husayn, and for what are known as the *arba'een* rituals 40 days later.

My meeting with the Ayatollah of Karbala was completely different from the earlier encounter with the Grand Ayatollah. The Ayatollah of Karbala is younger and takes an altogether more relaxed approach. Rather than restricting the people he was prepared to meet, everyone in my team—both men and women—was invited to take tea with the Ayatollah in the complex of the shrine of Imam Husayn.

We were led upstairs, through a labyrinth of corridors and into a large meeting room lined with bookshelves filled with scholarly tomes. The floor was covered with traditional rugs, which were predominantly red and featured intricate patterns. In the middle was a large, formal wooden table surrounded by leather chairs. The entire room had an atmosphere of calm and learning.

We were given glasses of tea as we waited for the Ayatollah. When he came into the room and started talking to us, the Ayatollah was focused not only on the work we were carrying out in Iraq but also on the technology and techniques involved. I showed him videos of osseointegration patients walking within a few weeks of undergoing surgery. He seemed fascinated and asked plenty of questions.

After spending around twenty minutes with us, the Ayatollah rose, shook my hand and told me that he would be delighted to see me again. With a cheeky laugh, he added, 'And I don't say that to everyone!'

Each member of my team was given a gift bag that included a watch, a square of marble from the shrine of Imam Husayn and a large ring featuring marble from the tomb of the Prophet Mohammed. The marble items had been removed from the shrine and the tomb and replaced during repair work. These are absolutely priceless mementoes of our visit. The reception we received illustrates the different approach of radical Islamist groups in different countries. In Iraq, foreigners, people of different faiths, non-believers and women—even atheists and infidels like me—were not just accepted but welcomed. I don't believe radical clerics in Saudi Arabia or Egypt would afford us the same levels of hospitality.

On the way back to Baghdad, I noticed that stretches of the highway from Karbala to Baghdad have a distinctly Australian appearance. In a number of places, large stands of gum trees line the roadside. They were planted after the First Gulf War, because they grow quickly and can rapidly provide a richer, greener landscape. But there's nothing Western about the images placed along extended stretches of the road's central reservation. Posters feature the faces of soldiers who are regarded as local martyrs. In other spots, there are images of leading clerics. I don't see either idea catching on along the freeways and motorways of Australia.

12

INTO THE RED

You feel safe in the Green Zone—but the price you pay for that sense of reassurance is that it's pretty sterile. And not by chance. The primary consideration in the Green Zone is the security of the nation's leading politicians and public servants, plus the foreign diplomats. What was once the centre of Saddam Hussein's power base—with many of the largest and most luxurious of his palaces—is now dominated by Iraq's parliament, government departments, residences for political party leaders and embassies.

The Green Zone is located on the western bank of the Tigris River, which snakes through Baghdad and is spanned by fourteen bridges. The permanent civilian population of the Green Zone is around 10,000 people—a large proportion of them working for the government. They pay a premium to live in the security of the Green Zone's houses and apartment blocks.

Their protection is provided by the heavily armed soldiers and military vehicles at the checkpoints on all roads in and out of the area. Concrete blast walls topped with razor wire line the roads. Everyone needs identification papers and permits to access the Green Zone, and there's also a midnight curfew. No one comes in and no one leaves from the witching hour until 5 a.m.

There are reminders of the Saddam era throughout the Green Zone. Many of his palaces are still intact, but they have been put to fresh uses. The famed military parade ground, with its pair of arches featuring towering hands holding crossed scimitars, remains a major landmark and was the centre of the official celebrations to commemorate the defeat of ISIS in late 2017.

The roads in the Green Zone are strangely quiet. The traffic—mostly government cars and SUVs—is sparse. It's a long way from the peak-hour traffic snarls of Sydney, Melbourne and Brisbane.

You won't see many people walking along the main roads, especially during the ferocious heat of summer. In the residential areas, small groups of people will walk—or even jog—through the narrow streets, particularly after dark when temperatures are cooler. Shops and other retail outlets are few and far between. There's an occasional restaurant or super-market. Generally, Iraqis will venture outside the Green Zone for shopping.

Many diplomatic staff from the various embassies stay in their compounds during the week, with some making a weekend visit to another diplomatic mission—probably the well-equipped US or British Embassy compounds—for rest and recreation. Gym classes and swimming in an Olympic-size pool are available at the US Embassy.

Despite the sense of security in the Green Zone, guards—usually former soldiers from various countries, including Australia and the United Kingdom, who are armed with handguns—accompany diplomatic staff when they leave their compound. The feeling is that, even now, diplomats could be targets. They can't be too careful.

The Red Zone is the name used by foreigners for the part of Baghdad that lies outside the Green Zone. Iraqis simply call it Baghdad. The Red Zone is authentic Baghdad, but with a surreal atmosphere created by military and police checkpoints and the obvious presence of the army and other security forces. A drive through the Red Zone is a journey through the city's history, as well as its various political and cultural influences.

Originally, Baghdad was a village on the Tigris River. In 762 AD, Caliph Al-Mansur chose it as the site for the new headquarters of the caliphate. It held that status for less than 75 years, before being abandoned in favour of Samarra. Within another 60 years, the caliphate had moved back to Baghdad.

By that stage, the city had been known by various names, including Madinat al-Salam—the City of Peace. The name, of course, is hugely ironic considering the regular conflicts that have marred the city's history—especially over the last 40 or more years.

On the eastern bank of the Tigris River is Baghdad's central business district, which is like most contemporary city centres—multistorey commercial buildings, unit blocks and hotels. North-east of the city centre is the Army Canal, an open waterway that Saddam built to take the city's sewage. On the other side of the canal is Sadr City—unofficially named after the murdered Grand Ayatollah Mohammad Sadeq al-Sadr. In the past, it has been known as al-Thawra—Revolution City—and Saddam City.

Sadr City is easily recognisable because of its run-down public housing, which was built in 1959 to accommodate the vast influx of poverty-stricken farmers who were flocking into the capital. The slums also provided homes for others who were previously living in appalling conditions in poor neighbourhoods of the capital.

The farmers brought their traditional tribal beliefs and way of life with them—and didn't adapt well to their new surroundings. The clash between their rural lifestyle and the rest of urban Baghdad has been a source of tension ever since.

These days, Sadr City is home to up to 30 per cent of Baghdad's population. With its low socio-economic profile, it has established a daunting reputation as a hotbed of violence and crime. I've only been there twice in my life—once to buy a sheep, and the other to look for a stolen car.

Fortunately, not all of Baghdad is like Sadr City.

At the other end of the Iraqi social scale is the palace complex in the west of the Red Zone, not far from the airport, known as Radwaniyah Palace, and originally built as a luxury estate for Saddam Hussein. The development incorporates lakes, landscaped hills and two buildings. One is called Al Faw Palace, the other—ironically, considering the enormous influence the neighbouring nation now has over Iraq—is the Victory Over Iran Palace.

The palace complex reflects the luxury that Saddam enjoyed. The buildings feature soaring reception halls lined with marble decorations and statues. Back in the day, many of the statues were of Saddam. Now they're less politically focused.

The grounds of the palace complex are extensive and carefully maintained. But they are not a rare oasis in the Red Zone. Large parks and gardens—many in need of additional care and maintenance—are spread throughout the city. The people of Baghdad love nothing more than a family picnic or a game of football—often a combination of the two—in the open spaces. On Fridays—the holy day in Muslim countries—you'll see Iraqi family groups doing the same thing as other families across the world. They'll be spread across the city's open spaces, playing games, eating food and enjoying each other's company.

The Grand Ayatollah had invited us to Najaf again during our visit in December 2017—and this time he was prepared to meet all the men in our group. But a couple of days before we were due to make the trip, I was informed that he was sick and was cancelling all engagements. We discussed other options with our contacts in the Prime Minister's Department, and they organised a day exploring some of Baghdad's most fascinating sites.

Even though security has improved massively in recent times, I was still apprehensive about leaving the heavily protected Green Zone and venturing into the rest of the city. The Prime Minister's Department wasn't taking any chances with our safety. No fewer than sixteen officials and plain-clothes security guards escorted us. I didn't specifically ask, but I believe that most, if not all, of them were carrying guns in case of any incidents. As usual, our two SUVs were bookended by utes equipped with machine guns and highly trained soldiers.

From the Prime Minister's Guest House, our convoy drove to the edge of the Green Zone, snaking through a maze of narrow streets flanked with concrete blast walls, through military checkpoints and, after ten to fifteen minutes, into the Red Zone. The hustle and bustle of daily life in this part of Baghdad is in complete contrast to the artificial calm of the Green Zone. However, what struck me most about the Red Zone was how dirty and dishevelled it looked. Baghdad had always been a clean and neat city when I was growing up there. Not any longer.

Going Back

We headed through the main roads on the western bank of the Tigris River north of the Green Zone, crossed a bridge over the river and entered the historic area of old Baghdad. As soon as you reach the old city, the streetscape changes. The wide roads built during Saddam's regime give way to narrow streets and alleyways; domes of mosques rise high above the streets in some places. Gone are the tall, contemporary structures, replaced with often centuries-old, traditional two-, three- or four-storey buildings. There are still examples of historic town-houses in the area of Al-Rashid Street. They're easily identified by the wooden balconies on the first floor and latticed windows.

The traffic is chaotic. Roads simmer with crowds of people. There are covered souks—selling everything from leather to copper and even birds—alongside makeshift street-front market stalls, with hagglers jostling and bargaining for the best deal.

What used to be the bus station has now been taken over by street traders, who've created a shambolic open-air market. The unofficial roadway through the stalls appears to be dictated by the traders and the spots they occupy. It's up to any vehicles to avoid the improvised stalls.

To complicate matters, buyers wander amid the traffic largely oblivious to any cars or trucks that are trying to nudge their way through the teeming mass of humanity. There seem to be few, if any, road rules. And those that do exist are generally ignored.

In the open-air markets, the goods are displayed on the ground or on shaky tables. There are also some formal shops in the down-at-heel buildings lining the area. Anything and everything is on sale, from car and machinery parts to clothing and food. Buyers and sellers gesticulate and argue as they negotiate over prices. Other people are sitting at small cafes, drinking coffee or tea from traditional Iraqi glasses, which are tall and narrow.

This area of the Iraqi capital is home to the palaces where many of the ancient rulers of Baghdad lived. There are also other historical places, including Al-Qushla, that was originally built as a military barracks by the occupying Ottoman Empire in the mid-nineteenth century and now houses the Baghdad Cultural Centre. One of its features is a celebrated clock tower, complete with a clock given to the Iraqi people by King George V during the British mandate over Iraq, which lasted from 1914 until the military coup in 1958.

A few metres inside the main entrance to the Al-Qushla grounds, the vista opens to reveal a park on the eastern bank of the Tigris River. Each Friday, the park is a meeting place for poets, musicians and political speakers. In a lively scene, visitors from all over Baghdad and other parts of Iraq swarm through the grassy area. Vendors in traditional clothing and turbans stand at strategic locations holding tall and elaborately shaped brass teapots, offering glasses of tea. For a price, of course.

One of the main features of the park is a statue of tenth-century poet Abu Tayeb al-Mutanabbi next to the river. Al-Mutanabbi is a revered Arab poet who often wrote about the many kings and tribal leaders he visited. He was also regarded as something of a prophet. As well as being the source of his livelihood and fame, poetry was also his undoing. Al-Mutanabbi was kidnapped and killed by Dabbah al-Asad near Baghdad in 965 AD because the poet had included a personal insult about al-Asad in one of his works.

In the main courtyard, where poets read their works, one of the centrepieces is a gazebo protecting the king's carriage. It's a piece of Iraqi history and I believe it should be respected as such. Sadly, it's now being used as a political statement and has a Hashd flag draped across it.

I was livid. I saw the flag as a desecration of a historic object. I wanted to intervene and remove the flag and asked the senior representative of the Prime Minister's Department if he would allow me to take matters into my own hands. He was horrified. 'We have only fifteen security guards with us,' he told me. 'To remove the flag, we'd need a whole army!'

I took his advice that such action would seriously endanger our safety. But I remain determined to request another visit to Al-Qushla with the specific intention or taking the paramilitary flag off the carriage.

Opposite Al-Qushla is a branch of the National Museum that focuses on the more recent history of Iraq. An aunt of mine used to run another branch of the museum, which featured priceless artefacts from the region's ancient history. She was in charge when the US troops invaded Baghdad towards the end of the Second Gulf War. As the American soldiers approached, she simply locked the front doors of the museum and walked away. There was nothing more she could do to protect the unique contents.

The US military was ordered to search the museum. So they blew off the front doors, stomped through the exhibitions with their heavy army boots, found nothing and withdrew. They left a gaping hole where the front doors should have been, with one of the world's most valuable museum collections standing unprotected inside.

It didn't take long for the looters to sweep through. Up to 33,000 items went missing. Many of them were later seized at London's Heathrow Airport, en route to the United States. Only a very small portion of the items that had gone missing were ever recovered.

A few metres from Al-Qushla is Mutanabbi Street, which has been there for hundreds of years. It's famous as another gathering point for Iraq's intellectuals, artists and poets. On Fridays, book buyers and sellers dominate the narrow roadway, which is about 300 metres long but less than ten metres wide. Whether they're looking for an ancient embossed copy of the Koran or something more contemporary, everyone is focused on reading, learning and culture. Stallholders spread their goods on tables or on sheets outside the old brick buildings. Many of these buildings are decorated with traditional columns, but some are in desperate need of repair. In street-front cafes, men—and it is mainly men—drink black tea, typically heavily laced with sugar, and smoke tobacco flavoured with anything from mint to orange in large ornate hookah or shisha pipes.

Sadly, like much of Baghdad, Mutanabbi Street has a deadly past. On 5 March 2007, it was shattered by a car bomb that killed 26 people. It took eighteen months of repair work before the street was opened to the public again.

Nearby is a traditional souk—a covered market with a maze of alleys no more than a couple of metres wide. It's packed with people elbowing their way past the huge variety of goods. Stallholders carry out a range of exotic activities—carving leather to make into bags, working with copper and stocking everything from books to old-style globes on a stand. Interestingly, while the others found it an intriguing experience, I was thoroughly uneasy and couldn't get through the souk fast enough.

I had never hung out in areas like this when I was growing up in Baghdad. And all the time we were there, I was supremely conscious of the vulnerability of the market. Many of the terrorist attacks in Baghdad have involved planting bombs in souks. The closely confined crowds offer the maximum potential for death and destruction.

Just down the road from the souk is Baghdad Museum, which offers a snapshot of historical scenes from Iraq over the centuries. It's not a high-tech institution, but it does illustrate traditional Iraqi religious and family events through mannequins dressed in costumes from bygone days, plus streetscapes, photographs and items from Baghdad's past. There's also a sign proclaiming, 'One who lived and died in Baghdad. As if he had been moved from heaven to heaven.' The words must have been written some time ago!

Into the Red

When I was growing up, the bubbling social heart of Baghdad was the hotel, restaurant and nightclub precinct further south on the eastern bank of the Tigris River. Especially during the cooler evenings of summer days, which regularly peak at 48 degrees Celsius, people would flock to the river with their families, friends and business associates. Restaurants lined the riverbank on Abu Nuwas Street, next to Abu Nuwas Park. Both are named after a poet who wrote in the late eighth and early ninth centuries about all the taboo subjects of Islam, such as sex, alcohol and blasphemy.

The park once featured all sorts of attractions, including grassed areas for family picnics or barbecues, as well as small lakes with paddling boats. The park hasn't been maintained at the previous standard and the lakes are now empty. On the other side of the park was the hotel quarter and nearby night-clubs. Some of the hotels are still there, along with a handful of restaurants. But something about the area has died. It's not the throbbing heart of entertainment that it used to be.

One of the more renowned restaurants that has remained is an open-air establishment not far from the river on the edge of Abu Nuwas Park. It specialises in the prized local delicacy known as *masgūf*—fish caught in the Tigris River and barbe-cued next to a huge fire. It's an acquired taste. The fish looks like a large carp and, as river fish do, tastes distinctly muddy. The bones are left in and need to be carefully negotiated as you pick through the flesh with your fingers. With no alcohol available, the drink of choice to accompany the fish is chilled freshly squeezed pomegranate juice. It's a staple of Iraq and absolutely delicious.

There was hardly anyone in the restaurant when we arrived. But, all of a sudden, it became crowded. Initially, I was puzzled by the sudden influx of customers—until I realised that they were the security and other officials who were accompanying us!

After eating at the restaurant, we took an impromptu walk along a path that meandered around the park before carefully making our way through one of the many holes in the barbed wire fence protecting the riverbank. That gave us access to Abu Nuwas Street.

The road that I remember as bustling and busy, especially at night, with the latest American cars and taxis ferrying in the upper echelons of Baghdad society, now lies derelict. Little remains of those heady days before the Iran-Iraq War and the Gulf Wars.

The decline began in the 1990s, as the economy collapsed and conflicts sparked a huge slump in business. Leading hotels closed. Cafes and restaurants also pulled down the shutters. Finally, the area was declared off limits to the public because it was deemed to pose a security threat to one of Saddam's major palaces on the opposite side of the river.

As we walked a few hundred metres along the road, we found a surface of crumbling concrete. Clearly, it's been left to decay over the last 25 years. Now, only military vehicles are allowed access. You can still find a handful of sad reminders of the glory days—the rusting remains of two or three walkways that had once led to restaurants on the banks of the Tigris River. Everything else has been demolished. In place of the flourishing social centre is an overgrown riverbank with a couple of cranes, each appearing to be lying idle.

Individual Iraqi soldiers armed with machine guns are stationed at irregular intervals along the largely disused road. As we approached one soldier, he barked, 'You're not allowed to take photographs here.' His challenge brought our security guards and Prime Minister's Department officials scampering to our defence. As soon as he saw the official badges on their lapels and was instructed that the visitors shouldn't be denied photo opportunities, the soldier feared the worst. 'Does this mean I'm going to lose my job?' he asked nervously.

'Not if you allow them all to have a photograph taken with you,' was the reply.

The soldier stood and posed with each of us, brandishing his weapon, for a series of memorable images. And frankly, after his initial reluctance, he seemed to enjoy his moments of fame in front of our camera lenses.

For me, though, this was a sobering return to a place that had once been a celebration of Baghdad's thriving culture. It no longer shows any signs of its previous prosperity. Now it stands abandoned, offering a tragic commentary on how much times have changed in the Iraqi capital. I was shocked and almost brought to tears by the decay that surrounded us, as this place held such happy memories for me.

Going Back

Arts, culture and intellectual pursuits are a deep-seated tradition in Iraq—although the world's knowledge of this heritage has long been lost among the violence and slaughter of successive wars over the last four decades or so. A remnant of Iraq's artistic history is the number of statues in public places. Abu Nuwas Park is a living reminder of this cultural heritage and features a few large statues—one of them created by my Uncle Ismail, my mother's brother, who was a famous Iraqi sculptor. It depicts Abu Nuwas seated in a large chair on top of a marble plinth and raising a glass of wine in his left hand.

The most famous statues in the park, though, were created by my uncle's rival, Mohammed Ghani Hikmat, who was also responsible for other important statues in Iraq. Many of his works depict characters from the *Arabian Nights* stories. Before his death in Jordan in 2011, he made an equally significant contribution to Iraqi culture as one of the leading figures in the recovery of artworks looted from the National Museum following the fall of Saddam's regime.

His statues in Abu Nuwas Park are large metal figures of fictional Sassanid king Shahryar and his wife, Scheherazade— the two central characters in the *Arabian Nights* stories. The legend tells of Shahryar discovering that his first wife had been unfaithful and ordering that she should be killed. His brother's wife was also unfaithful—and the combined experience persuaded Shahryar that no woman was to be trusted.

As a result, Shahryar married a succession of virgins and ordered that they should be beheaded on the morning after their nuptials to ensure they couldn't be unfaithful. Eventually, the political adviser who doubled as the king's matchmaker ran out of prospective wives, and his own daughter, Scheherazade, put herself forward as the ruler's next bride.

On the first night after their wedding, Scheherazade told her husband a story. But she didn't finish it by the time he fell asleep. When he awoke the next morning, he was so curious to hear the end of the tale that he allowed her to live. The next evening and morning followed the same pattern. Another unfinished story meant another decision to delay her execution. This occurred for the next 1001 nights. By this time, Shahryar had fallen in love with his bride and had learned to trust her. The sculpture in the park depicts Shahryar reclining on a bed, with Scheherazade standing in front, deeply involved in telling one of her stories.

Probably the most famous statue in the recent history of Iraq was erected a few hundred metres from Hikmat's Shahryar and Scheherazade. The statue of Saddam Hussein was erected in Firdos Square to celebrate the dictator's 65th birthday in 2002. It captured the Iraqi leader with his right arm raised in a gesture of generosity and authority.

A year later, as US troops advanced north towards Baghdad, Iraqis started attacking the statue. When the invasion force arrived, in a symbolic gesture indicating that the Battle of Baghdad was over, US soldiers attached a chain around the neck of the statue and toppled it with an army vehicle. The demolition was screened live on television around the world, and it became one of the enduring images of the campaign.

Saddam's statue was replaced by another that was intended to celebrate Iraq's unity. But it was pulled down in 2011, and Firdos Square is now unadorned—a grassed roundabout near the heart of Baghdad.

More recently, the square has become a centre for demonstrators protesting about anything from corruption to high unemployment and homelessness. It remains an important place in Iraqi society—but these days it represents the harsh realities of Iraqi life and the divisions that face the nation.

13

THE PLOT THICKENS

On our first three visits to Baghdad, we'd been welcomed with open arms, often feted like rock stars. Prime Minister Haider al-Abadi had visited the Ibn Sina Hospital wards to meet many of our patients and talk to them about their experiences. The Prime Minister's Department had been instrumental in organising everything associated with our visits: accommodation, food and trips to Najaf, Karbala and the Red Zone.

The government and Hashd had presented us with plaques and other memorabilia to recognise our contribution. The Minister of Health Dr Adila Hammoud—who will shake my hand if we meet one on one, but, when members of Hashd are present, follows the hard-line Islamist custom that forbids men from touching unfamiliar women—and the deputy leader of Hashd, Abu Mahdi al-Muhandis, had arranged a special dinner and reception for us.

The then Iraqi President Fuad Masum—a short, stocky, veteran Kurdish politician with a head of white hair—had staged a special morning tea at Al-Salam Palace in Baghdad to thank us for our humanitarian work. He was effusive in his acknowledgement of our activities.

But by our fourth trip, in April 2018, the atmosphere at Ibn Sina Hospital had changed dramatically. This time, the reception was at best lukewarm and at worst actively hostile. The attitude of senior officials had hardened significantly. Administrators who'd enthusiastically offered to help in any way they could were now distant—barely even greeting us when we arrived each day.

I discovered that three senior surgeons at the hospital were each being paid US$300 for every operation we carried out. As this was a humanitarian mission, I had paid for my team's travel to and from Iraq, and picked up the tab for transporting all of our equipment—90 kilograms of excess baggage for one visit alone. And we hadn't charged a cent for performing 322 operations.

Some of the other more established surgeons who previously had been desperate to learn new techniques also seemed to have lost interest. They were scrubbing in only for the elective hip and knee replacements on individuals with connections high in the Ministry of Health. They were really only focused on money-making ventures. They weren't interested in joining us for serious trauma cases—such as soldiers with severe injuries.

The only surgeons who stuck with us were the residents, the juniors. Their thirst for knowledge has remained constant throughout the time we've been going to Baghdad. Often we didn't finish until the early hours of the morning, and we would be back at the hospital by 8 a.m. The residents were prepared to work all hours of the day and night just for the experience. One, for example, managed only three hours of sleep one night and a solitary hour of sleep the following night. But he was still there when we started work the next morning.

On our fourth visit to Baghdad, the political shenanigans—particularly over operating on civilians—that had scarred our previous work at Ibn Sina Hospital took on new and altogether more disturbing proportions. Exactly why, I'm not sure.

The fact that the national elections were approaching in a matter of weeks may have had something to do with it. Uncertainties surrounding the outcome of the elections could well have brought on a paralysis of decision-making. The frantic schedule we adopted on the previous visits might also have been a factor. Some Iraqi hospital staff probably didn't want to work as hard or as long as we required.

In April 2018, surgeons and anaesthetists were putting limits on the hours they would spend in the theatre, and they refused to prepare anyone for an operation after the early evening. It meant that we were finishing by ten o'clock at night—rather than in the wee small hours, as we had before.

Instead of concentrating on surgery, much more of my time was spent in meetings negotiating with the powers that be at the hospital, health officials and senior figures in the paramilitary. In fact, I was called to so many protracted meetings on one day that I had time for only three operations. It was enormously frustrating. I hadn't gone to Baghdad to attend meetings!

The demon of money emerged, too. One of the main reasons for going to Iraq in April 2018 was to fit the robotic legs to patients who'd undergone osseointegration. As far as I knew, the Prime Minister's Department had handed over the US$3.5 million for the new legs to the Ministry of Health. But when we arrived, there was no sign of the prostheses. I asked the Ministry of Health representative where they were.

'You need to provide them,' was the answer, which came as a complete bolt from the blue to me.

'And who's going to pay for them?' I asked.

'You are,' they bluntly informed me.

'But I don't have that sort of money,' I replied. The response wasn't sympathetic. A number of proposals were put forward. One was that I should pay for the prostheses up front, and the Ministry of Health would reimburse me however much—or little—they wanted. Another was that I should foot the initial bill, and the Ministry of Health would pay me 50 per cent at the start and another 50 per cent a year later.

Then there was a third option. 'Just arrange for an agent to organise buying the legs. You pay 50 per cent to the agent, and he'll organise for the Ministry of Health to hand over the money.'

It wouldn't take anyone terribly long to figure out what was going on. This was corruption writ large. The proposal was that I should find someone with friends in high places, pay them a whole heap of money—which they would pocket and probably share with others who were in on the racket—and then the government money would be handed over as had been agreed in the first place.

Incredulous, I spoke to a senior official in the Ministry of Health. Rather than expressing outrage, he simply informed me, 'Yes, I can arrange for all that to happen. You give me the money, and I'll do it!'

Soon after, I was told that the agent's price had dropped to 15 per cent of the total bill for the prostheses. And I've even been asked by a number of people, 'Why are you so worried? It's only $3.5 million!' But, of course, there's no way I will ever be involved in any scam. The agreement had always been that the government would pay for the new legs of all the osseo-integration patients from counterterrorism, the army and the police. But this arrangement had now been thrown into doubt. Separate from that, Hashd had said it would pay for the new limbs of all the paramilitary patients. Hashd remained committed to keeping its part of the bargain. But there would be no government subsidy for civilian patients. They would have to purchase their own robotic legs.

Going Back

On our previous two visits, we'd taken a rest day on the Friday—the Muslim holy day. However, as this was a shorter mission of just one week, every hour we could spend in the operating theatre was vital. We wanted to continue operating on the Friday, but the senior staff members weren't having a bar of it. I was informed that I wouldn't be allowed to operate at Ibn Sina Hospital that day.

The paramilitary officials were much more collaborative, though, and were keen for their personnel to undergo surgery. They made a number of calls on the Thursday and located a private hospital in the huge Medical City facility in Baghdad, where I'd done my initial training and had been due to operate on the day the Republican Guards delivered the cargo of army deserters to have their ears removed.

The project was approved by the hospital manager, and a theatre and staff had been organised. Then, in the early hours of Friday morning, I received a phone call from a senior medical figure in the paramilitary, saying, 'Unfortunately, the hospital manager has called and told us, "I'm sorry, it can't be done."'

The arrangement had been cancelled. But the hospital manager wouldn't give a detailed explanation of what had changed—he simply stated the fact that the operations wouldn't be going ahead. It was very clear that the Ministry of Health and Hashd were fighting each other. Hashd was devoting all its time and resources to ensuring its wounded soldiers were treated. But the Ministry of Health wanted to take control and dictate what was happening.

The Ministry of Health insisted that Hashd should provide only one-third of patients. The other two-thirds were provided by the Ministry. And most of them were elective-surgery patients who knew people in high places—not the chronic trauma patients with war wounds.

Despite the late-night cancellation of Friday's surgery, paramilitary officials were still determined that I should see their patients and operate. They quickly arranged a clinic for 30 or so paramilitary patients at the Hashd hospital in the Red Zone, at the Razi Centre—named after the Persian physician who built Baghdad's first hospitals in the ninth and tenth centuries—in the working-class suburb of Utafiyah.

Hashd provided the security for us as we were inside examining some extremely complex cases. While we were involved in the clinic, behind the scenes Hashd medical officials were desperately trying to come up with another hospital where I could operate. It took a few hours. But through the paramilitary's extensive network of contacts, they came good.

Hashd protected our convoy as we set off through the Red Zone—this time headed to the Red Crescent Private Hospital in Mansur City, close to the airport in the west of Baghdad. The paramilitary organised for its patients to be transferred from Medical City to the Red Crescent facility.

Red Crescent staff welcomed us warmly and were obviously thrilled to work with us. I managed to complete eight operations at the hospital.

Outside, Hashd had mobilised a small, heavily armed

militia—which remained on duty protecting the entrance, the operating theatres and the corridors of the hospital while we were operating.

We found out later that, during the evening, a Sunni leader's bodyguard, who'd been shot, was brought into the Red Crescent Emergency Unit, surrounded by his own small army. The two military units—the Shi'ite Hashd and the Sunnis—are massive rivals. And, by all accounts, there was a grave danger of tensions between the two groups erupting into open warfare at the hospital. In the end, they managed to keep a lid on it. But it was a close-run thing.

We completed the theatre list at around 2 a.m.—two hours after the midnight curfew for getting back into the Green Zone. Fortunately, the Prime Minister's Department managed to organise for our permits to be extended.

Even while I was operating, the political wheels were turning. Officials at the Ministry of Health weren't happy that we'd managed to defy their ban on Friday surgery. On Saturday morning, the Red Crescent Private Hospital was bombarded with accreditation inspectors, who were led by the brother of Ibn Sina Hospital's director. They wanted to see every single document and made life extremely uncomfortable for the administration.

I was targeted as well. Until then, I hadn't been required to fill out much paperwork about the operations. I just provided a brief summary to demonstrate what we'd done, along with any specific health issues facing each patient.

After operating on the Friday, I was instructed to fill out detailed accounts of each and every procedure I'd carried out that day. It was a complete waste of time—and it meant that I could treat fewer patients. But the authorities were perfectly happy to sacrifice the patients as they played their petty political games.

The politicians and bureaucrats weren't finished there, though. We went back to Iraq for a fifth visit in August 2018 and at almost the exact same time we landed, the Ministry of Health ordered the Red Crescent Hospital to close for the duration of our stay. Closing a hospital is a major exercise and was another act of sheer bastardry, clearly indicating that the Ministry of Health was more focused on playing politics than looking after patients.

The message was clear, and it contained a certain amount of menace. Officialdom wanted to flex its political muscles and demonstrate that it holds the real power in the country's health system—and that it shouldn't be messed with.

—-—

The former prime minister, Nouri al-Maliki, remains a significant powerbroker in Iraq, despite dwindling public and international support. Towards the end of our fourth visit to Baghdad—as I was growing increasingly frustrated by the Ministry of Health's refusal to release all the money to pay for the new robotic legs of the osseointegration patients from the military—I was to discover just how pervasive that power could be.

Al-Maliki arrived as a patient at Ibn Sina Hospital. He headed straight into a meeting in the hospital director's office, located opposite the clinic I was running on the ground floor. If that had happened on previous visits, I'm sure I would have been invited to the meeting. This time, I was pointedly locked out.

I decided to confront al-Maliki about the money for the robotic legs. As I approached the director's office, the former prime minister's bodyguards immediately intervened and ushered me away. Determined not to be thwarted, I waited until one of the senior hospital doctors emerged from the meeting. In a loud voice so that I could be heard inside the office, I insisted that the money for the new legs should be released.

Not long after that, al-Maliki left the meeting and entered the ground-floor corridor. I approached from the clinic on the opposite side of the corridor. Simultaneously, a barrage of around 30 patients closed in on al-Maliki and confronted him. One of the patients was Nadhum Abbas Abid Ali, who was in a wheelchair after osseointegration on one leg and ankle fusion on the other. One of his legs was sticking straight out, blocking al-Maliki's exit. On the other side, the hospital director was inadvertently preventing his retreat. So, the former prime minister had no choice but to address the throng of discontented people.

Everyone was jostling, pushing and shoving. It was like being in a mosh pit. As I made my way to the front of the

The guard room at the entrance to Ibn Sina Hospital. This hospital was the site of my work treating amputees and others who'd suffered trauma injuries while repelling ISIS. Before my arrival, word of my clinic had spread, and the reception area and hospital corridors were heaving with people hoping to be seen.

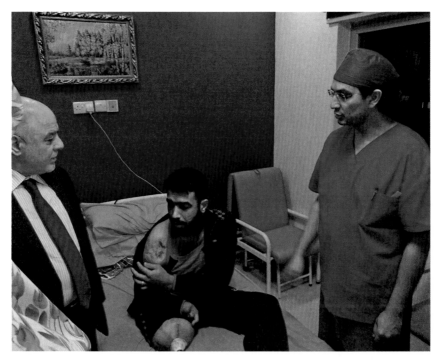

Iraqi prime minister at the time Haider al-Abadi visits patients at Ibn Sina Hospital, where I explain the reverse shoulder operation I performed on Ahmed Abd Alrahman Yosif.

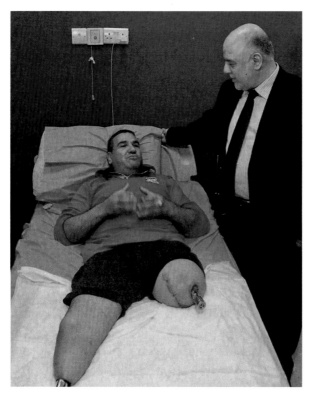

Fityan Hussein Ali discusses his recovery with then Prime Minister Haider al-Abadi.

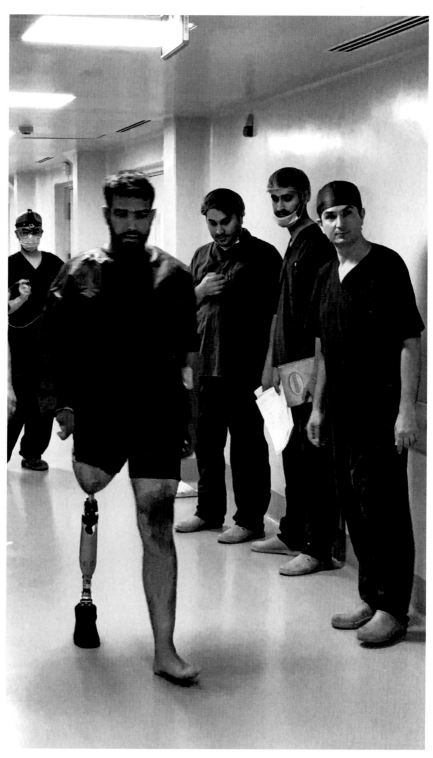

Ahmed Abd Alrahman Yosif takes his new leg for a trial walk along the corridors of Ibn Sina Hospital, with me and other surgeons looking on.

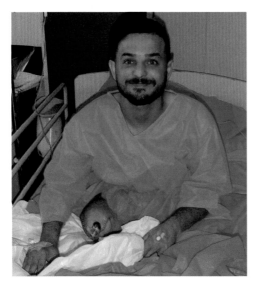

Left: Haithem Jabbar Raheel—
the Dancing Man—the day after
undergoing osseointegration on his
amputated right leg.

Below: Haithem is being fitted with
his new robotic leg. He became the
first patient in Iraq to walk on a
robotic leg.

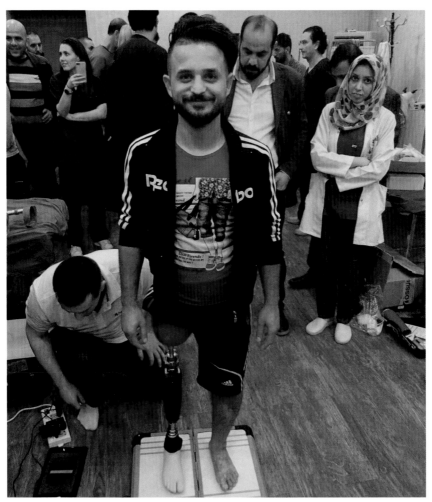

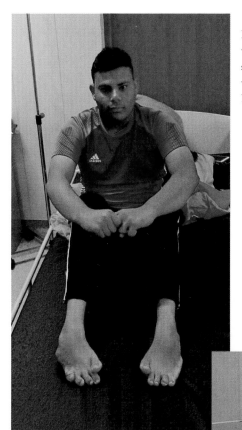

Left: Seventeen-year-old Yasser Nabeel was born with two club feet, which severely restricted his mobiity. For him, to walk 50 metres was a major undertaking. He is shown here before his surgery.

Right: Yasser pictured after the surgery that attached an Ilizarov frame to his right leg. Another frame was later attached to his left leg. The frames are gradually adjusted to change the angle of his feet. His prognosis for greater mobility is good.

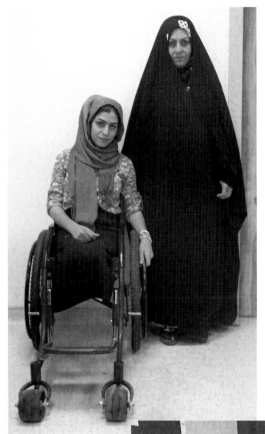

Left: Amani Nasser Jaber before undergoing osseointegration, with her mother, Allia Hamed Ali. Amani lost both her legs at the age of ten, when an exploding mortar shell sent a kerosene heater crashing down on her. After she recovered, she became a champion para-athlete.

Right: Amani presenting me with one of the gold medals she won as a para-athlete to thank me for giving her the most precious gift—the ability to walk again.

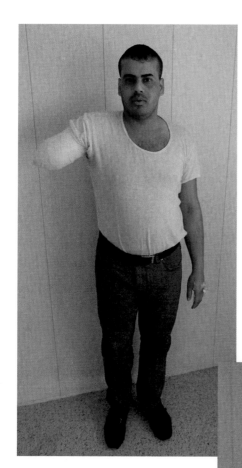

Left: At the age of twenty-three, Abbas Jasim Humood was wounded when an ISIS rocket struck his arm during an advance through Anbar Province. After osseointegration surgery, he is preparing to be fitted with a new arm.

Right: Mohammed Khareem, a member of the Iraqi police force, was fighting ISIS terrorists in a Mosul street when an IED went off, taking his right leg with it. Osseointegration would grant him one of his greatest wishes: to carry his children.

Final adjustments are made as Ali Basim Jabbar Shareef receives his new leg. He lost his leg after being surrounded by ISIS for two days in a battle that killed more than 70 of his fellow paramilitary fighters. Life before his surgery held unemployment, financial hardship and constant struggle.

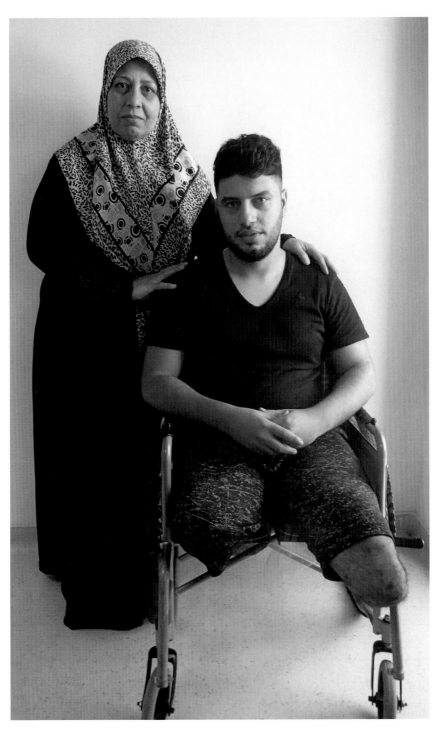

Ghadban Subhi Mahmood before undergoing osseointegration, with his mother Amira Najeeb Saleeh. Her commitment to her son was unshakable and admirable. Before his surgery, she would haunt the hospital corridors with a mournful expression from morning to night.

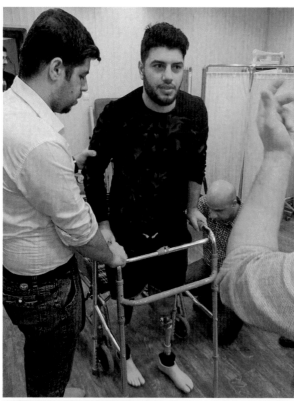

Left: Ghadban Subhi Mahmood starts walking on his new legs.

Below: Ghadban in August 2018, standing on his own two feet. The dramatic transformation in both mother and son is unmistakable.

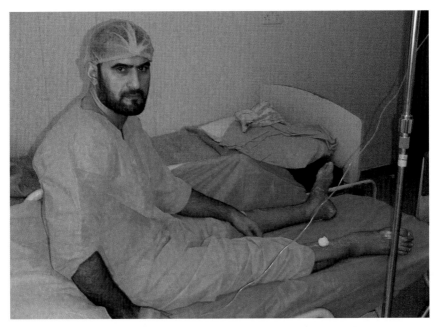

Mohammed Salah Salman before surgery to amputate his damaged right foot to prepare for osseointegration. He later took his amputated foot for burial in Najaf. When he eventually dies, the rest of his body will be buried in the same grave, in the belief that the whole of a person's body must be interred in the same place.

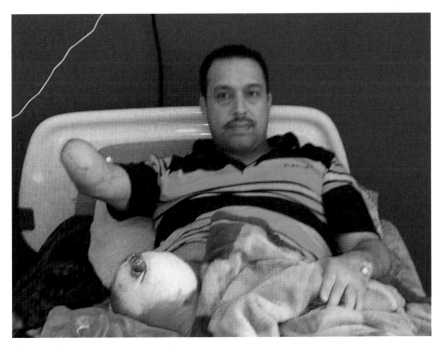

Former policeman Aetham Abdul Hussein Mohammed after osseointegration surgery on his right leg. He wanted the surgery in part because, as he explained, 'I don't want to be a burden on my community'.

Baghdad was one of the most dangerous places on earth in 2009. Fityan Hussein Ali was a major in the Iraqi police force during those dark days. 'It was terrifying to be in Baghdad,' he remembers. 'Everyone was frightened. The police couldn't keep control. Even the American soldiers couldn't stop the killing.' Here he is after osseointegration surgery.

In Iraq, a lot of things are improvised. Here, a patient travels home in improvised transport after having surgery the previous day.

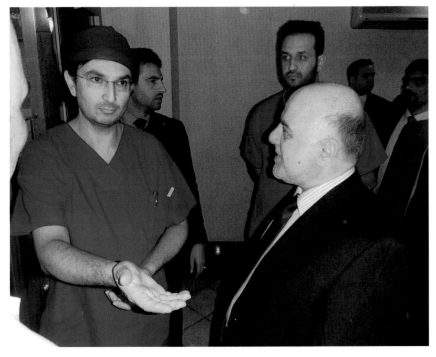

With then Iraqi Prime Minister Haider al-Abadi, who visited Ibn Sina Hospital to meet our patients and find out more about our humanitarian work.

Al-Salam Palace, the presidential palace in Baghdad, where we were received by the then president Fuad Masum.

My team, plus two officials from Ibn Sina Hospital in Baghdad, on the steps of Al-Salam Palace after meeting then Iraqi President Fuad Masum. Left to right: Dr Kevin Tetsworth (surgeon), Dr Solon Rosenblatt (surgeon), Claudia Roberts (physiotherapist), Michelle Nairne (personal assistant), me, Patrick Weaver, a member of the president's staff, Dr Ash Sehgal (anaesthetist), Dr Wejdi Ali (urologist from Ibn Sina Hospital), Dr Yasser al-Timmimi (Director, Ibn Sina Hospital).

Hashd Deputy Leader Abu Mahdi al-Muhandis and Iraqi Minister of Health Dr Adila Hammoud present me with mementoes recognising my humanitarian work in Iraq.

Celebrating a lifelong friendship: my old school friend Mohannad Yusef and his wife's family treated us to some fabulous Iraqi feasts in their home. Left to right: Mohannad, his wife Israa, Israa's mother, Mohannad and Israa's son Ali, me, Mohannad and Israa's daughter Lara, and Israa's father.

With UK-based reconstructive surgeons Norbert Kang (in scrubs, centre) and Alex Woollard (far right) and three members of the Iraqi surgical team.

The Australian Embassy in Baghdad has been wonderfully supportive of our humanitarian project. Left to right: Patrick Weaver, Claudia Roberts, me, the then Australian Ambassador to Iraq Christopher Langman, American surgical Fellow Matt Weldon, Simmy Masuku and Michelle Nairne.

group, one of the resident surgeons extracted Claudia from the mob and escorted her to the safety of the operating theatres.

When I was face to face with al-Maliki, I stretched out my hand and introduced myself. Reluctantly, he shook my hand. Then I said, 'We have a problem.'

'What is the problem?' he inquired.

'I have 48 patients who I've operated on, but they have no legs. The government promised they would be given new legs,' I explained in full earshot of the gathered patients. 'We need to fit them with legs.' I was trying to provoke him into responding.

He took the bait. 'This is not my problem.'

Spontaneously, I fired back in a loud voice, 'You're telling me this is not your problem? These people lost their limbs fighting for you when you were prime minister and for your country against ISIS. This *is* your problem. It's also my problem, and we have to fix it.' As impartial as I tried to be, I couldn't hide the fact that I despised this guy for what he'd done to Iraq.

The look on al-Maliki's face was one of amazement. I don't think anyone has ever spoken to him in that way. As he took a step back, I heard one of the patients shout something like, 'God curse you. You stole our money.' Then the whole mosh pit moved forward and chaos erupted. People were screaming. Some were swearing at him. Others bellowed, 'Burn in hell!'

Realising the potential danger of the situation, al-Maliki's bodyguards moved in and shielded him from the angry crowd. They virtually dragged him out of the corridor.

The minister of health and the hospital administration are strong supporters of al-Maliki, so this was their worst nightmare. I remember glancing at the hospital director. He was horrified and looked like a small, scared mouse.

The rest of the surgical team could hear the shouting two storeys above. 'Be prepared,' I warned them when I returned to the theatre area. 'They might send a death squad to come and kill us!'

The following day, dozens of people came up to me, asking, 'What have you done to al-Maliki? You insulted and humiliated him in front of everybody.' Even the Prime Minister's Department staff wanted to know what had happened. Clearly, word had spread quickly.

The majority of responses were favourable. But when the deputy leader of Hashd asked me about it, he said, 'You know he's a good friend of mine.'

I responded, 'I don't care. I stand for what's right, even though I know he might send his death squad to kill me.'

When I returned to Sydney, I was contacted by members of the Iraqi community who'd also been told of the clash. Among the messages was one from senior supporters of the powerful Shi'ite cleric Muqtada al-Sadr—who had formed and led the rebel Mahdi Army and was gaining significant political power—assuring me that they would guarantee my safety if there was any future threat from their old enemy, al-Maliki.

14

THE CHANGING FACE

First impressions count—and my first impression on returning to Baghdad after 18 years was that the city where I'd grown up had changed dramatically. Baghdad was once renowned for its wealth, culture, security and sophistication, while, during my childhood, Iraq had been one of the most successful economies and societies in the Middle East. Those strengths had vanished by the turn of the 21st century. It was like returning to the Dark Ages.

The economic and social decline was largely brought on by the war with Iran, which lasted from the autumn of 1980 until the summer of 1988. It is estimated that between 500,000 and one million people—half of them soldiers, the rest civilians—were killed. Thousands more were wounded.

Although Iraq nominally won the war, the conflict effectively ended in a stalemate. No land was gained or lost on either side. But while there were no changes to the borders, there were other dire consequences.

Iraq was financially ruined by the war and the subsequent sanctions backed by the United Nations. Among the symptoms of the decline, food and petrol were rationed and unemployment ballooned. Academics and highly qualified professionals were faced with poverty—their jobs disappeared, and many couldn't find meaningful work.

Even those who were employed found it tough making ends meet. To maintain their incomes, they would work at their day jobs in the morning, then run a shop in the afternoon and evening. Others would go home for a siesta in the afternoon before heading out to a second job.

The old society that celebrated intellectuals, education, discussion and debate was replaced by a new breed of decision-makers and influencers—many of them little more than thugs who'd become wealthy on the spoils of war. They were often hangers-on and henchmen who based their power and riches on corruption and nepotism.

After that, the two Gulf Wars left Iraq in chaos. The First Gulf War started after Iraq invaded Kuwait in the summer of 1990 and ended in early 1991, while the Second Gulf War began with the invasion of Iraq by the US-led Coalition of the

Willing in early 2003 and finished only with the withdrawal of troops in late 2011. The George W. Bush administration may have won the second of those military conflicts, but it had absolutely no idea how to win the peace.

The country was plunged into civil war, and the emergence of dozens of insurgent groups opened the way for the fragmentation of Iraqi society and the bitter internecine battles between various heavily armed groups. No one felt safe in Baghdad—and with good reason. Despite more than 210,000 Coalition soldiers pouring into Iraq, armed militia groups still ran the city. Car bombs, suicide bombs, gun battles, kidnappings and executions all became part of daily life in the Iraqi capital.

Even after the US withdrawal and the establishment of a civilian government, there was no respite for the people of Iraq. ISIS invaded and occupied around one-third of the country, including a number of major cities in the north and west. The jihadists launched raids just a few kilometres from the capital and came terrifyingly close to capturing Baghdad. Happily, following the defeat of ISIS in late 2017, security has improved. Baghdad is now safer than at any time since the overthrow of Saddam Hussein.

In August 2018, one official observer estimated that there had been around 50 killings in the Iraqi capital over the previous month. Most of them were due to gang attacks and street violence rather than organised terrorism. If you think the number is frighteningly high, compare it to the statistics from some of the biggest cities in the United States. From the start of the year through to mid-August 2018, 305 people were shot and killed in Chicago—an average of almost 40 each month. Another 1585 people were shot and wounded. In Los Angeles, 607 people were murdered in the year to mid-August 2018. That's more than 50 each month.

Around four million people live in Los Angeles, while almost three million reside in Chicago. The population of Baghdad is eight million. So, despite its reputation, Baghdad is relatively safer than both of those American cities.

Like Los Angeles and Chicago, Baghdad has areas that are acknowledged as being no-go zones for the average person. One Iraqi police officer explained that around 80 per cent of Baghdad was considered safe by mid-2018. Law enforcement authorities have identified the other 20 per cent—places such as Sadr City—and isolated the incidents to those neighbourhoods.

Aside from violence, the other major crime in Iraq is corruption—which is systemic from top to bottom. Inevitably, that will hamper any broadening of the economic base.

Politically, there's a huge difference between today's Iraq and the country I left. These days, Iraqi politics is a tangled mess, with Iran exerting a heavy but covert hand on Iraq's Government.

Iran had been supporting opposition groups in Iraq since the war of the 1980s. With the overthrow of Saddam, Iraq's Shi'ite neighbour identified an opportunity to rapidly increase its power in the country. In the internal political vacuum that followed the invasion in 2003, Iran boosted its role, encouraging

Shi'ite factions to improve their structures and prepare to take part in elections.

Iran now controls much of the Iraqi Government. Al-Maliki, the prime minister from 2006 to 2014, created much stronger links to Iraq's neighbour. He also purged Sunnis and former Ba'ath Party members from the government, replacing them with Shi'ites. His successor, al-Abadi, also owes his position to Iranian patronage, but he took a more moderate line. He brought Sunnis back into the administration and increased contact with Saudi Arabia.

Outside the government, Iran became involved with the Kurdish population in the north of Iraq and has maintained links with their two main political parties—the Kurdistan Democratic Party and the Patriotic Union of Kurdistan.

At the same time, Iran positioned itself as the military protector of the Shi'ite population in Iraq, backing various armed militia groups to fight the US-led forces and counter the growing attacks on Shias by terrorist units such as Al-Qaeda. These activities escalated after the ISIS invasion in the summer of 2014, and Iranian-backed militia groups became a cornerstone of the paramilitary force Hashd.

The growing influence of Iran and its Islamic philosophies on Iraq is seen in the rise of religion and tribalism in the country, especially following the overthrow of Saddam. The Iranian Revolution of 1979 installed Ayatollah Ruhollah Khomeini as the Supreme Leader, and since then clerics have held the government reins in Iran. The Supreme Leader remains a religious figure and sits on top of the chain of power, above the president and the elected representatives.

Evidence of the rise of Islam in Iraq is everywhere. In Saddam's Baghdad, most men were clean-shaven. In contemporary Baghdad, most men have beards. And it's not just a fashion statement, as it is in Western nations.

In Saddam's Iraq, very few women wore head coverings. These days, very few aren't covered. And there are regions where women are required to be covered even if they're not Muslim. In those areas, like Najaf and Karbala, there's no tolerance for anything other than strict observance of Islamic practices.

When I was growing up, the general greeting between Iraqis was 'Hi', 'Hello' or 'Good morning'. Now, it's 'As-salamu alaykum'—which literally translates to 'Peace be upon you'. The Prophet Mohammed created this greeting as a sign that he was coming in peace. Ironically, Islam's history is bloodier than the history of just about any other religion. Indonesia and Malaysia are among a handful of modern countries that adopted Islam without coming under the threat of the sword.

Another common expression in Iraq is 'insha Allah'—which literally translates to 'God willing'. It annoys the hell out of me. Often you'll ask an Iraqi to do something, and they'll say 'insha Allah'. In effect, it means they're not remotely interested in fulfilling your request. It's the equivalent of 'Yeah, maybe' or 'Whatever'—but leaves the outcome to the benevolence of God rather than individual responsibility. It's a massive cop-out. And I make no apology for pointing out every time I hear the phrase that, in fact, God's will has absolutely nothing to do with it!

At least in part, I attribute the rise of religion to a decline in the educational standards caused by the collapse of the economy. As a general rule, the lower the educational standards, the more people turn to religion.

While religion has been on the rise, if you delve beneath the surface of Iraqi society you'll discover that many people are not as committed to Islam as you might think. When you talk in more detail to many Iraqis, you find their religious beliefs are often only skin-deep. Plenty will tell you, 'We have to appear religious to go along with the crowd.'

Others will demonstrate their piety by praying every day. But when you ask them how long they pray, they'll say, 'Maybe two or three minutes.' That's not a massive commitment to the faith.

Along with the return of religion has come a resurgence in tribal values. The tribal system was very limited when I left Iraq. It had thrived under British rule, but was suppressed after the military coup in 1958. Saddam had courted the tribal leaders to win their support, but they started to flex their muscles again once the dictator was overthrown.

These days, tribal customs and laws are being observed by a growing number of people—often fervently. And this is not just confined to remote areas. Tribal customs and laws are imposed everywhere in Iraq, even in major cities such as Baghdad. It's an alternative to the government and civil structure, and is evident in a number of ways. For example, tribal traditions are used to solve all sorts of conflicts.

If there's a dispute, the people involved can ask for a *majlis*—which literally translates to 'a sitting'—of the tribal leaders, who will meet representatives of the victim and the offender, and negotiate the damages that should be paid. Usually a financial penalty will be imposed on the offender. If they can't or won't pay up, the victim's tribe will attack the offender—maybe even killing them.

The system is used in all areas of life—from motor-vehicle accidents down to something as trivial as a cow walking over to the wrong side of the road and eating another farmer's grass. This latter example could quite easily end up with the cow—or even the farmer—being slaughtered. Minor incidents have sometimes even resulted in the outbreak of tribal wars, especially since the collapse of the economy.

I have firsthand experience of the rise of tribal traditions in Iraq. I've always been close to one of my female cousins, Lenaz. She was a year behind me in medical school and I often drove her to university while we were studying. Recently, she called me from Baghdad in despair. She had been driving on a highway when a pedestrian illegally tried to cross the road immediately in front of her vehicle. Lenaz hit the pedestrian, who subsequently died despite her best efforts to revive him. The man's tribe called a *majlis* and demanded retribution—in this case, the payment of the equivalent of US$60,000. Even though she works as a radiographer, Lenaz's family circumstances are modest and she didn't have access to that sort of money. The alternative was that she would face whatever consequences the tribal leaders chose. Her home may have been attacked, or even worse, she or one of her family could have been murdered. I lent her the money to resolve the crisis.

Another area of Iraqi life that has changed dramatically is the consumption of alcohol. I estimate that during my childhood days up to 80 per cent of Iraqis drank alcohol. One person I spoke to put the number as high as 99 per cent. The favourite drink was arak—the aniseed-flavoured liquor that often reaches 50 per cent alcohol content. In some parts of Iraq and Iran it's made out of dates, raisins or sugar cane and doesn't actually contain aniseed.

At the peak of his powers, Saddam's son Uday made the consumption of alcohol in bars illegal. But, as with prohibition in the United States, the move backfired. People set up illegal stills at home, leading to frequent cases of individuals being hospitalised with various forms of poisoning. Before long, the regulation was overturned.

Now, as a result of the rise of Islam, although Iraqis still drink alcohol, the practice isn't as widespread as it once was—and it's certainly not as open. It's not easy to buy alcohol in Iraq, and more than once I've been asked to purchase grog for locals or bring it into the country duty-free when I'm visiting.

On one trip to Baghdad, we were taken to the Al Rasheed Hotel on the edge of the Green Zone, where alcohol is available—largely for the international visitors who stay there.

After we asked if they had any wine, we were ushered into a private room big enough for a sizeable function. There was a lengthy delay while the staff searched the vaults, but finally we were offered two bottles of French wine. They'd been stored in unsuitable conditions for so long that the wine was undrinkable.

In Iraq, it seems that alcohol consumption has been replaced with smoking cigarettes, as far more Iraqis smoke now than when I was a kid. And not only do more people smoke but they also smoke more.

One of the standard questions we ask patients before we operate is whether they smoke. In Baghdad, the vast majority said they smoked—some of them as many as three packets a day! Plenty of our hospital patients frequently headed outside for a cigarette before or while they were recovering from surgery. Others would simply close the door to their room, open the windows and hope the breeze would blow the tobacco smell away.

Shisha or hookah pipes are also widely smoked—especially in cafes and restaurants, but also in homes. They're usually filled with tobacco that has been flavoured with one or more herbs or fruits. Mint and orange are popular choices.

— —

Baghdad was once a clean, green city with plenty of well-manicured parks. Not anymore. Now, it looks unloved. Like many Middle Eastern capitals, it's dirty and dusty. Visitors are immediately struck by the number of military and police checkpoints on the major roads through the city. And the overnight curfew for people travelling in and out of the Green Zone adds to the feeling that the city is still on edge.

Military vehicles—ranging from M1 tanks to utes armed with machine guns—are a regular sight. Personnel in camouflage uniforms are spread throughout the city and are visible along the major roads across the country. For all that, there's not a constant sense of menace—but there is a need to be aware of local conditions.

On the drive to Najaf and Karbala, I raised the prospect of a brief visit to some of the ancient ruins of Babylon. Security personnel from the Prime Minister's Department quickly scotched the idea. 'It's not safe for visitors,' they bluntly told us.

Further north, near the border with Syria, there are still consistent reports of bomb blasts in places around Mosul. The war against ISIS may have been won in late 2017, but small pockets of terrorists remain.

By now, you may have the impression that Iraq is a basket case. In terms of its politics and economy, the country certainly is struggling. But there are upsides.

At the time I escaped from Baghdad under Saddam's rule, freedom of speech simply didn't exist. Most people couldn't challenge even junior officials or police officers without the fear of reprisal. Questioning anyone from Saddam's regime or the ranks of the Ba'ath Party could easily be interpreted as directly questioning the validity of the president. Troublemakers weren't tolerated, and retribution was severe.

There's much less repression these days, and anti-government demonstrations aren't uncommon. They're reluctantly tolerated, and zones have been set aside for protests. These are managed, but not attacked, by the military and police.

Some aspects of life haven't changed. The people of Iraq are strong and retain their sense of humour and generosity amid all the adversity they've faced. They still know how to laugh and joke about their situation. The ability of Iraqi people to simply plough on regardless was highlighted when I met up with a couple of old school friends during my time in Baghdad.

Haider Inthar Khuther had been with me through medical school. Despite all the turmoil of the intervening years, he has managed to become head of emergency services at Baghdad University Hospital. He came to see me at Ibn Sina Hospital on my second visit to Baghdad. We sat in the boardroom and chatted for about an hour.

He hadn't altered in the slightest—he's still a rogue and remains very flexible with his religious beliefs. When he talks to me, he says God doesn't exist. But when I look on his Facebook page, he's talking about going on a pilgrimage with groups of Shi'ites.

I've been friends with Mohannad Yusef since we met in the first year of primary school. With his wife, Israa, Mohannad came to see me to ask for help with their ten-year-old son Ali's feet. He was constantly walking on his toes with his heels raised.

The treatment was straightforward. In a simple operation, I released his Achilles tendons and put him in plaster for a few weeks. Ali has come to see me a couple of times since, and the difference in his condition is remarkable. He's now walking normally, with no sign that he ever had a problem.

On my subsequent visits to Baghdad, I had the opportunity to spend time with Mohannad, his wife, Israa, and children. They live with Israa's extended family in a two-storey house that sits off a laneway in the Green Zone. Three generations live together—Mohannad, Israa and their children, Lara and Ali; Israa's parents; her brother; and her younger sister and brother-in law, with their infant son. That living arrangement is common in Iraq—extended families residing under the same roof and closely supporting each other.

Israa's father was a general in the Iraqi Army, which is how he came to occupy a house in the Green Zone. His greatest claim to fame, which he's proud to point out, is that he was the only general to remain in his post after Saddam seized power. His status is probably the reason for the presence of the armed soldiers stationed in a small demountable in the laneway opposite the entrance to the house.

The traditional hospitality of Iraqis has been evident during a couple of occasions when we've been invited to an evening feast at Mohannad and Israa's home. Even with fourteen of us at the table, we've been treated to a generous spread—with enough food for two or three times that many people!

Israa and her mother would spend most of the day preparing

the food, which was absolutely beautiful and took me back to some of the very best flavours of my childhood and adolescence. Despite the enormous effort it took to prepare such a glorious spread, Israa's family was always delighted to entertain us.

This is another aspect of life in Iraq that hasn't changed. The food is superb. Just as it used to be, everything is fresh. Tomatoes actually taste like tomatoes because they haven't been kept in cold storage for months before being stacked on supermarket shelves. Cucumbers are equally fresh. If you crack a cucumber, you can smell its fragrance at the other end of the room. And the olives are rich with flavour.

Salads are served with every meal, including breakfast. And there's always bread, which is similar to—but, in my opinion, superior to—Lebanese bread. This might explain the expanding waistlines of many of the local population!

My favourite breakfast remains *gaymer* (thick buffalo cream) served with a sweet pastry, sugar syrup and honey or date sauce.

For lunch and dinner, it's hard to beat lamb—whether roasted or in a kebab. A common Iraqi dish is a quarter or third of a lamb roasted and presented on top of flavoured rice and noodles, with almonds scattered across the top. But my personal favourite is *margat bamya*—an okra stew with lamb, tomato paste, garlic, pomegranate syrup and hot peppers.

Iraqi lambs are different from other breeds. They don't have a tail. Instead, where the tail would be located in other breeds, there's a large piece of fat. Of course, when it comes to meat, fat equals flavour. That gives Iraqi lamb its distinctive taste.

Years ago, Iraqi lamb used to be regarded as a delicacy across the Middle East, and carcasses fetched high prices for export. Unfortunately, in more recent times, live sheep have been exported and neighbouring countries now have their own flocks. It's essentially killed off the lucrative Iraqi export trade.

Beef is another popular meat, and it is often served in kebabs or grilled. *Makluba* is an upside-down dish made from beef, mixed vegetables, tomato, capsicum, zucchini and eggplant. Its precise origin is not clear but it's certainly Middle Eastern. (In Australia the influence of the Lebanese community is very evident in the Middle Eastern food. The majority of Lebanese restaurants serve Middle Eastern food that originates from many parts of the Middle Easter other than Lebanon. For example, falafel is claimed to be Lebanese but in fact is an Egyptian dish.)

Desserts are rich, sweet and creamy, and they regularly feature chocolate. There's also a wide variety of cheeses—many of them unlike anything I've tasted in Western nations. And the fruit is fabulous. The dates are the best in the world, the figs are fantastic, and there's an array of fresh tropical fruit available—from pineapple and bananas to pomegranates, cherries, plums, greengages and all varieties of melon.

Traditional Iraqi beverages include short black Turkish coffee with plenty of sugar, as well as *chai noomi basra*—tea prepared from dried limes simmered in boiling water. It's beautiful, but be aware of the pile of sugar at the bottom of the glass.

Pomegranate juice is another joy that remains. Freshly produced and chilled pomegranate juice is a staple refreshment, especially during the searing summer months. I have to be honest—just thinking about some of these dishes and drinks makes my mouth water!

— —

It's not only internally that Iraq has changed. Its international reputation has also plummeted—most recently fuelled by the policies of the Trump administration. In 2017, Trump announced the withdrawal of Electronic System for Travel Authorization (ESTA) access to the United States for anyone who had recently visited Iraq, among other countries.

The ESTA system is convenient because it's a short cut that avoids the potentially protracted full visa application process. Plenty of commentators have identified its withdrawal as lowest-common-denominator politics designed to win the hearts and minds of the disillusioned and disaffected white working class in the United States.

I ran headlong into Trump's politically convenient executive order in January 2018. Along with Claudia, I was due to fly from London's Heathrow Airport to Hawaii to deliver presentations to the 2018 Pac Rim Prosthetic/Orthotic Conference.

As I checked in my bags, the woman behind the counter announced that there was a problem. 'There's a note on the computer saying US Homeland Security wants to talk to you before you can board the aircraft,' she informed me. We waited a few minutes for a woman from Homeland Security to emerge and approach us.

On the forms we all had to fill out, one of the questions asked whether we had visited any of a list of countries—Iraq included. I had ticked Iraq. 'When were you in Iraq?' the Homeland Security officer asked.

'I've been there three times in the last year.'

'I have bad news for you,' she informed me. 'I can't let you on this plane. You'll have to apply for a full visa, and you'll need to explain why you've been to Iraq.' This didn't seem to make much sense as I'd been to the United States three times since I first returned to Iraq. The Homeland Security officer was unmoved when I informed her.

Interestingly, Claudia had been on exactly the same trips to Iraq and had filled out the same forms as me. But there was no suggestion that she would also be excluded from the flight. Indeed, she'd already been given her boarding pass by the time I was pulled aside. I pointed out the discrepancy to the Homeland Security official.

'We'd have stopped her before she got on the plane,' she replied unconvincingly. 'They would have stopped her at the boarding desk.' The upshot was that we weren't allowed on the aircraft, and we missed the conference.

The whole incident raised an important question. What was the difference between Claudia and me? There could be only one reason why I was blocked at the check-in desk and Claudia wasn't. Claudia is a tall, blonde Caucasian. I'm clearly of Arab appearance. It was plain and simple racial profiling.

Subsequently, I have successfully applied for a visa to visit the United States and have been there for professional activities. But there's no warm welcome from security officials for anyone of an Arab appearance.

On my next trip to the United States, I flew into Dallas and was again hauled aside by Homeland Security for a fifteen-minute grilling before I was allowed into the country. As I was being quizzed, the words of the deputy leader of Hashd in Iraq rang in my ears.

Abu Mahdi al-Muhandis was one of my main contacts in Iraq while I was arranging to operate on injured paramilitary soldiers. When I met him to discuss my plans, he chuckled and told me, 'You'll never be allowed into America now you've met me!' He was pretty close to the truth.

In 2018, I went to the United States to introduce my osseo-integration techniques to the nation's leading orthopaedic surgeons. Initially, the project is on a trial basis, because the US Food and Drug Administration hasn't fully approved the procedure. Still, I can't help but raise an eyebrow at the irony of the situation—an Iraqi-born surgeon introducing the latest osseointegration techniques, which in the near future are likely to be used on US soldiers who lost one or both of their legs fighting against Iraqis. What goes around comes around.

15

THE SHAPE OF THINGS TO COME

It's almost impossible to confidently predict the long-term future of Iraq. The challenges are immense. The economy's a mess, relying almost entirely on revenue from the nation's ailing oil industry. Iraq is the world's twelfth largest producer of oil, with the world's fifth largest petroleum reserves. The industry is centred on Basra, the Baghdad region, Ramadi and Baaj in the north-west, close to the Syrian border. Baaj—and its oil wealth—was under ISIS control until mid-2017 and was a major source of income for the terrorist group.

Despite the wealth generated by the oil industry, years of conflict and sanctions have meant that the industry's infrastructure is run-down. Experts estimate that as much as US$100 billion is needed to bring the sector up to contemporary standards.

The war with ISIS was also enormously expensive, and it continues to be a drain on Iraq's finances. The government is still dealing with small pockets of ISIS sympathisers, who remain active in the remote and sparsely populated provinces of Diyala, Kirkuk and Saladin to the north and east of the capital.

On top of that, tens of thousands of people have been displaced from the war zones and are living in camps sponsored by the United Nations in various parts of Iraq. Most are faced with awful conditions in tents or makeshift shelters, with little or no sanitation. They must deal with summer temperatures that reach the high forties, and winter nights that can plunge to single figures.

These refugees escaped the carnage of the conflict in search of safety and security. Now, many can't go back home. For some, it's because their neighbourhoods—especially in eastern Mosul—were destroyed by the sheer power of the Iraqi Army, paramilitary and Coalition air strikes that finally overwhelmed the terrorists. Others have family links with ISIS. Retribution awaits if they attempt to return now that the rebels have been defeated. Most of the refugees are Sunnis.

The other major issue facing the country is corruption. It's everywhere—as shown by my struggles to prise open the coffers of the Ministry of Health to pay for the robotic legs of osseointegration patients.

Corruption appears in all layers of Iraqi society—from the government and the public service right through to the lower echelons. It's a source of serious unrest and a cause of the continuing political instability. While some people are ripping off hundreds of millions of dollars and are becoming unspeakably wealthy, a significant proportion of the Iraqi population is struggling to make ends meet. Mass demonstrations have been staged in Baghdad and other major cities to protest against the status quo.

Politically, there are so many diverse powerbrokers meddling with Iraq's future. The United States has a major influence over the choice of the country's leader. Iran also has a powerful role—especially through the paramilitary forces, which it trains and equips. Iran wants to keep Iraq stable, but relatively weak.

Religious leaders have an important say in decision-making in Iraq. While the Grand Ayatollah generally believes in a separation of religion and politics, he has made a number of crucial interventions. By demanding early democratic elections, he effectively ended the US administration of Iraq and brought forward the withdrawal of American troops. He also issued the fatwa against ISIS, which led to the creation of Hashd. And, as ISIS threatened to overrun Iraq, he openly moved to prevent the country from breaking up completely by opposing a separate Kurdish state in the north.

Then there are the various militia groups—Shi'ites, Sunnis, Christians and glorified street gangs. Tensions between them are constantly simmering. The more popular of those groups also want to have their say about who runs the country.

With so many factions influencing the government of Iraq, consensus is almost impossible. Add to this the fact that the reputation of most politicians who lead or aspire to lead the country is at rock bottom. Their wells of credibility with the long-suffering people of Iraq have almost run dry.

Iraq now has its fourth prime minister since the Americans handed over the running of the country to an elected government. The first was Ibrahim al-Jaafari, from the Shi'ite Islamic Dawa Party, who was sworn in as the head of the transitional government in 2005. His leadership was marred by sectarian violence between Shi'ites and Sunnis, which escalated towards a civil war. The United States and key sections of the Iraqi parliament decided there was an urgent need for change.

There weren't many alternatives, but Nouri al-Maliki eventually emerged as al-Jaafari's successor in May 2006. He was another senior member of the Islamic Dawa Party and was viewed as hardworking.

Al-Maliki had risen to prominence as a vocal opponent of Saddam Hussein and was forced into exile for nearly a quarter of a century after being sentenced to death by the dictator in the 1970s. He spent time in Iran and Syria, and forged close links with the regimes of both countries.

During the eight years of his government, al-Maliki became an increasingly divisive figure. He worked with the Chief Justice to bar a number of leading opponents from the 2010 national elections. But he still lost the ballot to a moderate coalition that maintained a pro-Western stance.

Even in the face of defeat, al-Maliki wouldn't relinquish power. He accused the United States, the United Kingdom, the United Nations and Saudi Arabia of fixing the vote. Iran became involved in the tense stand-off, backing al-Maliki. The Chief Justice then gave him the first opportunity to form another government, so he set about creating a new leadership group—which included most of Iran's favourites. Sunnis were nominated for positions much further down the food chain and were soon intimidated out of those roles when al-Maliki sent tanks to their homes and ordered their arrest.

Early in his second term as prime minister, and particularly after the US troop withdrawal of 2011, al-Maliki tightened his grip on the country and formed strong alliances with Washington and Tehran. All the while, the disintegration of Iraq continued.

One of the first major cities to fall to Sunni rebels was Fallujah, just 75 kilometres from Baghdad. At the end of 2013, the Iraqi Government had closed a Sunni protest camp outside the city, sparking attacks by armed militants on army check-points and patrols. Al-Qaeda took control of the city centre before morphing into ISIS.

Six months later, 1500 ISIS soldiers crossed the Syrian border and attacked Mosul. Although the Iraqi Army and police force outnumbered them by as much as fifteen to one, ISIS caught the military and police by surprise and managed to break through the city's western defensive lines. They launched a guerrilla campaign through the streets. Sunni militants and underground ISIS cells in the city joined the regular fighters and captured substantial parts of Mosul.

Within three days, two Iraqi generals had ordered their troops to make a strategic withdrawal across the Tigris River. The sight of the convoy heading away from the front line started rumours that the army had collapsed and soldiers were deserting—which became a self-fulfilling prophecy.

Before long, the terrorists controlled the second-largest city in Iraq, plus the light and heavy weapons the Iraqi Army had abandoned. They also had access to nearly half a billion dollars in cash, which was stored in Mosul's central bank.

There was a massive collapse of morale in the Iraqi Army. This opened the way for ISIS to advance across Iraq, capturing large areas of the country, including major settlements in the country's north and west. The rebels even launched raids on Abu Ghraib—which was infamous as the site of the gaol where US soldiers tortured and humiliated Iraqi prisoners—on the western outskirts of the capital. Repressed Sunni provinces welcomed ISIS because they felt it would free them from the sectarian actions of the al-Maliki regime.

The events of the summer of 2014 shook al-Maliki's power base. While Iraq was in turmoil, hundreds of millions of dollars disappeared from the nation's oil revenue. Al-Maliki's government was accused of extreme corruption, and his leadership was terminally weakened. The United States, his own party, large swathes of the Iraqi population and Iraq's Middle Eastern neighbours finally lost confidence. After eight years in power, al-Maliki reluctantly announced he would stand down.

His replacement was Haider al-Abadi, another opponent of Saddam. He had spent twenty years in exile and completed his university education in the United Kingdom. Al-Abadi had returned to Iraq in 2003.

He sat in complete contrast to his predecessor. He's a technocrat who, as a member of the Governing Council, had a tetchy relationship with the Coalition Provisional Authority and the US administrator, Paul Bremer. Al-Abadi was an adviser to Prime Minister al-Jaafari and was elected to parliament in December 2005. He was even considered for the top job in 2006.

When he did finally take over as prime minister, al-Abadi was handed a poisoned chalice. Iraq was a divided nation—the paramilitary controlled the south, ISIS occupied large sections of the Sunni provinces, and the Kurds ran an almost separate state in Erbil, Duhok and Sulaymaniyah. With control of Kirkuk, the Kurds had the oil resources to seriously bolster their claim for independence.

In Baghdad, al-Abadi faced strong dissent—the slums of Sadr City were dominated by supporters of the Shi'ite cleric Muqtada al-Sadr, who had formed and headed the Mahdi Army militia group that had battled the United States-led occupation forces. Al-Sadr's supporters from the Saraya al-Salam faction, along with their leader, Qais al-Khazali, were accused of carrying out a stream of kidnappings and political assassinations.

Regardless, al-Abadi ran his own race. He refused to be a rubber stamp and reintegrated Sunnis into the Iraqi Government. He also reached an agreement to share oil revenue with the Kurds. Internationally, al-Abadi set about increasing links with Saudi Arabia, Egypt, Turkey and even Russia during the battle to oust ISIS, rather than relying solely on Iran.

His measures against corruption included efforts to cut the generous benefits to senior government figures and the removal of the bodyguards who surround those officials. This didn't win him many friends in the corridors of power. And, in the meantime, his predecessor, al-Maliki, was exercising considerable influence behind the scenes.

The fragmentation of government in Iraq was graphically illustrated by the saga surrounding the elections in May 2018. Both al-Abadi and al-Maliki stood at the elections, but lost considerable popular support. Regardless, they were both prominent in the horsetrading for power that followed.

The elections reflected the nation's disillusionment with the political system. There was a record low turnout—officially just 44.5 per cent of registered voters bothered to cast a ballot. This was a massive drop of 17.5 per cent from the previous election. Uncorroborated rumours on the streets—and in some diplomatic circles—claim the actual turnout was about half the official figure.

The initial results came under challenge almost immediately—especially from the pro-Iranian groups that had lost the most ground. The election was the first time an electronic vote-counting system had been used, and, alongside claims of corruption by political groups, there were allegations it wasn't an accurate reflection of the actual voting. The Korean company that had provided the technology refuted the claims. Despite this, the Iraqi parliament ordered a manual re-count. It also suspended the board of the Independent Election Commission and replaced it with a panel of judges.

To further complicate matters, there was a fire at a storage depot holding half of Baghdad's ballot papers. Fortunately, reports indicated that no votes were damaged. Four people were arrested in connection with the blaze—three policemen and a worker from the Independent Election Commission.

Another indication of the political crisis facing Iraq was the result of the election. The re-count showed no major changes to the original numbers. This meant that populist cleric Muqtada al-Sadr's Alliance Towards Reforms party ended up with the largest number of seats—54—which was twenty more than at the previous parliamentary elections. The Fatah Alliance party, which is closely aligned with Iran and was led by Hadi al-Amiri, finished second with 47 seats.

Al-Abadi's Victory Alliance—a newly established group— lost ground, winning 42 seats and finishing third. The State of Law Coalition led by al-Maliki was the biggest loser, winning just 25 seats—down 67 from the previous election.

All in all, it meant that no group had secured enough support to form a majority in the 329-seat Council of Representatives. A period of intense bargaining followed, with the major parties all trying to knit together a coalition that could create the necessary numbers on the floor of the parliament. Being Iraq, this didn't happen quickly.

Media reports indicated that various factions had agreed to work together to establish an administration with an effective majority. But months after the election, no new government was in place. So why hadn't it happened within a few weeks at most? One observer summed it up with the words: 'In Iraq, everything is under the surface. Up front, everyone is smiling. Everything looks happy. But beneath the surface, out of sight to the public, is where things are really going on.'

The rise of Muqtada al-Sadr was significant. He's a nationalist and a populist who opposes United States and Iranian influence in Iraq and is the champion of the lowest Shi'ite socio-economic groups—including the people living in the slums of Baghdad, Sadr City. The Iraqi Communist Party is one faction involved with his Alliance Towards Reforms group.

In recent times, al-Sadr has railed against corruption and has organised mass anti-corruption and anti-government demonstrations. Among his election platforms was a call for the new government to establish a firm policy agenda, and then appoint key ministers who can deliver on those policies. To complete the leadership team, he urged the appointment of a prime minister who can provide the direction and drive to deliver change. But al-Sadr himself won't be directly involved in running the country as he made a conscious stand—even though he is the party leader—not to nominate for election to the parliament. From the start of the election campaign, he made it clear that he has no interest in becoming prime minister and that he wants to remain in the background.

Al-Sadr has an interesting history. At various times he has been labelled by the foreign media as a 'radical' and a 'firebrand'. He comes from a high-profile Shi'ite religious family. He's the fourth son of the Grand Ayatollah Mohammad Sadeq al-Sadr, who was assassinated along with two of his older sons in Najaf in February 1999 after leading Friday prayers. The Grand Ayatollah had been a prominent critic of Saddam's government, and the word on the street was that he was on the dictator's hit list.

The cleric responded defiantly to the rumours that he was about to be killed, wearing his funeral shroud for his final appearance at the mosque to indicate that he wasn't afraid of dying. When he and his sons were driving away after prayers, they were attacked by gunmen. His sons were killed in the spray of bullets, and the Grand Ayatollah died in hospital. Saddam was considered at least complicit in the murders—if not directly responsible.

Following the US-led invasion and the overthrow of Saddam, Muqtada al-Sadr organised a Shi'ite political group to oppose the occupation and raised the Mahdi Army militia to actively fight against the foreign troops. His militia soon began launching sporadic attacks on US and other Coalition forces. Although the Mahdi Army was mainly equipped with IEDs and light weapons, over five years it still managed to capture parts of Najaf, Karbala, Kufa and Kut in the south of Iraq, as well as maintaining control of Sadr City in Baghdad.

After the withdrawal of British forces from the centre of Basra in 2007, the Mahdi Army—which, at the time, could muster as many as 60,000 fighters—took significant areas of the city. Over the next seven months, three militia groups grappled to establish complete dominance over Basra. The occupation was seen as a direct challenge to the national government in general and Prime Minister al-Maliki in particular.

In March 2008, the prime minister dispatched 15,000 soldiers from the Iraqi Army, with support from the US and UK air forces, to suppress the uprising. Six days after the battle started, al-Sadr declared a ceasefire, and the prime minister claimed victory. Later that year, al-Sadr ordered an end to the Mahdi Army's military operations.

He reversed the decision in 2014. Amid another security crisis, al-Sadr re-mobilised his army—this time known as the Peace Brigades—as part of the new paramilitary force fighting ISIS. But that wasn't its only aim—al Sadr also wanted to use the Peace Brigades to force the resignation of Prime Minister al-Maliki.

Al-Sadr's show of power, and the potential implications for the regime, added to the growing pressure on the nation's leader to quit. When he did, the Sadrists initially supported al-Abadi's new government. But, in the ever-changing world that is Iraqi politics, al-Sadr later switched positions and organised high-profile protests against the government.

In February 2016, he gave the prime minister 45 days to appoint a new cabinet of skilled professionals rather than career politicians. He also wanted the Peace Brigades to be incorporated into the Iraqi Army. The ultimatum was that if al-Sadr's demands weren't met, he would order his supporters to stage a mass demonstration in the Green Zone.

Hundreds of thousands of al-Sadr's backers set up a make-shift camp outside the heavily protected government area, ready to breach the security cordon if there was no action from al-Abadi. But when the deadline expired, instead of ordering the throng of people into the Green Zone, al-Sadr walked through the checkpoint alone, dramatically declaring that he was prepared to sacrifice his life for the people.

As events unfolded, it became clear that he wasn't in any danger. Rather than confronting al-Sadr, the army commander in charge of the checkpoint kissed the cleric's hand and allowed him to pass through unmolested. Once inside, al-Sadr hunkered down in a tent until, five days later, al-Abadi announced a cabinet reshuffle. Al-Sadr decided that this was enough to satisfy his demands and called off his sit-in.

That wasn't the end of the anti-government demonstrations, though. In April 2016, a state of emergency was declared when protesters—many associated with al-Sadr—climbed over the blast walls surrounding the Green Zone and invaded the Iraqi parliament. In another flamboyant gesture, al-Sadr declared, 'Today the people announced their revolution. History will record the birth of a new Iraq from the ashes of corruption and the corrupt.'

While he is hugely popular among poverty-stricken Shi'ites, critics of al-Sadr point to his blurred and inconsistent vision for the country, his failure to deliver on promises and the failure of his party representatives to make a substantial difference when they've been elevated to ministerial positions. Significantly, it's also doubtful whether either Iran or the United States would support a government following the lead of al-Sadr.

It wasn't until October 2018, five months after the elections, that the independent and reputedly secularist Shi'ite politician Adil Abdul Mahdi was appointed prime minister. He was a compromise candidate, and not the first choice of either of the two major outside influencers, the United States and Iran. Washington wanted to continue with Haidar al-Abadi, while Tehran preferred either the discredited Nouri al-Maliki or Hadi al-Ameri.

Abdul Mahdi is a trained economist who was vice president from 2005 to 2011 and oil minister from 2014 to 2016. He's the first Iraqi prime minister since 2005 not to be aligned to the Shi'ite Islamic Dawa party.

My initial reaction to the appointment is one of cautious hope. The new prime minister has a reputation for being astute, competent and moderate. He comes from a good family, speaks English well and is a former pupil of Baghdad College, where I went to school.

The new Health Minister is Alaa al-Alwan, a technocrat

who I hope will be able to work more closely with my humanitarian project. My first priority will be to persuade him to order the release of the funds to deliver new prostheses for my osseointegration patients. It's absolutely unacceptable that many of them have been waiting for a year or more for their new legs because of the corruption within the Ministry of Health.

As for the future, questions still remain. In August 2018, one diplomat's assessment was, 'You could have all the crystal balls in the world, and you still wouldn't be able to pick it!' That's how politics works in Iraq.

It may come as a surprise to outsiders, but many Iraqis look back on the rule of Saddam Hussein as the good old days. There's a longing for the certainty of the years when he ruled the country. That's not so much a reflection of Saddam as a benevolent ruler. Nor does it indicate that everything was fine and dandy under his leadership. Rather, it's a sign of weariness with the chaos and the fragmentation of Iraqi society since he was ousted.

Sure, freedom of speech and actions were severely limited. And your life was potentially in danger the moment you spoke or acted against the dictator, the government or the Ba'ath Party. But many people believe that, during Saddam's rule, everyone knew where they stood and there was a decisive direction for the nation.

A significant proportion of Iraqi people are looking for a strong government—or even a strong individual—to take the reins and stamp out corruption. They want someone to broaden the economic base and create jobs, to help them lead more productive and rewarding lives. They just want security, certainty and the ability to put food on the family table.

What does that point to? Well, I've heard serious talk—both in Iraq and among the expat community in Australia—of a military coup. The rationale is that with military rulers, at least things would get done and the nation could move in a unified direction. At the moment, people say, Iraqis can march on the streets and shout, but they still can't find a steady and reliable income.

The festering dissatisfaction is clearly evident on social media. I've seen various posts urging the general population to rise up against the government—but only in a peaceful revolution. The posts insisted on no violence, and I had hoped it would stay that way. But, ominously, in the space of two days in early September 2018, six protesters were killed and another sixteen were wounded in clashes with security forces in Basra. Fourteen members of a security detail were also injured as homemade bombs were hurled at government buildings. The grievances of the demonstrators were familiar—government corruption, high unemployment and a lack of basic services, including clean drinking water.

Iraq has seen far too much violence. There's an urgent need to avoid more bloodshed.

The rumblings of a coup have been strong enough that the Grand Ayatollah al-Sistani felt it necessary, eight days before the 2018 election, to emphasise the need for a solution to be found at the ballot box rather than the barrel of a gun. He remains a steadying influence on a nation that has the potential to be extremely volatile.

Staging a military coup is not as simple as some advocates make it sound. One of the many dangers is that it could lead to another civil war within Iraq. In the worst-case scenario, a civil war could divert sufficient resources to encourage a resurgence of ISIS. That would be in the interests of no one but the Sunni terrorists.

Iran would perceive a military coup as a threat to its powerful influence over Iraq and, ultimately, a potential threat to its own border security. I doubt Iran would relinquish its current position of strength without a fight. Under those circumstances, the prospect of Iranian-backed militia taking up arms against the Iraqi armed forces is very possible.

As unpredictable as the Trump administration's policies are on anything and everything under the sun, the United States is also likely to oppose a coup. While having US boots on the ground isn't a realistic option, arms and other support could certainly be shipped in to assist loyalist fighters.

As a mark of the desperation of the Iraqi people, I've been asked a number of times to form a new political party. I think they want someone from outside the country and the political elite to come in and start with a clean sheet, rather like former cricketer Imran Khan in Pakistan. One patient even went as far as suggesting, 'Why don't you take over the country?'

'I can't, I'm an infidel and my heritage is Sunni,' I said.

'That doesn't matter,' my patient responded. 'They just want someone who cares for them to lead the country.'

The other problem, of course, is that I would have to live permanently in Iraq. While I do care passionately about Iraq and its people, I am now a proud Australian. My future is based in my new homeland.

The longer-term alternative is for everyone to work together to establish a firm foothold for democracy. But that takes a while, probably generations. You need to educate people about how successful democracies work.

The very minimum requirement as a first step is to address education across the country, eradicating illiteracy and ensuring that all children remain at school until a certain age—even if it's only until they're fifteen. Too often in the past, education has been seen only as an option if there was not a more pressing alternative. From an early age, many children have been forced to work on the family farm or sent to manual jobs to help provide food, shelter and clothing for the family. It's almost like Dickensian England.

Of course, democracy has to work for the majority of the people. Democracy as a concept is only as successful as the positive impact it has on the population. As we're seeing right now, if the majority of people in Iraq aren't benefitting from democracy, their heads will easily be turned by an alternative.

—-—

In 2018, my work in osseointegration and, I believe, my humanitarian project in Iraq have earned recognition on the international stage. In October, I travelled to New York to receive a Game Changer Award from the Asia Society at a ceremony led by Bill Clinton. The citation for the award read: 'For courage that led to his freedom—and then groundbreaking work to give patients new hope.'

Of course, I want to keep helping and improving the lives of the individual patients we're treating. But I also want to raise the standards of surgery in Iraq, effectively establishing a centre of excellence in orthopaedic and trauma surgery—at Ibn Sina or another suitable hospital—whenever we visit. Even just four visits a year will reinforce the high standards we expect in our operating theatres.

We started from a low base. The facilities were presentable, and the equipment—half of it from Baghdad, the rest donated by hospitals in Sydney—was first rate. But there were plenty of obstacles to overcome.

Because I speak Arabic and know the Iraqi way of thinking, I'm at an advantage. I can communicate with everyone in the operating theatre and bring staff into line if standards are slipping. I'm very direct and will raise my voice if I feel it's necessary to achieve the best result.

My approach is completely task-orientated, and I don't take prisoners if things aren't working to my satisfaction. If the equipment or procedures aren't correct, I'll let the Iraqi theatre staff know in no uncertain terms.

For example, one of the most basic lessons you learn early in surgical training is that, in an operating theatre, you always keep your hands above the waist. It's simply because there's more risk of contamination below the waistline. In the beginning, many of the surgeons at Ibn Sina Hospital didn't seem to be aware of this straightforward precaution, or chose to ignore it. It soon became a practice that everyone followed.

I never give in to suboptimal standards, so the Iraqi staff learned very quickly that I wouldn't put up with slackness. Not surprisingly, during our fourth visit to Baghdad, the theatre was run very close to the way I operate in Sydney. However, working in Iraq has been more complicated—professionally and culturally—for some of the other surgeons.

My colleague and friend Dr Kevin Tetsworth—an orthopaedic surgeon who lives and works in Brisbane—adopts a different approach to mine. Kevin is very polite, quiet and agreeable to all suggestions given to him by the local Iraqi consultants. He encourages them to take charge of his equipment and play a full role in whatever procedure he's carrying out. But it doesn't always make things easy for him.

In one operation, Kevin completed an 18-centimetre resection of a distal femur close to the patient's knee at around 1.30 in the morning. He'd let down the tourniquet and given the assisting registrar instructions to pack the wound with gauze before coming to meet me in the other operating theatre.

Within a minute, he had walked back to his theatre . . . to find that all hell had broken loose. Everyone in the theatre—four anaesthetists, a consulting surgeon and a registrar—was rushing round, screaming at the top of their voices. Quickly, they started suctioning the wound and repositioning the gauze.

'What's happening?' Kevin demanded.

'He's losing blood.'

'From where?'

'Everywhere!' The Iraqi staff had taken out the compression, and the patient's blood pressure had plummeted.

Kevin immediately looked at the monitors to check the patient's heartbeat, blood pressure and temperature. He saw two flat lines and heard the sound of several monitors blasting out alarms. The heart rate indicator showed a large zero, while the blood-pressure monitor was registering 46 over 35. Any medical professional will tell you that this is not good!

The Iraqi team dropped the patient's head below the rest of his body to increase the blood supply to the brain.

As the final stage of the operation, one of the Iraqi surgeons was about to mix some bone cement with large amounts of antibiotics, which can cause patients to become more hypotensive. In the midst of the chaos, the assistant piped up, 'I'm ready to mix the bone cement!'

It was the last thing Kevin wanted to hear. 'Stop,' he instructed.

But the consulting surgeon was insistent. 'It's about fifteen minutes of work that I don't want to waste.'

Kevin turned around to now see five anaesthetists staring at the monitors. None of the screens was showing any sign of life.

At that stage, the assistant surgeon called out, 'The cement's ready!' No one else in the theatre was speaking, which isn't a good sign.

Kevin broke the silence. 'Is this guy dying?' he asked.

'No,' came the reply from the one specialist in the room who seemed to know what was going on. 'He's just hypotensive.'

'What about the monitors?'

'The monitors are broken. Sometimes they work, sometimes they don't. He had a pulse and blood pressure all along.'

An anaesthetist pumped fluids into the patient, and his condition stabilised. They completed the operation, and the man who at one stage appeared to be slipping away made a solid recovery. But Kevin was convinced that it would have been better if the theatre staff had told him about the dodgy monitors at the start rather than at the end!

Another complicating factor in a non-English-speaking country such as Iraq is language difficulties. In the intensity of an operating theatre, plenty of concepts can get lost in translation.

One of the standard pieces of equipment is a pulsed lavage—a device commonly used during operations to pump pressurised irrigating fluid into a wound at high velocity. It debrides the area, effectively washing out debris, reducing bacteria and preventing the risk of infection.

One time, Kevin asked the Iraqi theatre staff for a pulsed lavage. The registrar and the anaesthetist looked at him blankly and said they'd never heard of it. Kevin thought this was odd because he'd used one the day before.

The Shape of Things to Come

In the absence of the correct equipment, Kevin had to use a 20cc syringe to manually irrigate the wound while he was operating. It meant that every twenty minutes he was pumping in 200 millilitres of irrigating fluid—instead of the 6 litres he could apply with a pulsed lavage. It was tortuous.

I only found out about this when I walked into his operating theatre and saw what was going on. 'Where's the pulsed lavage?' I screamed in Arabic.

One of the theatre staff reached out no more than arm's length and handed it to me. It had been there all the time. But the staff couldn't understand Kevin's American accent!

Another day, Kevin was about to operate on a patient who'd suffered a significant head trauma. The patient was already on the operating table and was covered in drapes and gowns. Kevin examined the chest X-rays and saw a tracheostomy tube, which had been inserted into the throat to help the patient's breathing.

To double-check that the patient on the table was the right one, Kevin turned to the anaesthetist and asked, 'This guy has a tracheostomy, right?'

The anaesthetist shook his head and replied, 'No.'

Kevin was a little taken aback and asked, 'Are you sure?'

This time, the anaesthetist lifted the drapes, looked at the patient and again shook his head and said, 'No.'

By now, Kevin was completely nonplussed, so he consulted one of the Iraqi surgeons. 'Does this patient have a tracheostomy?'

The surgeon responded quickly, 'No.'

293

Bewildered, Kevin took the surgeon to look at the chest X-rays, pointed to the evidence and said, 'Isn't that a tracheostomy?'

The surgeon responded, 'That's a breathing tube. They put it in when someone's been badly injured and needs help breathing.'

Kevin resisted the temptation to point out that he's a highly experienced surgeon, and to him a tracheostomy and a breathing tube were one and the same thing! It transpired that both the anaesthetist and the surgeon had thought Kevin was asking whether the patient had taken any aspirin!

To put the icing on the cake, during a later visit to Ibn Sina, Kevin was operating on a completely smashed femur. He spent a significant amount of time and effort putting all the pieces of the bone together—it was like working on a complex jigsaw puzzle. After he asked for a plate to fix the fracture, the nurses scrambled and brought him a suitable plate. Kevin then followed up with, 'Now, can I have a drill?'

One of the nurses said, 'Oh, you need a drill?'

'Yes, I need to use a drill to put the screws in.'

'Oh, you need screws?'

Kevin was physically holding the leg together with his hands and, because of the delay, was beginning to lose his grip. At that point, he finally lost his temper. 'What the fuck? Of course I need screws to hold the plate in place,' he bellowed in frustration. His yelling was so loud that I heard it in the other theatre.

I immediately rushed across the corridor to see what was

going on. As I burst in, I could see that his verbal explosion had achieved the desired outcome. Sometimes it pays to be forceful—especially when you want the theatre staff to be thinking ahead at the same rate as the surgeons.

There's no doubt that what we're doing—albeit slowly—is raising the standard of surgery and surgical care in Iraq. The improvement each time we visit Baghdad is noticeable. We haven't yet achieved the standards of a centre of excellence among the Iraqi staff, but there are encouraging signs from most quarters—except perhaps the senior surgeons.

The hope for the future lies with the young Iraqi doctors—the residents and junior surgeons. They're as keen as mustard to learn the latest techniques. They have an almost unquench-able thirst for learning, which makes their future prospects extremely positive. Hopefully, they will be at the forefront of vastly improved standards of patient care, and will develop rewarding and successful careers for themselves along the way.

It's not easy for these young doctors. Most of them live outside the Green Zone and face extended journeys to and from the hospital due to delays at the checkpoints. Despite working long hours and sleeping little, the young surgeons don't complain. They turn up bright and early each morning, raring to find out more from working with us.

The physiotherapists have been equally enthusiastic. They regularly contact Claudia for advice on rehabilitation programs.

Although there's still a way to go, the nurses have proved that they can learn and apply new methods. A young male nurse named Haider comes to mind. He's quiet, polite and will always look at the ground when he talks to you. He's very shy and doesn't speak fluent English. For all that, he's every bit as good as the Australian nursing staff I work with. It's a pleasure to operate alongside him.

— —

I want Iraqis to know that people outside their country care enough about them to go to their homeland and attempt to make a difference. I'm frequently asked, 'Are you an Iraqi doing this for the people of Iraq?' or 'Do you feel as though you're coming home?' I have to be honest and tell them, 'No, I'm an Australian who's coming here to help you because I care about you and the country.'

I know that we are having an impact. Although our initial progress has been slow, I aim to return to Iraq four times a year so that we can gain momentum. Every patient we treat will tell others about our work. Word will spread—and from my experience at Ibn Sina Hospital, word spreads quickly in Iraq. Increasing numbers of people will find out that we care enough about them to make regular visits to repair the physical wounds inflicted during the various conflicts in Iraq over the last 40 or more years.

But it's an almost never-ending task, because there are more than 150,000 amputees in Iraq. Around 90 per cent of them have no artificial limbs—not even the old-fashioned socket prostheses. In a seven-day stay in Iraq, we can perform up to 50 operations—and only about one-third of them are osseointegration. You don't need to be a genius to figure out the size and scale of the task that confronts us.

I accept surgery—and particularly osseointegration—isn't for everyone. Around 50 per cent of the people I see in the clinics at the hospital decline the procedure. I think it's largely because of a fear of the unknown. Those who go ahead with the operation are happy with the results and the huge improvement in their mobility and lifestyle.

That in itself is satisfying. We go to Iraq to transform people's lives, and there's clear evidence that we're achieving this goal. But there are ongoing complications—especially surrounding financial support for our humanitarian work, and obstructionism by the powers that be. I just wish the authorities in Iraq would realise that this is all about the patients—not about the politics, the self-interested politicians or the bureaucrats.

I believe there is an opportunity for Australia to make a much more meaningful—and mutually beneficial—contribution to the development of Iraq, without falling foul of the corruption that is rife in the Middle East.

Instead of providing bottles of water or milk or other staples—which are inevitably sold on at inflated prices by corrupt officials, Australia could help develop the skills of Iraqis in vital areas such as water supply, sanitation and medicine.

Australia has a wealth of skilled professionals and educators in these areas. I am proposing that the Australian Government send necessary infrastructure equipment to Iraq, along with professional trainers who would be paid to run courses for the locals. When sufficient numbers have been trained, the equipment would be left in Iraq for locals to operate. Over time, more equipment and trainers could go to Iraq to help the country become self-sufficient in the most important aspects of its economy and social services.

A program of this kind would also provide long-term employment prospects for the newly trained professionals and possibly allow for Iraqis to take over the training roles.

Overcoming the obstacles isn't easy. But I'm a persistent individual—I fight for what I believe in and I don't give up.

I have been invited to speak to the Iraqi parliament about our work. I hope my address will open the eyes of the politicians and bureaucrats to the validity and necessity of our humanitarian project.

The patients desperately need funds to be released so they can be fitted with new robotic legs. I remain optimistic that, sooner or later, even the most cynical of Iraqi politicians will place the needs of their people above their own interests. Certainly, I will be doing everything in my power to make sure that happens.